PENGUIN BOO

MOURJO

After reading classics and modern languages at King's College, Cambridge, Peter Graham emigrated to France – lured, say his more malicious friends, by the attractions of good French food. He has since compiled a film dictionary; written *The New Wave*; directed two short films; translated Jacques Médecin's *Cuisine Niçoise* (Penguin) and several other books (on film, art and the history of psychoanalysis); written *The International Herald Tribune Guide to Business Travel and Entertainment: Europe*; co-written several guide books; contributed articles on food and wine to the *Sunday Times* Magazine, *The Times*, the *Guardian* and the *Good Food Guide*; and written *Classic Cheese Cookery* (Penguin), which won the 1988 André Simon Memorial Fund Book Award.

Peter Graham has lived for the last twenty years in Mourjou, a small village in the Châtaigneraie, part of the southern Auvergne.

Mourjou

The Life and Food of an Auvergne Village

Peter Graham

Illustrated by Peter Campbell

PENGUIN BOOKS

PENGUIN BOOKS

Published by the Penguin Group
Penguin Books Ltd, 27 Wrights Lane, London w8 5tz, England
Penguin Putnam Inc., 375 Hudson Street, New York, New York 10014, USA
Penguin Books Australia Ltd, Ringwood, Victoria, Australia
Penguin Books Canada Ltd, 10 Alcorn Avenue, Toronto, Ontario, Canada m4v 3b2
Penguin Books (NZ) Ltd, Private Bag 102902, NSMC, Auckland, New Zealand

Penguin Books Ltd, Registered Offices: Harmondsworth, Middlesex, England

First published by Viking 1998
Published in Penguin Books 1999
1 3 5 7 9 10 8 6 4 2
Copyright © Peter Graham, 1998
All rights reserved

The moral right of the author has been asserted

Set in Monotype Bembo
Printed in England by Clays Ltd, St Ives plc

Contents

THE CHÂTAIGNERAIE

Preface

It was exactly twenty years ago that I first set eyes on the house where I live in the Auvergne. Overlooking a tiny square next to the church of the small village of Mourjou (Cantal), it had been for most of its life (it was built in 1817) one of those hotels/restaurants/cafés/groceries rolled into one that used to be, and in some cases still are, the backbone of French rural life. It was there that generations of children had bought their sweets and farmers' wives the staples they did not produce themselves; there that the menfolk would go for an *apéritif* or two after church services and funerals, while their wives waited outside in cars, or to play endless disputatious games of *belote*; there that village dances and wedding feasts had been held. No doubt because of all that, the vibes felt good as I followed the notary who was selling the house into the two huge ground-floor rooms that used to serve as café and dining-room; they felt even better by the time I had finished looking the house over, and a week later I managed to raise a mortgage and buy it.

Over the two decades I have lived in my house, I have come to know and love the village and people of Mourjou and the surrounding communes. Acquaintances sometimes ask me (friends do not need to be told; they know) whether I feel I have fully integrated into the local community. It is a difficult question to answer, and perhaps best turned on its head: what do the people of Mourjou think?

At first I was probably seen as something of a curiosity: the previous occupiers of my house were two mini-skirted women with a *soixante-huitard* lifestyle influenced by the libertarian ideas in fashion after the 'events' of May 1968, and since the car I drove when I moved in was a Citroën *traction-avant* (a 'Maigret car'), a vehicle then widely associated by the older generation with '*les gangs des tractions*' of the forties and fifties, many assumed that Mourjou had acquired another eccentric resident. Some villagers, puzzled by the lack of any visible signs of industry on my part (they could not see me hunched over my typewriter in a back room), even speculated that I might be a drugs dealer. But it gradually sank in that I worked with words, and that my 'equipment' was a typewriter, then a word processor, and that my 'produce' was dispatched initially by mail, then by fax or modem.

It was in my capacity as a writer and journalist that in 1993 I was asked to become a member of the Confrérie du Pelou, a confraternity created to add some folklore to Mourjou's Foire de la Châtaigne (chestnut festival), which had been started four years earlier. Each member was given a title in Occitan (p. xxi). As the title of Writer (*Escriveire*) had already been taken up by the founder of the Confrérie, they decided to call me Grand Master (*Grand Mèstre*) – a title possibly seen as appropriate because of my height and girth. I was naturally delighted and honoured to have become, in this way, 'one of them'.

Mourjou lies at the heart of an old region known as the Châtaigneraie (literally 'chestnut grove'), much of which is indeed carpeted with chestnut woods. It centres on the area between Aurillac and the River Lot, and occupies the south-western lobe of the Cantal *département*, as well as the fringes of the neighbouring Lot and Aveyron *départements*. In the twenty years I have lived in Mourjou, I have naturally had a chance to get to know the food of the Châtaigneraie very well, both from eating at friends' homes and dining at local restaurants of every category, from the most basic to the Michelin-rosetted. But I have also, in the course of writing articles on food for newspapers and contributing to guidebooks, travelled and eaten extensively in the rest of the Auvergne (roughly speaking the Allier, Puy-de-Dôme, Haute-Loire, Cantal and upper sections of the Aveyron and Lozère). What this has brought home to me is the great homogeneity of Auvergnat cuisine. While each part of the Auvergne may have its local speciality – the Bourbonnais its *gigot de sept heures*, Saint-Flour its *rissoles*, Aurillac its *tripoux*, Le Puy its *petit salé aux lentilles*, the Cantal its *truffade* and the Aveyron its *aligot* – that does not stop those dishes being eaten on occasion throughout the region along with such universal Auvergnat stalwarts as *soupe aux choux*, *farinette*, *potée*, *chou farci*, *coq au vin*, *falette*, *truite au lard* and *millard*.

This book does not set out to be exhaustive. In other words, I have restricted the recipes to those that are specifically Auvergnat and preferred not to include all the classic dishes of *cuisine bourgeoise* and *cuisine fermière* that Auvergnats also eat. I have naturally drawn on much of the existing printed material on the food of the Auvergne. But I have also relied on numerous conversations with Auvergnat men and women, mostly from the Châtaigneraie, who described to me their culinary memories, attitudes and practices, and in some cases gave me their version of a traditional recipe. I also interviewed several professional chefs, who kindly provided me with recipes of their own invention which use typically Auvergnat ingredients in new and imaginative combinations – a style sometimes described as '*le terroir réinterprété*'.

Peter Graham, 1998

Acknowledgements

I am primarily grateful to Peter Campbell, who first suggested many years ago that I should write a book about the village of Mourjou; to Mary and Philip Hyman, who argued that there was a need for a book in English on Auvergne cookery; to Tag Gronberg, Paul Overy and Ginette Vincendeau, who bullied me to get down to writing it; to Michèle Canet, an unfailingly helpful source of local culinary lore; and to Eleo Gordon, of Penguin Books, who patiently shepherded the book through its various metamorphoses.

I would like to thank all those cooks, both 'amateur' and professional, who kindly gave me recipes: Louise Aymar, Michèle Canet, Théodore Carrière, Mauricette Cayron, Jeanne Chabut, Jean-Pierre Courchinoux, Claudine Croutes, Yvonne Croutes (of Lestrade), Yvonne Croutes (of Le Seriès), Nicole Fagegaltier, Fernande Faven, Yvonne Figeac, Christian Gaudel, Yvette Gazal, Germaine Lacoste, Joseph Pétry, Marie Pétry, Eliette Pons, Yvonne Puech, Louis-Bernard Puech, Sylvie Ratier, Pierre Ratier, Colette Rouquier, Nicole Saldana and Juliette Vigier (references to the recipes concerned will be found under their respective names in the index).

I am also grateful for sundry information, tips, cuttings, documents, reminiscences, encouragement and advice from – in addition to those already mentioned – John Ardagh, Geneviève Aymar, Louis Bedel, Matthew Bennett, Mireille Biedermann, Roger Biedermann, Anne Boston, Richard Boston, Marie-Louise Bouquier, Jane Campbell, Winifred Campbell, Mimi Cantarel, Elizabeth Carmichael, Richard Castle, Simon Caulkin, Jean Cayron, André Chabut, Marcel Chabut, Lesley Chamberlain, Maria Coudere, Marcelle Coudon, André Coudon, Germain Croutes, Raymond Croutes, Caroline Davidson, Alan Davidson, Paulette Delannes, Henri Delannes, Colette Delclaux, Yvon Delclaux, Patrick Ensor, Michèle Fagegaltier, Eugénie Fau, Paul

Faven, Renée Fenby, Jonathan Fenby, Jules Figeac, Marcelle Fleys, Victor Fleys, Nicholas Garnham, Jean-Marie Gaston, Marie-Christine Gazal, Michèle Gire, Michel Gire, Anne Graham, Denise Guy, Carola Haigh, Nigel Haigh, Bronwyn Hipkin, Christine Ife, Tom Jaine, Catherine Kemmet, Gerald Kemmet, Tony Kitzinger, Marinette Lacoste, Jean Lacoste, Robert Lacoste, Jean Lapeyre, Henri Lavigne, Jean-Pierre Lebrun, Annie Lee, Odette Loubières, Jean Loubières, Timothy McFarland, Marie-Andrée Marre, Arthémy Mazars, Pierre Ménini, David Morgan, Maguy Morin, Jean-Pierre Morin, Nicole Mousset, Laurent Mousset, Gérard Moussié, Brian Oatley, John Parry, Joseph Périer, Lucienne Pétry, Carla Phillips, Bernard Phillips, Joshua Phillips, Pascal Piganiol, Solange Piganiol, Marinette Robert, Pierre Robert, Nicky Roberts, Keith Roberts, Marie-Claude Roques, Robert Roques, Sylvie Roualdes, Marie Rouquier, Roger Rouquier, Jean-Marc Saldana, Pierre Soissons, Josette Vigier, Raymond Vigier, René Vigier, Daniel Ville, Keith Walker and the staff of the Archives Départementales du Cantal in Aurillac.

Introduction

Visitors to the Auvergne countryside often come away with the impression of a land overflowing with milk and honey. There are few outward signs of poverty. Houses and gardens are well-kempt. Animals in the fields look sleek and healthy. There is plenty of modern farm machinery. Many people, including the elderly, drive gleaming new cars. Food shops are well stocked and well patronized. Most restaurants do a thriving trade.

This impression of well-being is broadly correct, though there are one or two pockets of poverty. But what needs to be remembered is that the prosperity of the Auvergne is a fairly recent development. It was ushered in by the so-called '*trente glorieuses*' (France's thirty years of swift economic growth from the end of the war until the first oil shock of 1974), the introduction of the welfare state, and the European Union's generous treatment of hill farmers. Before that, the Auvergnats, like people in many other rural areas of France, were poor; before that again, they just about survived at a subsistence level; and before that, in the eighteenth and early nineteenth centuries, they often starved. Tourists would do well to remember this as they tuck into mountains of *cuisine paysanne améliorée* at knock-down prices in cosy country inns, browse at the tempting stalls of *marchés de pays*, or trek up the mountains to 'eat the ambiance' of the *burons*, the austere stone huts where cowherds used to toil away making cheese during the summer.

Tourism in the Auvergne predates its prosperity. In the first issue, dated March 1898, of *L'Auvergne Pittoresque*, a quarterly bulletin put out by the Syndicat d'Initiative de l'Auvergne, the improbably named Desdevises du Dézert urges the reader to get on his or her bicycle (touchingly known at the time as *la petite reine*) and explore, with camera at the ready, the Auvergne's 'grandiose views, volcanoes that seem to have become extinct only yesterday, picturesque valleys, quaint characters, old costumes and magnificent ruins of former feudal castles'.

The 'quaint characters' he was referring to exactly 100 years ago would mostly have still been surviving on an extremely frugal diet. As for the 'feudal lords', they were probably still indulging themselves as much as they had in earlier centuries. Paul Charbonnier tells us, in the journal *Annales* (March–June 1975), that Auvergnat *seigneurs* living in the region of Vic-sur-Cère in the fifteenth century got through 664 litres of wine and 187 kilos of meat per head and per year!

In the last half of the eighteenth century, a succession of failed harvests resulted in famine in the Auvergne. On occasion people were reduced to eating ash leaves to supplement their diet. Their health suffered as a result. In his invaluable first-hand account of life in the Auvergne in the 1780s, *Voyage Fait en 1787 et 1788, dans la ci-devant Haute et Basse Auvergne*, Pierre-Jean-Baptiste Legrand d'Aussy – a typical product of the Age of Enlightenment who later became head of the Bibliothèque Nationale – gives a grim description of the Châtaigneraie (p. viii) as it then was:

[The Châtaigneraie] is perhaps the part of the Auvergne where there is the most extreme poverty and the worst food: this is all too clearly attested by the inhabitants' gaunt and swarthy features, their thinness, the bilious and splenetic attacks to which they are prone, and finally the visible deterioration of their physical constitution.

Food shortages throughout France were of course one of the major causes of the French Revolution. They were also, interestingly, responsible for the French language's borrowing of two English words: roast beef. It may seem odd that the French should use this culinary term, re-spelt as *rosbif*, as a familiar noun to denote Brits – *rosbif* carries the same pejorative connotation as Frog or Kraut (from *sauerkraut*) in English. After all, it is in France that the national Sunday lunch dish, especially in urban areas, is *rosbif*. The word *rosbif*, like *bifteck* and *romsteck*, gained currency in the late eighteenth and early nineteenth centuries as a result of French visitors to England returning to underfed France with reports of the leisured English classes consuming gargantuan quantities of beef (cf. James Gillray's and William Hogarth's caricatures). England's agriculture before the industrial revolution was easily able to support its population, which at the time was much smaller than that of France.

Meanwhile, food shortages in the Auvergne were aggravated by a rising population. Something had to give: Auvergnats began migrating in large numbers to Paris, Toulouse, Lyon and South America. The trend gathered momentum in the nineteenth century, partly assisted by the building of railways, when a very large Auvergnat community put down roots in Paris. The hard-working Auvergnats were prepared to do all manner of arduous jobs. They soon found a niche as water-carriers and coal and wood merchants, two activities that complemented each other seasonally: in summer they would carry water up several flights of stairs in sufficient quantities for their customers to have a bath; in winter they supplied the same customers with heating fuel. Their *bois-charbons* shops often had a *zinc* (bar counter) on one side and were known as *bougnats* (a corruption of the word Auvergnat). These *bougnats* eventually stopped selling fuel and turned into fully-fledged cafés. The tightly-knit Auvergnat community quickly dominated Paris's expanding catering trade. At the height of their success, soon after the last war, Auvergnats ran some 90 per cent of Paris cafés and restaurants.

Those who stayed at home continued to work as farmers, struggling to feed their large families. Until about fifty years ago they lived in a state of almost complete autarky. Any little surplus that could be sold was sold (eggs, poultry, ham, veal, chestnuts) to help pay for such staples as oil, wine, salt, matches, seeds and coffee. Their everyday diet was extremely frugal and monotonous, consisting of bread and soup at most meals and very little meat. And the meat they ate was usually something that could not easily be sold – for example, an old hen (turned into *poule farcie*) or a meagre breast of veal (*falette*).

The potato was introduced into the Auvergne by the government in 1771, after two years of food shortages and high grain prices. It caught on only slowly. The Auvergnats are notoriously conservative when it comes to what they eat. A farmer's wife I know does not tell her husband when she slips a few young nettle shoots into the soup – in his mind, nettles are what you mash up and give to chickens, rabbits or pigs. The potato was initially regarded as a '*légume du diable*'. But once accepted it became a pivotal part of Auvergnat cuisine. The

Auvergnats' considerable energy requirements, caused by the strenuous manual labour that was the rule before machines came in, were largely satisfied by salt pork fat, often eaten on its own with a crust of bread, and cheese. Fat was not, as it is nowadays, regarded as something to be avoided. Its positive image lingers on in the Auvergnat word *graillou* (a fatty scrap of cooked meat), which in familiar parlance means 'grub' in general. Auvergnat cuisine 100 years ago was certainly much greasier than it is today. And for economic reasons it was also very basic. But hardship can stimulate the resourcefulness and imagination of the cook. The ability to exploit cheap and mundane ingredients to best effect is a quality that Auvergnat cooking shares with Italian cuisine.

Although in my experience it is true that the Auvergnats, like most country-dwellers, keep a close eye on what they spend and how much things cost (the legacy of grinding poverty in the past), they are, like the Scots, an extremely hospitable people. And that does not just mean inviting you for a drink or a meal. Legrand d'Aussy again:

Rarely will [an Auvergnat] refuse to give a poor man alms. Truth to tell, it will not be money he will give; but he will share his bread and his soup with the poor soul, and he will even lodge him in his cowshed, even though such hospitality may sometimes have dangerous consequences – there are many examples of thieves who have used that method to get into a farm and then bring in their accomplices to ransack it.

The generosity also extends to neighbours. Edouard Laforce, in his *Essai de Statistique du Département du Cantal* (1836), notes:

If a farmer has some major work to undertake, such as building a house, a barn or a cowshed, help is lavished on him [by his neighbours] that he could not get by paying for it: people give him wood, bring him his materials and erect the frame of his building. All he needs to provide is food for the oxen, the drivers and the workmen. This kind of get-together of neighbours to help one of their number is called a *bouade*.

Not so long ago, before combine harvesters and maize-munching machines came in, such *bouades* used to be organized on a rota basis at harvest and threshing time. Each day was rounded off with a hearty meal, washed down with plenty of wine, which was provided by the farmers on whose land the work had been done. The *bouades* season would culminate in a huge and often al fresco banquet. Another tradition which has virtually disappeared – thanks to television – is the *veillée*, a gathering of friends at this or that person's house, where they would crack walnuts and jokes, husk maize, exchange seeds, play cards, tell stories, sing songs and dance.

When a locally based charitable organization asked the people of Mourjou if they would be prepared to take in a family of Cambodian refugees, the answer was immediately yes. One of the village's two 'squires' lent the family a little eighteenth-century mill, and we all donated blankets, linen, pots and pans, crockery, cutlery, a radio set, a record-player and so on. A rather over-directive but well-meaning woman in whose charge the Cambodians had been put decreed that they should eat potatoes instead of rice, because they were cheaper – overlooking the fact that, in terms of calories provided, the two staples were roughly equivalent in price, and that rice was their traditional food.

Before going on a trip to Paris, I asked the Cambodians if there was anything I could get them from a Cambodian shop I knew of in the capital. Yes, they said, some fresh lemon grass, plenty of rice and 2 kilos of monosodium glutamate! They eventually found a more congenial home in the Cambodian quarter in Marseille, which was warmer than the frost pocket in which their mill nestled, and safer in their eyes – when asked why they barricaded their front door at night, they replied it was to prevent a tiger crashing into the house.

Before leaving Mourjou, they cooked a Cambodian meal for those who had helped them out, a moment of culture shock for many villagers which I unfortunately missed. But by all accounts it went down well with some people. Curiously, it was the men, generally more hidebound in their attitudes than the women, who enjoyed the Cambodian meal more, apparently because, in the course of doing their national service or fighting in Algeria, they had had more experience of foreign cuisines.

Women, as is only to be expected, are the repositories of Auvergnat cuisine. They have also long been the backbone of the rural Auvergnat household. As in many other regions of France, it is only relatively recently that they have ceased to be exploited. As for the more distant past, the word 'exploitation' would be an understatement.

Even Legrand d'Aussy, who was certainly no proto-feminist, was shocked. Having noted that women retired later and rose earlier than the rest of the household so they could cope with their very heavy workload, he was scathing about their menfolk:

A man would think it beneath him to go and fetch water; and he would most certainly become the laughing stock of the village if he did so. These mountain peasants have, as regards women, the profound contempt and despotic disdain peculiar to all savage or semi-barbarous peoples. They regard them as slaves, whose job it is to do all the work which they deem base and which they despise.

An Auvergnat legend tells of the suffering of the womenfolk in one village, where they had to go down into the valley to fetch water. It was difficult enough going down a path covered with loose pebbles, but even harder trekking up again with a bucket on their heads crushing their neck vertebrae. One day they decided enough was enough: they came rushing up the hill screaming that they had seen a many-headed dragon at the spring. The menfolk puffed up their chests and said: 'We're not afraid of a dragon. We'll get the water.' This they did for a few days, but then got fed up. The women still refused to go down. Then one man had the bright idea of digging a well. It was only when the well had been dug that the women admitted the dragon story had been a hoax.

Some of those attitudes persisted until fairly recently. Twenty years ago, when I moved to the Auvergne, I witnessed a ritual in a remote farmhouse in the Cantal mountains that has now almost completely died out: that of a farmer's wife remaining standing during the meal, serving her husband and sons their food at table, and herself eating afterwards in a corner of the *cantou* (large fireplace).

The *cantou* is the focus – if you will excuse the etymological tautology – of life on the farm. It is usually located in the living-room (*salle commune*), a large space that serves as both a kitchen and a dining-room. The *cantou* usually contains only a few smouldering logs, and is brought to a blaze only occasionally. Country people in general, and the Auvergnats in particular, are used to living at much lower temperatures than city-dwellers. I remember going to fetch some milk at a farm down the road at 8 a.m. on a very cold day. The farmers had never bothered to weather-strip their front door, which had a good one-inch gap at the bottom that helped to draw the fire. When I entered, they were having their breakfast with their backs to the *cantou* and plumes of steam coming out of their mouths. As I walked across the room I noticed that the dog's water bowl had frozen over. Yet I have never known those farmers to go down with a cold.

Keeping out the cold is a major preoccupation of the Auvergnats, particularly of course in the higher and colder areas. In the past, when central heating was unknown, one way of keeping warm was to exploit the heat of farm animals. On the windswept highlands of the Puy-de-Dôme, many farmhouses have an adjoining cowshed through which you walk to enter the house. The warmth of the cows forms a barrier against the cold, rather like the blasts of hot air that are directed down at you when you enter a department store in winter.

There is a higgledy-piggledy house in my village which long puzzled me because, however cold it was, its front door and all its windows were always kept wide open throughout the day. It turned out that the *salle commune* was situated above the pigsties, with nothing but an old and not very tight-fitting chestnut-wood floor as a separation. Conversation during meals, I was told by a regular visitor to the house, would be interrupted by the occasional envious grunt from below. The deeply grooved chestnut floors of many of the houses in the

Châtaigneraie are perfect crumb traps, and I have visited farms where chickens are occasionally allowed in to do some housework. On the whole, however, the *salle commune* is out of bounds to farm animals, and sometimes even to dogs and cats, and its floor, whose chestnut planks have often been replaced by tiles, is kept immaculately clean.

The typical *cantou* is very deep and wide, often with little benches on either side reserved for *papi* and *mamie* (grandparents, most of whom spend their final years in the house where they raised their family rather than in an old people's home). One of the benches, a *banc à sel*, has a hinged seat and contains that most vital ingredient before the advent of deep-freezes: salt. A ham or two and maybe some *saucissons secs* are suspended from a hook on the side of the *cantou* or in front of it (which gives some idea of how little fierce heat the fire produces). Hanging from the mantelpiece is the *bofador*, 'bellows' in the form of a stick about 75 centimetres long with a small hole bored through its centre (the wood used is elderberry, because it has a pithy centre). When it is blown through at one end, the thin jet of air that shoots out of the other end fans the embers very effectively. During the winter, yeast is kept in niches in the *cantou*.

In front of the *cantou* is the kitchen table, a long, imposing piece of furniture with a foot-rest running along the middle, two huge end-drawers for keeping bread and cheese in, and a narrow transversal drawer half-way down one side for cutlery.

Suspended above the table in some households there is a *posse* – one or two shelves attached to the ceiling by two wooden arms, on which anything vulnerable to domestic animals or rodents can be safely stored (bread, cut *saucisson* and so on). The *posse* is also a convenient place to keep salt, pepper, mustard, jam and other regularly used foods.

The living-room might also contain one or more relics of the past: closet beds with little curtains that look like a row of Punch and Judy stages. Nowadays their short, high beds with hemp sheets and mattresses made of beech leaves or straw have been abandoned in favour of larger beds in bedrooms proper. A grandfather clock, whose case may have been made by the farmer himself, stands against a wall facing a window (in the days before watches came in, this position enabled people to look through the window and see what time it was). On one side of the *salle commune* in many houses there is a *souillarde*, a vaulted, north-facing and often windowless recess with a low stone sink; in the old days the dish-water was drained off directly outside via a hole in the wall.

Much cooking used to be done directly in the *cantou* (it was a way of economizing on fuel), by placing the casserole or frying-pan either on a large trivet sitting among the embers, or on a kind of grid with a handle, called *andrilièras* in Occitan,* suspended from a rod or hooked on to the trammel. It was an ideal place to cook dishes like *potée* (p. 91). And even today many people still fry their *farinettes* (p. 23) in the fireplace, which, once the logs have been revived with the *bofador*, can generate far more heat than the biggest gas burner and thus brown the *farinette* to their satisfaction. Sadly perhaps, in households where central heating has been installed, *cantous* have usually been closed off and their inside walls covered with brick-patterned wallpaper.

In most households, a new piece of furniture now stands in one corner of the *salle commune*, or in an adjoining room: the deep-freeze. Whereas in the past many products of the kitchen garden used to be

---

* Occitan, or *langue d'oc*, was the language of educated Europe at the time of the troubadours in the Middle Ages. It was spoken for two centuries in Spain, Italy and England as well as in France. Richard Coeur de Lion wrote poems in *langue d'oc*. Northern Occitan, one of the two remaining principal branches of Occitan, is still widely spoken in the Auvergne. In Mourjou, it survives as the language that people over fifty prefer to use among themselves. It is not all that long ago that children going to school for the first time, after being brought up for the first few years of their lives in a completely Occitan linguistic environment, found they had to learn a new language – French – and would get literally rapped over the knuckles by their teacher if they were caught whispering a few words of what was dismissively referred to as *patois*. Many Auvergnats under fifty are able to speak Occitan but tend to use French, while members of the younger generation often understand Occitan but do not speak it (except when they choose to learn it at school, as they are now allowed to do).

The sharp decline in Occitan speaking dates exactly from the time, thirty to thirty-five years ago, when television sets started beaming the French language into almost every rural home. As the older generation dies out, Occitan looks doomed to wither away within a decade or two, despite the efforts of militant Occitanists to promote it – though it will no doubt linger on after that as a semi-'dead' language studied in schools and universities.

Occitan is a rich language. It is claimed to have 160,000 words (only slightly fewer than English), but many of these are dialectal synonyms. It is also a complicated language from the spelling/pronunciation point of view: this has resulted in two distinct schools of thought on how it should be spelt – the 'Mistralian', which spells Occitan more or less as it is pronounced, and the 'classical', or normalized, spelling, in which there is often a discrepancy between spelling and pronunciation. This discrepancy explains why some Occitan words have a different spelling when transliterated into French. Common examples are the Occitan words *canton* (fireplace), *secador* (chestnut-drying chamber), *tripons* (a tripe speciality) and *estofinada* (a dried-cod dish), which, when transliterated into French, are spelt as they are pronounced in Occitan, i.e. *cantou*, *sécadou*, *tripoux* and *estofinado*. On the whole, I have adopted the French transliteration of such common words, because that is how they appear on menus, food labels, postcards and so on. In the case of rarer words I have retained the classical Occitan spelling.

sterilized, and haricot beans and chestnuts dried, they are now often deep-frozen. The deep-freeze has revolutionized attitudes to meat. Whereas in the past poultry would be killed as it was needed, nowadays farmers' wives prefer to do their slaughtering, plucking and gutting in batches of five or six, so they can put the birds that are not eaten straight away into the freezer. The annual slaughter of the pig has been affected, too. Cuts that used to be put in salt or sterilized are now frozen. The Auvergne countryside is now combed by vans bearing names like Argel, Toupargel and Gel 2000. They are insidiously changing eating habits with their selection of *quiches*, *friands*, fish *gratins* and fingers, stuffed pancakes and so on. As more and more mothers go out to work – thus contradicting the old Auvergnat adage: 'Women don't bring in any money' – such foods are of course very convenient. Not every mother bothers to drop in at the local butcher's on her way back from work (my local butcher now stays open till 8 p.m. to cater for such customers). The cook at the Mourjou school canteen says that children's tastes are being increasingly perverted by what they eat at home: they will not touch real mashed potatoes or real chips any more – they prefer the deep-frozen variety. Her grandchildren will not eat green vegetables. She gets pestered by the men selling frozen food, and enjoys telling them to get lost.

So does this trend mean that Auvergnat cuisine is doomed in the long term? Are the little girls attending the local school going to grow up into microwave dependants? Despite various efforts to hold back the tide (through the organization of 'Semaines du Goût', government-sponsored operations designed to raise awareness of the taste of food), the future looks bleak. Gone are the days when teenage girls learnt the techniques and composition of Auvergnat dishes by watching their mothers and grandmothers at the stove.

It could be that restaurants will replace women as the repositories of traditional Auvergnat cooking. Now that the Auvergnats are relatively prosperous, they like nothing more than an expedition *en famille* or *en groupe* (ex-servicemen, OAPs) to a local restaurant. They expect the restaurant to replicate, in more abundant form, the meals they eat, or used to eat, at home. They are ruthless in their criticism, or lavish with their praise, of the chef. On the whole, the standard of Auvergne restaurants and the value for money they offer are very high, though one can have the occasional disappointment. Bryan Morgan claims, in his *Fastness of France*, that 'the ordinary level of Auvergnat cooking [is] rather worse than the ordinary level of cooking in French rural hotels, and decidedly worse than the ordinary level of cooking in English country inns [*sic*]'. He was writing in the 1960s, a decade during which I visited the Auvergne extensively; I therefore feel qualified to dismiss his judgement as rubbish. But then perhaps we do not share the same culinary values. Morgan goes on: '[Beef] usually comes to the table mooing. The French, like the Americans, have yet to learn that *cooking* is one of civilization's achievements and that meat tastes better than blood.'

Perhaps I should explain why I beg to differ with Morgan and why I so like the food of the Auvergne, whether sampled in the home or in restaurants. First, there are raw materials of the highest quality: tasty vegetables from kitchen gardens that are organic in all but name, delicious eggs with deep orange yolks, strong-legged chickens that spend much of their time foraging in the hedgerows, pampered family pigs which are also sometimes allowed to comb the woods for acorns and chestnuts, and which produce superb ham, *saucissons secs* and *saucisses fraîches*, veal from calves that are innocent of crates and beef from animals that have never touched meat-and-bone meal, cheeses, most of them unpasteurized, that are few in number but rank among France's finest, fruit of incomparable flavour (Sainte-Germaine apples, Paquette chestnuts, Ente and Sainte-Anne plums, bilberries, green-gages), and bread in which wheat flour and rye flour are perfectly combined.

Secondly, as I have already mentioned, Auvergnat cooks have a knack for getting the very best out of those excellent raw materials. The final reason why I like the food of the Auvergne and why I have lived happily in the Auvergne for the past twenty years is that I often eat it in the company of Auvergnats. Need I say more?

Soups

One of the first typically Auvergnat phrases I heard on moving to Mourjou was: '*Vous allez manger la soupe avec nous.*' The words were spoken by Mimi Cantarel, whom I had driven to the Thursday market in Maurs, the nearest small town, fifteen kilometres away. Her husband was away and she had no means of transport except a tractor. Although we had met only once before, the Auvergnat principle of *donnant donnant* was already in force: I had done her a service, and she felt the need to return it. I enjoyed a good basic lunch with her and her children, which despite the phrase '*manger la soupe*' comprised, on top of soup, *pâté*, roast veal, salad, cheese and fruit. This was quite normal, as the phrase in fact means 'to have a meal'.

Soupe is a curious word. It is generally agreed it comes from the Low Latin *suppa*, but further back than that its etymology is disputed. Some contend that *suppa* comes from the Gothic family *supôn*, 'to season' (cf. the English 'sop'); others see it as originating from the classical Latin *suppus* and *supinus*, 'turned on its back' or 'laid out'. However that may be, *soupe*'s first meaning in French, in the twelfth century, is 'a slice of bread'. That meaning has survived in phrases like '*tremper la soupe*' (to pour broth over – literally 'soak' – slices of bread) and the figurative '*être trempé comme une soupe*' (to be drenched like a slice of bread). It was only in the fourteenth century, by metonymy, that *soupe* came to mean the broth itself, thickened with mashed-up bread. From the seventeenth century on, as soup became an increasingly vital feature of the diet, the word *soupe* took on the meaning of 'a meal' or just 'food' – as in '*manger la soupe*'. Interestingly, another Mourjou woman, Marie-Louise Bouquier, still uses the phrase '*une soupe dans un café au lait*' in the old sense ('a slice of bread in white coffee') when referring to what she ate for breakfast as a child seventy years ago. This is because in Occitan, the language spoken among themselves by most Auvergnats over fifty, the old sense of *soupe* has lingered on: *far sopas* means to cut bread for soup.

Nowadays most of us do not put bread in our soup, except in the form of *croûtons*, whose purpose has less to do with nourishment than with providing a pleasantly crisp texture to contrast with the liquid. But in the Auvergne lining one's soup bowl with bread remains a common practice, left over from the period before bakeries came in, when each household baked its own bread every fortnight or so: soup was an ideal vehicle for making stale bread edible.

Because of its importance in the Auvergnat diet, soup has always been invested with great symbolic, almost ritualistic, importance, as it has in other regions of France where it is commonly eaten (cf. *garbure* in the south-west). In the patriarchal society of the Auvergne, it was traditional for the head of the household to serve soup, and the practice survives in some families today. For an outsider to be invited to serve soup is a great privilege: Patricia Auger-Holderbach, in her *La Cuisine paysanne en Rouergue* (a mine of information about the Rouergue and its culinary traditions), describes how the producer of the film *Farrébique*, Georges Rouquier's masterpiece about peasant life (1946), was given that signal honour.

'*La soupe fait l'homme, et la femme fait la soupe*' ('Soup makes the man, and the woman makes the soup') goes the proverb. Making soup was and indeed is one of many tasks allotted to womenfolk in the Auvergne. In the old days, when *cantous* (open fireplaces) were still used to heat the living-room, much cooking was done on wood logs. The soup would brew gently over the embers in an *oule*, a large stockpot with a swivelling handle which was either hung directly from the chimney-hook or placed on a flat grid, called *andrilièras* in Occitan (p. xxi), which was suspended from a rod running across the chimney or hooked on to the trammel. Those who remember tasting soup cooked in an *oule* claim its flavour was enhanced by its smoky environment.

Nowadays such soups are usually cooked on top of the stove, but their composition has not changed much. In most cases the basic flavour is provided by the pig, in the form of a hunk of *lard* (solid back fat with the rind on), a ham bone, or pieces of pork rind (these are sold by some charcutiers rolled up like mini-Swiss rolls and held together with string). Any vegetables in season are then added: leeks,

carrots, potatoes, turnips, swedes, cabbage. Sometimes the pork contribution is as meaty as a chunk of *petit salé*, and the dish becomes a *potée*
(p. 91), which is eaten in two stages, liquid first, solids afterwards, with
any leftover liquid forming the basis of the next day's *soupe aux choux*
(p. 10).

In the past soup was eaten at every meal. Today it still forms a very
common start to the meal. During the hard work of harvesting and
threshing before mechanization came in, when people commonly ate
extra meals in the fields at 10 a.m. and 4 p.m. − *les dix et les quatre* −
even soup was carried out to them by wives or, more often, daughters
strong enough to lift the heavy baskets, cutlery, soup plates and pots
of soup. Several Mourjou women, now middle-aged and older, have
unpleasant memories of coming back from school and being forced
to carry such weights up hill and down dale for a kilometre or so to
the hungry workers in the fields. One in particular remembers the
terrible wigging she got after she tripped and fell, losing the contents
of the soup pot in the process.

The starkest of all Auvergnat soups are *les papes* and *coufidou*. *Les
papes*, or *papas* in Occitan (p. xxi), is just what it sounds like: pap, in
other words flour (often half buckwheat, half wheat) cooked in milk
until it thickens, then salted or, more usually, sweetened. In the
Margeride region of the Auvergne, people used to eat a version of

papes called *bulhidas*; this called for flour that had been pre-cooked in a bread oven, which made it more digestible.

Coufidou was a standard breakfast dish for children in Mourjou sixty years ago. It was a mixture of bread (preferably crust) and milk, sometimes covered with grated chocolate, and left to cook very slowly in the fireplace until it had a kind of crust. Like *farinette* (p. 23) and *fogassons* (p. 177), it is a dish whose cooking smells are something that many local people treasure in their often rose-tinted memories of childhood. (Basic though *coufidou* is, it cannot beat the Welsh Milk Soup, from Lloyd George's Favourite Dishes – quoted in *Farmhouse Fare* (Countrywise Books) – in which a little oatmeal is soaked in water overnight, the water drained off, more water added and left overnight, the oatmeal strained off – and presumably thrown away – and the resulting liquid boiled with a little milk and eaten with toast.)

Lastly, mention needs to be made of the widespread Auvergnat custom of pouring a little red wine into the last few remaining spoonfuls of soup. The practice is known as *faire chabrot* or *chabrol*. The mixture is sometimes even administered in small quantities to infants and very young children in the belief – corroborated by recent research – that a little red wine is very good for you. Jeanne Chabut, who gave me her recipe for *soupe au fromage* (p. 6), certainly thought so. The wine she took in her *chabrot* was the only alcoholic beverage she ever drank. Older menfolk traditionally drink their *chabrot* by holding the soup plate itself up to their mouths (a practice represented on postcards). Normally the soup into which the wine is poured will be a clear broth, though I am told that a local man, invited to a ceremonial banquet, poured a little of the vintage wine in his glass into a *crème d'asperges*.

⊰ Aïgo boulido ⊱

Nothing could be more basic than this *aïgo boulido* ('boiled water' in Occitan). It is a classic example of the Auvergnats' ability to produce something delicious out of the humblest ingredients – in this case, water, garlic, bay leaf, clove, eggs and walnut oil. Because garlic is the ingredient with the most pronounced flavour, it is also known as *soupe à l'ail*. According to an Occitan proverb, '*l'aïgo boulido sauvo la vido*' ('boiled water is a lifesaver'). Reputed to be an effective cure for a hangover when taken at breakfast, *aïgo boulido* is also sometimes served to newly-weds instead of *soupe au fromage* (p. 6). It is also recommended to those of delicate digestion.

There are various versions of this dish: in the southern Auvergne, no eggs go into the soup, and olive oil is used instead of walnut oil and fresh sage or thyme instead of bay leaf. In other versions, only egg yolks are used; they are beaten into the hot soup.

[*For four*]
1 litre (35fl oz) water
salt
8 cloves garlic, peeled, halved and slightly crushed
1 clove
1 bay leaf
4 slices stale rye bread
1 tablespoon walnut oil
4 eggs
freshly ground pepper

Bring the water to the boil, add a large pinch of salt, the garlic, clove and bay leaf, and simmer. Put the slices of bread into soup plates and dribble a little walnut oil over them. After the soup has simmered for 15 minutes, poach the eggs in it one after the other and reserve on a warm plate. Check the seasoning of the soup and strain over the bread. Add a little pepper, gingerly place one poached egg on each slice of bread and serve immediately.

↔ Soupe de potiron ↔

Most kitchen gardens in the Auvergne find room for one or two pumpkin plants. In November, their vegetation begins to die back, revealing monstrously large, sculpturally ribbed pumpkins of an intense orange-red hue. They are harvested after the first frosts (which have the effect of making them sweeter), then taken to the cellar, where they can be kept for several weeks. Segments are carved off as required, usually ending up in this pumpkin soup. An especially flavoursome soup can be made if you use a smaller, redder-skinned variety of pumpkin called onion squash (*potimarron*) so called because of its shape, not its taste.

[*For six*]
50g (2oz) unsalted butter
1 onion, peeled and finely chopped
1kg (2lb 3oz) pumpkin, peeled and seeded
1 litre (35fl oz) milk
250ml (9fl oz) double cream
salt
freshly ground pepper
250g (9oz) stale half-rye bread, cut into small dice

Melt the butter in a thick-bottomed saucepan. Add the onion and sweat for 5 minutes over a low heat. Add the pumpkin, cut into chunks, and cover. If the pumpkin is fresh, it should give off enough liquid for no water to be added. When soft, liquidize. Add the milk and cream, and slowly bring to near boiling point. Add salt and pepper to taste. Distribute the bread in hot soup plates, pour the soup over it, and serve.

↞ Soupe au fromage ↠

Soupe au fromage is a highly restorative and filling dish whose aromatic vapours make the nostrils tingle in anticipation as it is served. Cheese soup is eaten not only in the Auvergne, but, in slightly different versions, in other mountain areas such as Savoie, Jura and Switzerland. Auvergne restaurants used to serve it first thing in the morning on market days (p. 109). Nowadays it often rounds off village dances, giving the flagging dancers a chance to recharge their batteries before setting off home in the early hours of the morning.

The soup's restorative qualities have given birth to a curious Auvergnat tradition, now fast dying out, that requires it to be served to a bride and bridegroom on their wedding night. The ceremony, which takes place in their bedroom, is accompanied by many predictable jokes, ribald songs and, sometimes, the wielding of a large *saucisson sec*. Since newly-weds tend to dread the ordeal, they try to slip away

6

from the wedding festivities, separately so as not to arouse suspicion, and flee to a safe house. Often someone who is in on their secret gives them away. Alternatively, a paper bag full of feathers may be tied to the bottom of their car, ripping open as the car leaves and leaving a tell-tale trail. Well-wishers who succeed in tracking down the newly-weds take them the cheese soup, up a ladder if they are locked out, and sometimes in a chamber-pot kept specially for that purpose, with a staring eye painted on its inside. Sticklers for realism sometimes jazz up the brew by throwing in a handkerchief smeared with melted chocolate. No wonder the bride and bridegroom prefer to take evasive action.

The following recipe for *soupe au fromage* was given to me by my late and much lamented friend Jeanne Chabut, who used to run a café, hotel, restaurant and grocery rolled into one in the house where I live in Mourjou. It was a gruelling job, for in addition to cooking for customers and serving in the shop, she had to milk the cows (she made and sold her own butter), feed the chickens and the pig, tend a large kitchen garden, take dirty clothes and sheets down a steep hill to be washed in a stream (and, worse, lug them up again when they were wet and twice the weight), and bring up four children.

People came a long way to enjoy her cooking, and especially her cheese soup. Her husband, Rémy, would go to the trouble of driving 100 kilometres to the little medieval town of Salers to get the top-quality grade of Cantal (called Salers). He kept his cheeses in the café cellar, conscientiously turning them over and brushing their rinds every few days. What with sales of Cantal to customers and Jeanne's mammoth cheese soups, the Chabuts used to get through two of the 42-kilo cheeses a week.

When they retired in the early seventies, the Chabuts moved to a house they had built down the road and let their café to two young Parisiennes. These were committed *post-soixante-huitardes* (in other words they belonged to a generation influenced by the May 1968 'events' in France), and became close friends of another Parisian expatriate living in Mourjou, a joky admiral's son who made what he called '*cabécous géants*' (an intentional contradiction in terms, as a *Cabécou* is always a small goat cheese). Locals were bemused by the women's mini-skirts, the 'outlandish' dishes they served (such as tabouleh), the name they gave their establishment, À la Toile d'Araignée (At the Spider's Web) – no doubt because of the abundance of spiders in the house – and their idea of interior decoration (they painted the café lime-green, orange and chocolate-brown and installed a bar counter made of unstripped silver birch logs). Just as Jeanne Chabut had before them, the two women organized well-attended dances in the large back room of the café. In memory of the enjoyment they provided, À la Toile d'Araignée is the name now given to any dance held in Mourjou's village hall – where the tradition of a final *soupe au fromage* has been maintained.

[*For four*]
50g (2oz) salt pork belly or green streaky bacon
1 onion, sliced
1 litre (35fl oz) vegetable stock
freshly ground pepper
salt
250g (9oz) rye bread, sliced and lightly toasted
200g (7oz) young Cantal cheese
2 tablespoons double cream

Render the salt pork or bacon in a small frying-pan and fry the onion until golden. Bring the stock to the boil, add the onion, its cooking fat, some pepper and a little salt (allowing for the saltiness of the cheese). Simmer for 20 minutes. Put alternate layers of toasted bread and thickly sliced cheese into an ovenproof soup tureen, ending with a layer of cheese. Dribble the cream over the top and add the boiling hot stock. Put uncovered into a moderate oven (180°C/350°F/Gas mark 4) for about 20 minutes, then serve in hot soup plates or bowls.

⤙ Bajanat ⤚

One day at about 7 p.m. I dropped in on Jeanne Chabut (see previous recipe) down the road. She had just started her supper. In front of her was a bowl of hot milk with chestnuts bobbing up and down in it. This, she explained, was one of her favourite dishes when chestnuts were in season, as it strongly reminded her of her youth. People were much poorer in those days, she said, and relied more on chestnuts for nourishment than they do now. But she remembered them as happy times: 'We were tougher then and made do with less. There were very few cars. My friends and I would think nothing of walking, after a day's harvesting in the fields, to dance at the fête of La Vinzelle in mid-August, and then walking back again through the night, carrying straw torches, before going back to harvesting or threshing next morning.' The walk to La Vinzelle, a tiny village perched above the river Lot, is an 8-kilometre trek up and down steep hills through chestnut woods.

In Jeanne's youth, those woods were carefully husbanded for their valuable crop of chestnuts. The tree used to be known as '*l'arbre à pain*', and its fruit as '*pain d'hiver*'. As chestnuts do not keep well like walnuts, they were often dried by being placed on the floor of the upper compartment of little two-storey constructions called *sécadous* (drying huts). The floor consisted of wooden slats placed just close enough together to stop the chestnuts falling through. In the lower compartment, a slow-burning heap of twigs and bark was lit. Heat and smoke filtered through the slats and dried the chestnuts. The fire would be moved around the lower floor with a rake to ensure even drying.

The dried chestnuts were then either shelled for human consumption, when they became known as *auriols*, or given unshelled to the family pig(s), greatly improving the flavour of the resulting pork. There are today a number of up-market pig farms in the Auvergne that include chestnut meal in their feed.

Today, most of the geometrically planted *châtaigneraies* (chestnut groves) have been neglected as the now more prosperous local population no longer needs to rely on chestnuts as a food source. Many trees are sick with ink disease. But there is still an ample quantity of thriving trees to satisfy the needs of those, mostly middle-aged or older, who gather chestnuts with traditional chestnut-wood tongs (which prevent the hands from being painfully spiked by the husk). The chestnut still exerts a strong emotional pull, and not just among the older population, to judge from the success of the Foire de la Châtaigne (chestnut festival) held annually in Mourjou (p. 166).

Nowadays, when people want to keep chestnuts for another day they peel and blanch them, then put them in the deep-freeze – frozen chestnuts taste much more like fresh chestnuts than dried ones do. Almost all the fires in the *sécadous* have now died out for ever – except during the Foire de la Châtaigne, when one *sécadou* is ritually brought back into service. And several larger *sécadous* in the aptly named Châtaigneraie, the region where Mourjou is located, have been turned quite successfully into quaint, if rather poky, *gîtes*.

[*For four*]
20 fresh, frozen, dried or unsweetened tinned chestnuts
salt
1 litre (35fl oz) milk
freshly ground pepper

If using fresh chestnuts, make a circular incision round each of them with a sharp knife, boil for 5 minutes in water, remove and peel while hot. Put a pinch of salt into the milk and bring to a bare simmer. Add the chestnuts and simmer until soft (20 minutes will suffice for fresh or frozen chestnuts, 40 for dried, and 5 for tinned). Add a little pepper and serve immediately.

⊰ Soupe aux choux ⊱

Soupe aux choux contains more flavours than its name would suggest. It is the liquid in which a *potée* has been cooked, and is normally served as a first course to that dish of salt pork, turnips, carrots, potatoes and cabbage (p. 91). Any liquid left over after that is served at subsequent meals as a soup in its own right. When properly made (i.e. if the cabbage has been blanched), it has a complex and not too cabbagy taste. But many Auvergnats I have talked to remember with horror the sharp taste of *soupe aux choux* that fermented after being kept too long in the days before refrigeration.

Soupe aux choux is a dish as closely identified with the Auvergnats as haggis is with the Scots. The Auvergnats brought many of their eating habits with them when they migrated in large numbers to Paris from the eighteenth century on (p. xv). One of them was the custom of starting every meal with soup, often containing cabbage. As with haggis, the dish became an object of fun in vaudeville and *opéra comique* at the turn of the century, where the expected mention of *soupe aux choux* by Auvergnat characters always got an easy laugh. Often they would pronounce it *choupe aux choux* – and produce even greater hilarity – because in many parts of the Auvergne 's' was pronounced 'sh' (as indeed it still is by that most patrician of Auvergnat politicians, Valéry Giscard d'Estaing).

Louis Nadeau, in his *Voyage en Auvergne* (1865), describes how he turned up at the house of an Auvergnat man at just the wrong time: a wake was being held for the man, who had just died. His tearful widow was praising him in ringing tones. 'All the qualities he possessed, and all the faults he did not, were passed in review,' writes Nadeau. 'Her tone was heart-rending; but never was there a more bizarre funeral oration. Pathos was combined with absurdity: "Oh poor Jean!" she exclaimed. "You who were so good, you who never beat me, I'll never see you again! You who so loved bacon omelette . . . you'll never eat my good cabbage soup again!" '

But *soupe aux choux* was not always ridiculed. In the 15 March 1908 issue of *La Cuisine des Familles*, a fascinating cookery magazine containing 'a weekly collection of up-to-date, very clearly explained and easily executed recipes' aimed at bourgeois households, Albert Chevallier writes a flowery editorial in praise of *soupe aux choux*:

Soupe aux choux is not one of the sophisticated products of transcendent cuisine.

Gasterea, the deity created by the imagination of gastronomes to preside over the delights of the table, did not act as its midwife.

Soupe aux choux is a village girl whose only attractions are her simplicity, rustic perfume and appetizing mien.

Daughter of the fields, she nonetheless seduces poets, princes and potentates daily.

History tells us that one of her most ancient worshippers, the emperor Claudius, once told the Senate that he could not live without her.

The Conscript Fathers adopted the imperial favourite with enthusiasm, and for many a long year *soupe aux choux* was the delight of the king of peoples.

If *soupe aux choux* enjoys the privilege of being welcome in all classes of society, it owes it to the flavour and felicitous combination of its ingredients.

It is interesting that among the ingredients he mentions is parsnip, which has now virtually disappeared from French tables and is grown by the French, if at all, either 'for donkeys', as one farmer told me, or for a handful of adventurous modern chefs interested in using 'neglected' vegetables.

In a sonnet entitled 'La Soupe aux Choux', printed below Chevallier's editorial, a poetaster called Raoul Ponchon concludes:

> I can hear you say: 'This *soupe aux choux*
> Is what my concierge eats.' Good lord! Holy Mary!
> Your concierge? So be it. Now you remember this:
>
> You would still have the appetite of a doge
> As well as an incombustible stomach, if
> You took your meals more often in her lodge.

By 'incombustible', one assumes he means 'innocent of heartburn'.

[*For four*]
1.5 litres (53fl oz) liquid from *potée* (p. 91)
4 slices rye bread

Put the slices of bread – stale bread, if you want to be really authentic – into hot soup plates. Pour the liquid from the *potée* you intend to eat as a main course over the bread and serve.

Egg Dishes and Pancakes

For anyone like myself who has pristine memories of early childhood delight at going expectantly to the hen coop and finding a still warm, fresh-laid egg on its cosy bed of straw, a visit to an Auvergnat farmyard has a powerful mnemonic effect. Here are a dozen or so plump and healthy-looking hens, escorted by one or more macho cocks, freely going about their business of pecking grit (which they need to grind their food in their gizzards), feeding on what the farmer gives them (grain, meal, mashed nettles, household leftovers), using their strong feet to scrabble for grubs on and around the manure heap, or setting off for an excursion along the hedgerows and in the fields in search of other insect and vegetable fare. When they wish to roost, they return to the coop or climb ramps into little compartments built into the side of the barn or pigsty. Compare the fortunate lot of these birds with that of their battery-reared cousins, known in the poultry trade as 'layers', who spend their wretched two-year lives, debeaked and declawed to prevent cannibalism, eating 'grain, heavily dosed with egg-encouraging additives and antibiotics, moving by them on conveyor belts' (Margaret Visser, in her excellent *Much Depends on Dinner*).

The quality of the eggs that these jailed hens deposit on a sloping floor, down which they roll on to another conveyor belt, naturally bears no relation whatsoever to that of farmyard hens' eggs. These are incomparably richer and more eggy in taste; and their yolks are usually a deep orange that gives omelettes and sponge cakes a startlingly intense colour. There is an Auvergnat saying: '*Les poules pondent par le bec*' ('Hens lay through their beaks') – in other words the flavour of their eggs is conditioned by what they eat.

I am by no means alone in believing a boiled egg, laid by a farmyard hen – in the Auvergne or elsewhere – that enjoys a properly varied diet and an active life, to be one of the great gastronomic experiences.

The well-known French food writer Robert J. Courtine was unfairly pilloried some years ago by snobbish foodie journalists because he had chosen, as the dish he would take on to a desert island, soft-boiled farmyard eggs with *mouillettes* (fingers of bread, or soldiers) of toasted half-rye bread spread with unsalted butter from Echiré (Charentes), which has an *appellation contrôlée*.

Despite the scorn, he was in good company. In *A Little Tour of France*, Henry James describes taking luncheon in Bourg-en-Bresse: 'I had an excellent repast – the best repast possible – which consisted simply of boiled eggs and bread and butter. It was the quality of these simple ingredients that made the occasion memorable. The eggs were so good that I am ashamed to say how many of them I consumed. "*La plus belle fille du monde*," as the French proverb says, "*ne peut donner que ce qu'elle a*"; and it might seem that an egg which has succeeded in being fresh has done all that can reasonably be expected of it. But there was a bloom of punctuality, so to speak, about these eggs of Bourg, as if it had been the intention of the very hens themselves that they should be promptly served.'

Eggs of the Bourg-en-Bresse type, laid by identifiable and solicitous hens of the kind James had in mind, are of course commonly eaten in Auvergnat farming households nowadays – soft-boiled, hard-boiled or in omelettes and other dishes, such as *farinette* (p. 23) and *pounti* (p. 21), where they are ingeniously combined with flour and other ingredients. But there was a time, not all that long ago, when the relative value of eggs was so high that farmers mostly took them to market as barter or cash products. This practice was even more common in the impoverished farming society of the nineteenth century. In his *Description du département de l'Aveiron* [sic], Amans-Alexis Monteil tells us in 1884 that a dozen eggs could be sold at market for the equivalent of about a third of a casual labourer's daily wage, or for the same price as half a kilo of dressed lamb. One could say that in those days eggs were truly golden.

⤙ Omelette au boudin ⤚

Egg and black pudding is one of those concoctions that seem rather far-fetched, not to say repulsive, on paper. But it is a culinary combination which literally bears out that tired old cliché: 'The proof of the pudding is in the eating' (the origin of the word 'pudding' is '*boudin*'). It is only when you try *omelette au boudin* that you realize just how well the two flavours complement each other. Although not extraordinarily rich in calories, this omelette has a richness of taste that tends to cloy if it is served in main-course quantities, and therefore works better as an entrée. Scrambled eggs with *boudin* are also very good.

[*For four*]
150g (5½oz) *boudin noir*
6 eggs
salt
freshly ground pepper
30g (1oz) good lard or butter

Peel the *boudin* and mash. Incorporate the eggs and beat well. Add a little salt and plenty of pepper. Melt the fat over a high heat in a non-stick frying-pan, making sure it coats the whole surface and part of the sides. When it has completely melted and begins to foam, pour in the egg and *boudin* mixture and reduce the heat to low. As the edges of the omelette cook, lift them at various points and, tilting the pan, allow the uncooked egg on the surface of the omelette to run

over the edge and come into contact with the hot pan. When there remains only a thin layer of runny egg on top, fold the omelette over and transfer to a warm, but not hot, serving dish.

A fluffier version of this dish can be obtained by separating the eggs, mixing the yolks with the *boudin*, beating the whites until very stiff, and incorporating them into the mixture before proceeding with the omelette in the usual way. Some prefer the *boudin* used in this dish to have been crisped up by frying. But this is unnecessary, in my view, particularly as *boudin* is pre-cooked anyway.

⤙ Omelette du curé ⤚

This omelette, which is cooked right through instead of being kept moist in the centre, is more like a thick *galette* than a classic omelette and makes a hearty main course. It is apparently so named because the ingredients that go into it are those that parishioners most often offer as gifts to the village priest: eggs, ham, cheese and potatoes. Many curates, particularly those of the older generation, do not know how to cook, and therefore often arrange to take their meals at the village café.

In the old days, they sometimes had a *menette* to cook for them. *Menettes* were originally a lay order of nuns created by Jesuits in Aurillac in the seventeenth century. Their patron saint was Sainte Agnès. They took vows of celibacy but did not live in convents. In the eighteenth and nineteenth centuries, no bourgeois household in the Cantal was complete without its *menette*, who ruled the kitchen with a rod of iron and knew how to extract the very best out of the cheapest ingredients. Their services as cooks and housekeepers were also highly valued by the clergy. During the French Revolution, one *menette* even followed some non-juring priests into the *maquis* in the region of Mauriac.

By the time the last member of the order had died, in Aurillac in about 1950, *menettes* had become the stuff of legend. Not far from that town, in the valley of the Jordanne, there is a high rocky spur known as Menette's Leap: a *menette*, pursued by the devil, leapt off the rock and allegedly owed her salvation to God, who turned her skirt into a parachute. In the last 100 years or so, the word *menette* has also come to be applied to any pious spinster or widow who can be relied upon to help out in the kitchen in an emergency or on a more permanent basis.

When I asked him what he thought of *menettes*, my neighbour, Father Louis Bedel, threw his arms into the air and said: 'I wouldn't dream of having a *menette* in the house. They're dreadful nosey-parkers.' But then Bedel would not need a *menette* to cook for him. He learnt the basics of cooking from his mother, who lived with him until her death some years ago: as she grew older and he realized he would have to fend for himself in the kitchen, he made a point of watching how she cooked this or that dish. He is now a dab hand at *tête de veau vinaigrette*, *moules au curry* and other far from straightforward specialities. While his mother was still alive and able to cook, he received the occasional gift of eggs, cheese and so on, but this source has now dried up because, he says, his parishioners assume he does no cooking himself.

[*For four*]
50g (2oz) lard
175g (6oz) potatoes, peeled and diced
salt
100g (3½oz) *jambon d'Auvergne* (or similar raw ham),
    sliced and cut into strips
1 clove garlic, finely chopped
8 eggs, lightly beaten
freshly ground pepper
100g (3½oz) young Cantal cheese, cut in very thin slivers
100ml (3½fl oz) double cream

Heat the lard in a large non-stick sauté pan. Dry the diced potatoes and cook them in the lard over a high heat for a few minutes, turning them over frequently with a palette knife, then reduce the heat as low as possible, sprinkle with a little salt and cover. When the potatoes are cooked, turn up the heat a little, stir in the ham and garlic, and pour the eggs over the whole thing. Sprinkle with a little more salt and some pepper.

When the omelette has browned on one side, turn it over on to a warm serving dish, then slide it back into the pan so it cooks on the other side for 3–4 minutes. Lay the slivers of cheese very flat on the omelette while it cooks on the other side, so they come into contact with its hot surface and begin to melt. Heat the cream almost to boiling point, pour over the omelette and serve immediately.

⊷ Omelette à la Fourme d'Ambert ⊶

The subtle, unaggressive flavour of the blue cheese Fourme d'Ambert goes very well with egg. This omelette can also be made with Bleu d'Auvergne, but the quantity of cheese should be reduced somewhat to allow for its greater pungency.

[*For four*]
2 tablespoons double cream
80g (3oz) Fourme d'Ambert cheese
8 eggs
30g (1oz) unsalted butter
small pinch salt
freshly ground pepper

Put the cream and the cheese into a small thick saucepan, mash slightly and heat gently until the cheese has melted, stirring all the time. Set aside and keep warm. Break the eggs into a bowl and beat for 30 seconds. Melt the butter over a high heat in a large non-stick sauté pan, making sure it coats the whole surface and part of the sides. When it has completely melted and begins to foam, pour in the eggs and reduce the heat to low. As the edges of the omelette cook, lift them at various points and, tilting the pan, allow the uncooked egg on the surface of the omelette to run over the edge and come into contact with the hot pan. Sprinkle with salt and plenty of pepper. When there remains only a thin layer of runny egg on top, dribble the melted cheese evenly over the omelette, fold, and transfer to a warm, but not hot, serving dish.

⊷ Œufs à la cantalienne ⊶

This is the sort of dish that is best made with very fresh farm eggs of the kind described in the introduction to this chapter. Its fluffy lightness is uncharacteristic of Auvergnat cooking as a whole.

[*For four*]
4 eggs, separated
salt
pinch freshly grated nutmeg
pinch freshly ground pepper
20g (¾oz) unsalted butter
2 tablespoons double cream
100g (3½oz) Cantal cheese

Bring the eggs to room temperature. Separate the egg yolks from the whites carefully so as not to break the yolks, which should be set aside in their half shells. Whisk the egg whites with a small pinch of salt until very stiff. Gently fold in the nutmeg, pepper and some more salt, and transfer to a buttered soufflé dish. Make 4 little hollows on the surface of the beaten egg whites with the back of a spoon, and carefully place an egg yolk in each of them. Dribble the cream over the whole thing and strew with grated Cantal (if the Cantal is too soft to grate, cut it into very thin slices and lay them on top). Bake in a fairly hot oven (190°C/375°F/Gas mark 5) for 20 minutes or until puffed up and golden brown. Serve immediately.

⊷ Farçous ⊶

When Auvergnat cooks make *pounti* (p. 22), *chou farci* (p. 151) or a stuffing to go into a boiling hen (p. 116), veal breast (p. 136) or guinea fowl (p. 113), they often err deliberately on the generous side as far as quantities are concerned. That way they are certain they have enough to go into the dish or stuffing, and any mixture left over can conveniently be turned into a particularly moreish kind of green fritter – and great favourite with children – called *farçou*, or *farson* in Occitan

(p. xxi), which has the same pronunciation). Like the dishes and stuffings just mentioned, *farçous* may be made either with or without meat. The key to a successful *farçou* is plenty of greenery – without it, it becomes a *farinette* (p. 23). Its distinctive taste comes from near-charred fragments of chopped Swiss chard tops (no pun intended), plus parsley. Another important point is that the dollops of *farçou* batter that go into the sauté pan should not be allowed to bubble too fiercely to start with, as the holes thus formed as they firm up tend to act as fat-traps. The end result, while it may taste nice, is fattier than it needs to be.

[*For four*]
250g (9oz) lean sausagemeat
200g (7oz) Swiss chard tops
1 onion, finely chopped
1 clove garlic, finely chopped
1 tablespoon chives, finely chopped
1 tablespoon parsley, finely chopped
2 eggs
175g (6oz) flour
200ml (7fl oz) milk
large pinch salt
freshly ground pepper
50g (2oz) lard or butter

Mix all the ingredients except the lard or butter well until a fairly thick batter is obtained. Heat the fat, in 2 or more non-stick sauté pans if possible, until sizzling. Drop in dollops of the batter, flattening the fritters so they are not too thick. Turn the heat down low and fry gently for about 5 minutes on each side or until they feel firm. Repeat the operation until all the batter is used up. Put the fritters on a serving dish as they are made and reserve in a warm oven.

These fritters can also be made with chopped sorrel and/or dandelion as well as the Swiss chard tops.

⤙ Pounti ⤚

Pounti, a dish baked in a bread tin, includes ingredients that are as outlandish as its name is melodious (it derives from an Occitan word, *pontar*, meaning to chop coarsely). They include a typically medieval combination of meat (in some cases), eggs, parsley, Swiss chard tops and prunes. It can also be a dish that is pretty inedible in the hands of the ham-fisted cook: one *pounti* I ordered at an Aurillac restaurant was so greasy that when I put my fork in it and pressed the knife down to cut it a small pool of fat formed on the surface (reminding me, in a horrible flash, of the spam fritters I had to force down at school). I suppose it could have been described as an 'old-fashioned' *pounti*: my neighbour Marie-Louise Bouquier reminds me that in former and less weight-conscious times, when pork fat was an essential source of energy for hard-working, pre-mechanized farmers, greasy *pountis* were the rule. Another Cantal restaurant I went to once, but only once, produced a *pounti* that had neither greenery nor prunes – it looked like a charred Yorkshire pudding. Just occasionally, Auvergnat restaurant chefs can go badly wrong. Such experiences remain, however, very much the exception.

When well made, *pounti* is very different – a light, aromatic and refreshingly clean-flavoured dish with a crisp brown crust and a greenish-beige centre dotted with pleasantly mushy prunes. A proper *pounti* is also good cold, and often used to be included in the baskets of food and drink that were taken out into the fields for hungry harvesters and haymakers in the days when the fields had to be scythed and the crop gathered up with pitchforks.

As always with traditional recipes, there is a wide spectrum of variety in the choice of ingredients. Some claim that *pounti* should ideally be a vehicle for meat leftovers – and a very good one it is. Others argue that *pounti* should contain no meat. It is certainly true to say that in the last century, when Auvergnats could not afford to eat much meat, the meatless *pounti* was the rule (as was the meatless *chou farci*). Meatless, of course, does not necessarily mean vegetarian, as pork fat is used in recipes that call for no meat.

The following recipe, which includes a little meat, was given to me by Yvonne Figeac, who has run a *ferme auberge* with her husband,

Jules, at the hamlet of Cantuel (Cantal) since 1988. The idea behind *fermes auberges*, 'on the farm' restaurants which were introduced in 1978, was to boost tourist activity in the countryside. *Fermes auberges* differ from ordinary restaurants only in the following respects: the farmers enjoy a more favourable tax regime, but in return 80 per cent of what they put on the menu has to have been produced on the farm and they are not allowed to exceed a certain turnover.

Not all regular restaurateurs are pleased with what they regard as unfair competition from *fermes auberges*. It has to be said that the competition is not always unfair: the food offered by some *fermes auberges* is not up to scratch when they try to cut corners.

The Figeacs' *ferme auberge* is by far the best I have come across. Patrons eat in a small log cabin that would not be out of place in a Western. They sit at separate tables, but the menu on a given day is the same for everyone. It might include any of the following: soup, made with the best stock and vegetables, a platter of *charcuterie* (*pâté, saucisson sec* and ham), *pounti, chou farci, bourriols* (p. 27) *farcis au roquefort*, a wonderfully creamy *aligot* (p. 32) with an ivory gloss, roast chicken or duck (two pieces each), salad (lettuce straight from the kitchen garden), a well-chosen cheese platter, and a prune tart (p. 163) which, despite all that has gone before, slips down a treat.

[*For six*]

24 prunes
6 eggs
50g (2 oz) plain flour
30g (1 oz) cornflour
30ml (1fl oz) double cream
100g (3½oz) Swiss chard tops
3 sprigs parsley
1 small onion
200g (7oz) salt pork belly or green streaky bacon
salt
freshly ground pepper

Cook the prunes in water for 15 minutes, if very dry (the moister kind can be infused in boiling water or tea). Break the eggs into a bowl and add the flour, cornflour and cream. Chop the Swiss chard tops, parsley, onion and salt pork or bacon extremely finely and add to the bowl. Add a good pinch of salt and plenty of pepper. Mix vigorously. Incorporate the prunes. Pour the mixture into a 1.2-litre (2-pint) rectangular bread tin. Bake in a fairly hot oven (200°C/400°F/Gas mark 6) for 60 minutes, or until the top is well browned. Remove from oven and allow to cool for 5 minutes before serving.

An even more outlandish cousin of *pounti* is *picaucèl*, which derives from *picar*, another Occitan (p. xxi) word meaning 'to chop coarsely'. Made in the same way as *pounti*, its ingredients include buckwheat flour, ham (sometimes), Swiss chard tops, parsley, eggs, prunes and pears.

◂◂ Farinette ▸▸

Jeanne Chabut (p. 7) was proud of her *farinettes* to the point of pro-selytism. When I had friends to stay, she was keen for them all to sample what she called '*l'omelette du pauvre*' (the poor man's omelette). Sum-moned to her house – which she and her husband built after they had given up running their café (now my house) – for a kind of Auvergnat high tea at 5 p.m., we would troop into her cavernous 'kitchen' and sit down on benches at a long chestnut-wood table. The 'kitchen', as its rough concrete floor betrayed, had been designed as a garage for her husband's bus, which he continued to operate after they had moved. When he died, Jeanne, who had been used to spacious working con-ditions in her café, moved operations out of her tiny kitchen proper into the garage, a room the size and almost the height of a squash court that accommodated, with plenty of space to spare, a kitchen dresser, fridge, freezer, stove, boiler and various more decorative items such as the family's set of copper pans, a copper bed-warmer, a copper *fontaine* (a wash-basin topped by a small reservoir with a tap), and some potted plants. This arrangement was endearingly eccentric – Jeanne told me with relish how her bourgeoisified Paris cousins, who had made a fortune in the restaurant trade, reacted with a mixture of condescension and shock when they first set foot in her new 'kitchen'.

To make our *farinette*, Jeanne would take out her special *farinette* pan, a huge utensil with a non-stick surface of the pre-Teflon generation – a blackened patina that had resulted from decades of constant use (such *farinette* pans are sacrosanct in many households, and must not be used to cook any other dish). She heated generous quantities of lard almost to smoking point, poured the batter into the pan with a sploosh and left it to bubble audibly for three or four minutes. Then, commanding our attention with the authority of a ringmaster, she shook the half-cooked *farinette* with a circular motion so it slithered round the pan with a gently rasping sound that betokened crispness, and, without any further ado, tossed it expertly and confidently into the air so it fell back into the pan on its uncooked side, making the sound of a belly-flop and projecting droplets of lard in all directions. She claimed never to have mis-tossed a *farinette*.

When the *farinette* was cooked, she sliced it up cakewise and doled out our portions, which we then proceeded to wolf. On one memorable occasion, though, we ate our *farinette* with rather less gusto. In the course of a politically argumentative and therefore protracted lunch *chez moi*, we forgot about our 5 p.m. rendezvous down the road. As yet more wine was poured and second helpings of cheese eaten, we lost track of the time. Suddenly, at about 4 p.m., someone remembered we were going to have to eat a *farinette* in an hour's time. A walk was hastily organized in a desperate attempt to work off lunch, but by the time we turned up at Jeanne's house we realized we had not managed to work up any appetite and the *farinette* – a filling dish at the best of times – was going to be an ordeal instead of the usual pleasure. And it so happened that on that particular occasion Jeanne had also generously opened a jar of her home-made *pâté* for us to taste after the *farinette*.

It is ironic that a *farinette* should have played the central role in this anecdote of twentieth-century excess, for historically it is an emblematically frugal dish that was very often eaten by farming people and 'cost' very little to make (its cheap ingredients – flour, milk, lard, eggs – all came from the farm). It is a dish that is often remembered fondly by members of the older generation in Mourjou (hence Jeanne's proselytism), who insist that a *farinette* made on a stove does not taste the same as a *farinette* made over embers in the *cantou* (fireplace). I have heard husbands complain jokingly that their wives do not make *farinettes* 'as good as mum made them'.

Even such a 'modern' chef as Nicole Fagegaltier, of Le Vieux Pont at Belcastel (p. 84), says one of the fondest culinary memories of her childhood is of her mother and grandmother making *pascades* (the name for *farinettes* in the Aveyron) for supper, giving them extra flavour with herbs, or onions, or potatoes, or even meat leftovers. An irresistible dish that sometimes features on her menu today is lamb's sweetbreads served piled up on a small *pascade aux herbes*.

The variety of ingredients that can go into a *farinette* is matched by the variety of their respective proportions. Mostly, though, the *farinette* stands half-way between an omelette and a pancake – it is yellower than a pancake, and springier than an omelette. It has various names in various parts of the Auvergne. As well as *farinette* and *pascade*, it is also called *paschada*, *pachade*, *pascajous* (in which case it contains buckwheat flour) and *petarina*.

Most *farinettes* are meatless, and they have always been traditionally eaten on Fridays as a replacement for *ventrèche* (salt pork belly) and soup (made from meat broth), and during Lent. This custom is reflected in the Aveyronnais name, *pascade*, which derives from the Occitan (p. xxi) word for Easter, *pascas*. The Easter connection also explains why one of the classic versions of *farinette* contains dandelions, which are at their tenderest at around that time of year. Here are two versions of *farinette*. One, which uses yeast, a mixture of buckwheat and wheat flour, and white wine and water instead of the more usual milk, has a clean, sharp taste and almost the texture of a blini. The second, more commonly found version is an ideal vehicle for onions, ham, dandelions and even, if sugar is substituted for salt, cherries.

⊰ Farinette I ⊱

[*For four*]

4 eggs

12g (½oz) dried yeast

280ml (10fl oz) dry white wine

120ml (4fl oz) water

60g (2oz) plain wheat flour

60g (2oz) buckwheat flour

large pinch salt

freshly ground pepper

25g (1oz) butter or lard

Put the eggs, yeast, wine, water, flours, salt and pepper into a liquidizer and blend until a smooth batter is obtained. Check seasoning. Pour into a bowl, cover and leave for at least 2 hours, or overnight. Heat the fat in a large non-stick pan over a high heat until it begins to sizzle. Pour in the batter and continue to cook briskly for 3 or 4 minutes, then turn the heat down to low. When the batter on the upper side of the *farinette* has become sticky rather than liquid, turn it over with a palette knife or fish slice, or by pulling one side of it up towards you with your fingers and flipping it over. Toss only if you feel really confident. Continue to cook over a low heat until the underside is well browned (*farinette* needs to be cooked through, otherwise it is indigestible).

⤙ Farinette II ⤚

[*For four*]
4 eggs
300g (10½oz) plain flour
600ml (1 pint) milk
25g (1oz) butter or lard
large pinch salt
freshly ground pepper

Blend all the ingredients in a liquidizer until a smooth batter is obtained. Check seasoning. Cook following the procedure for Farinette I.

If you want to garnish your *farinette* with onion, ham, dandelions or cherries, proceed as follows:
Onion: peel and chop 1 onion finely, sauté gently in butter or lard in a large non-stick pan until soft, pour the batter over the onion and proceed as for a plain *farinette*.
Ham: cut 100g (3½oz) of raw or cooked ham into strips, sauté gently in butter or lard in a large non-stick pan for 5 minutes, pour the batter (which should be slightly less salted than in the plain version) over the ham and proceed as for a plain *farinette*.
Dandelions: wash 200g (7oz) of dandelions (if they are wild, wash very

thoroughly in vinegary water), blanch for 3 minutes in plenty of salted boiling water, chop coarsely and sauté gently in butter or lard in a large non-stick pan for 5 minutes. Pour the batter over the dandelions and proceed as for a plain *farinette*.

Cherries: proceed as in the general recipe for *farinette*, replacing the pinch of salt with 80g (3oz) of caster sugar. When the batter has been poured into the pan, dot the surface evenly with 200g (7oz) of washed and pitted cherries (if possible wild cherries).

◄◄ Bourriols ►►

Buckwheat (the seed of a starch plant, *Fagopyrum esculentum*, which is not a true cereal) was long considered a poor man's grain, partly because it cannot be made into bread, and partly because it is very hardy and thrives on poor soil. Whole, husked buckwheat grains go into kasha, the staple peasant food of Central Europe and Russia. In Russia, Brittany and the Auvergne, its flour is mixed with wheat flour and used to make leavened pancakes – blinis, *galettes* and these *bourriols*.

Bourriols (the singular and plural forms are the same) used to be commonly eaten in the Auvergne. In his book *Autour de la Ferme dans le Cantal* (1896), Henri Garnier describes *bourriols* as 'fresh and refreshing food' that country people preferred to bread. It was more likely that they ate *bourriols* because they cost less to make than bread. *Bourriols* certainly performed the function of bread and would be eaten with *charcuterie* and cheese. Nowadays when people in Mourjou make *bourriols* they tend to treat them like pancakes and serve them with cream or jam or both.

With the advent of modern fertilizers and farming subsidies, fields of undemanding buckwheat are now a rare sight in the Auvergne. But as recently as 1950, in the Châtaigneraie, buckwheat was an important enough element of the farm economy to feature in the lease of the Fleys family, tenant farmers who used to rent a farmhouse just down the road from me (a building now in the process of being converted into an '*éco-musée*' of the chestnut). Their lease stipulated that each year they give the landlord, or pay him the cash equivalent of, 365 litres of milk, 100 kilos of veal, five piglets, each weighing 20 kilos, and 50 kilos of buckwheat flour.

Few restaurants serve *bourriols* because they are so labour-intensive to make. However, *bourriols* generously stuffed with ham, or Tomme fraîche de Cantal (p. 192), or egg, or any combination of those ingredients, feature on the menu of Le Bouchon Fromager, an excellent little cheese restaurant that Jean-Pierre Morin has opened next door to his cheese shop (7 rue de Buis), by far the best in Aurillac. Rather than risk getting his *bourriols* made in the restaurant itself by a chef possibly unfamiliar with the technique, he orders large quantities of them from a farmer's wife up in the mountains above Aurillac.

She makes them in the traditional way, on a *bourriole*, a very large copper disc 30 centimetres (12 inches) in diameter with sides only 1 centimetre (½ inch) high, which is fixed to a handle 75 centimetres (30 inches) long. She holds her *bourriole* over the embers in her *cantou* (fireplace). As fewer and fewer people make *bourriols* at home, many *bourrioles* have, inevitably perhaps, started a new and highly burnished life as wall decorations. The yeast used for making *bourriols*, which used to be made with a mixture of flour, mashed potato and milk or water, was kept in miniature chestnut-wood barrels called *selhons*. These, too, have become collector's items.

[*To make ten bourriols*]
700ml (24fl oz) skimmed milk
7g (¼oz) yeast
175g (6oz) buckwheat flour
175g (6oz) plain wheat flour
large pinch salt
lard or butter for frying

Warm the milk to blood temperature, pour into a bowl and add the yeast. Stir until dissolved, add the flours and salt, and mix well. Cover and leave overnight in a cool place. Next morning add a little milk if the batter seems too thick. Melt a little fat in a 25-cm/10-in or larger *bourriole* or large pancake pan and spoon in enough batter to cover the surface. When little bubbles appear on the upper side of the *bourriols*, turn it over and cook for a minute or two on the other side. Serve hot or cold, either on the side like bread, or, as at Le Bouchon Fromager, stuff them with ham, cheese and/or egg and heat for 20 minutes in a hot oven (220°C/425°F/Gas mark 7).

Cheese Dishes

The Auvergnats consume very large quantities of cheese, both on its own and in cooked dishes. But, being culinary conservatives, they have evolved relatively few different varieties (p. 189). And of those, only Cantal and its unmatured, unsalted version, Tomme fraîche de Cantal, regularly find their way into cooked preparations. The use of Tomme fraîche in such cheese-potato classics as *truffade* (p. 36) and *aligot* (p. 32) grew out of the primitive kind of cooking that went on in *burons*, the stone huts where cowherds used to live and make (and mature) Cantal during their summer season in the mountains. A proportion of the unmatured Tomme would be consumed on the spot with potatoes from the small vegetable gardens next to the *burons*. Other dishes which call for cheese but which are included in other chapters are: *soupe au fromage* (p. 6), *omelette du curé* (p. 16), *omelette à la Fourme d'Ambert* (p. 18) and *œufs à la cantalienne* (p. 19).

⤙ Patranque ⤚

This concoction of bread and melted cheese is the ancestor of *aligot* (p. 32) and *truffade* (p. 36), both of which evolved when the potato was finally accepted for human consumption in the Auvergne in the late eighteenth century (p. xv). I first encountered it twenty years ago in a tiny restaurant run by two elderly sisters in the village of Salers, perched on a plateau above the valley of the Maronne (Cantal). The restaurant was a riot of lovingly polished wooden furniture. The menu consisted of a short list of local specialities, including *patranque*, which I had never heard of and therefore ordered, after inquiring what went into it. It came piping hot to the table, emitting a strong, tangy aroma that came not so much from the cheese (mild Tomme fraîche de

Cantal) as from the local bread that had been used, which is made from 50 per cent rye flour and 50 per cent wheat flour.

I have never seen *patranque* on a restaurant menu since. The sisters' establishment closed soon afterwards. Once a beautifully preserved, if dour, village of fine sixteenth- and seventeenth-century buildings built of volcanic stone (dark basalt, andesite and trachyte), Salers has since turned into a loud tourist attraction where souvenir shops jostle for space with restaurants, many of which, uncharacteristically for the Auvergne, are rip-off joints.

[*For four to six*]
600g (1lb 5oz) rye bread, fresh or stale
50g (2oz) unsalted butter
400g (14oz) Tomme fraîche de Cantal cheese, sliced
   thinly
4 cloves garlic, finely chopped
salt
freshly ground pepper

Slice the bread and soak it in a little water in a large flat dish. There must be enough water to soften it completely, including its crust. Squeeze out any excess water. Heat the butter over a low heat in a large non-stick sauté pan, add the bread, and stir until it has broken down into a kind of panada. Add the cheese and garlic. When the cheese begins to melt, beat vigorously until the mixture becomes elastic and smooth. Add salt to taste and plenty of pepper.

The *patranque* may be served at this point or left to cook until it acquires a crisp, golden crust underneath. If you choose the latter method, keep the heat as low as possible so as not to burn the garlic.

There exists a similar but more liquid dish, half-way between *patranque* and *soupe au fromage*, which is made with curd cheese instead of Tomme fraîche de Cantal. It goes by the evocative name of *cantamerlou* – 'sing-blackbird' in Occitan (p. xxi) – allegedly because the steam escaping the melted cheese makes a sound like the song of a blackbird.

⤙ Aligot ⤚

Driving through the Aveyron or the Cantal you may see a poster in a shop or café window advertising a mysterious event called an '*aligot géant*'. I say event, because although *aligot* is a dish (of mashed potato with cheese), and *aligot géant* a mammoth version of it, what is in fact being advertised is a rollicking dinner and dance. Such dances are as good an opportunity as any to get acquainted with this most spectacular of dishes.

The last time it was served in *géant* form in Mourjou was in October 1997, when, as usual, it rounded off proceedings at our annual Foire de la Châtaigne (chestnut festival – p. 166). We all packed into a marquee erected next to the village school and sat down at long trestle tables. The temperature outside was well below freezing, and there was no heating in the marquee. But it was soon warmed up by the sheer accumulation of body heat given off by the 340-odd diners. After two starters – soup and a plate of charcuterie – there was a mounting sense of expectancy as news filtered through from the school kitchen next door that the *aligot* was nearly ready. Then it made its triumphal entrance, borne by three strapping young men in one of those very thick, cast-iron cauldrons used for cooking pigswill in. The receptacle was hoisted on to a table, where, to cheers from the assembled company, the men plunged what looked like canoe paddles into it and raised them ceilingwards, trailing a mass of ivory-coloured rubbery strands that dangled down into the mixture below. This was the crucial moment when '*ça file*' (when the *aligot* becomes runny), before which it has not acquired its full creamy taste, and after which – if left on the heat for too long – the strands start breaking and the mixture turns oily.

An hour later, after we had chomped our way through the *aligot* (made with 145 kilos of potatoes, 42 kilos of cheese, 12 litres of cream and 4 kilos of butter), its accompanying *tripoux* (p. 128), a cheese course and an apple tart, the '*soirée dansante style musette*' (fast waltzes) got going. It was a village dance in the best tradition, where anyone was free to invite anyone else for a spin round the floor whether they knew them or not.

Although *aligot* has occasionally featured on restaurant menus in the Cantal for several decades now, it is only recently that it has become as popular in that *département* as in its region of origin, the Rouergue (an old province that corresponds roughly to the Aveyron), and more particularly on the windswept Aubrac plateau. Germaine Gros, of Chez Germaine, a famous restaurant in the village of Aubrac (alt. 1,300 metres), used, when the whim took her, to pour *aligot* over a selected customer's head to prove that '*ça file*' – more to her own enjoyment, it has to be said, than her victim's.

In his fascinating *Dictionnaire des Institutions, Mœurs et Coutumes du Rouergue* (1903), a book that discusses anything from medieval taxes and billiards to crockery and *aligot*, Henri Affre remarked on the muscular qualities required of *aligot*-makers:

It was a dish without which no wedding feast was complete; and it is curious to note that on such occasions its preparation was not the task of the mistress of the house or of her maidservant, but of two guests, of the stronger sex, who, skilled practitioners that they were, left the table at the required moment and went into the kitchen to take charge, with all due care, of that part of the menu.

Aligot is one of the very few dishes which, when made in large quantities, even today remains the responsibility of Auvergnats rather than Auvergnates. This may seem surprising in an area like the Auvergne, which has remained old-fashioned in so many ways. As I pointed out in the Introduction, womenfolk were conditioned to perform the role of beasts of burden up to about the time of the Second World War, and until recently it was customary at mealtimes in some remote mountain households for them to stand and serve their husbands and sons first, before dining themselves in a corner of the *cantou* (fireplace).

Even today, I know of some men of the older generation who would feel deeply uncomfortable about doing any of their wives' allotted tasks (washing, washing up, shopping, cooking, cleaning). If a wife happens to be absent (for an operation, say), her husband will often prefer to take all his meals at the local restaurant rather than cook for himself. When I and my partner split up some years ago, one concerned older villager, imagining that I would be quite helpless without her, asked: 'What are you going to do about meals now?'

The reason the making of *aligot* is an exception to this male-chauvinist ethos is quite simply – as you will have already guessed – that it requires a good deal of muscle power, and that stirring a big saucepan, let alone a pigswill cauldron, of the stuff has more in common with ploughing a field than with cooking.

Perhaps unsurprisingly in view of the almost 'tribal' nature of such events as an *aligot géant* (an excited gathering of people around a large stirred pot), the making of *aligot*, and more particularly worry about whether or not it will 'run' properly, has spawned two myths that are still half-believed by many: one is that *aligot* (like the charcuterie which is prepared just after the slaughter of a pig – p. 71) cannot be made successfully by a woman with a period; the other is that the mixture will not 'run' unless it is always stirred in the same direction.

There are many variants of *aligot*, including a sweet one without garlic and flambéd with rum. It can have chopped parsley in it, lard instead of butter, or, in its more sophisticated 'restaurant' version, much more Tomme fraîche de Cantal and butter as well as generous amounts of double cream. *Aligot* is basically a humble peasant dish which, like *truffade* (p. 36), cowherds used to eat quite often when they took their herds up to the high mountains for the summer (as the only company they had was two, or sometimes three, other men, they were forced willy-nilly to carry out the 'womanly' act of cooking).

Aligot is already a rather indigestible concoction when eaten in large quantities – the mind boggles at the digestive marathon faced by the man who ate a record 2.35 kilos of *aligot* in 15 minutes at an annual *aligot*-eating competition held in Tayac (Aveyron) – and is not, in my opinion, greatly improved by the extra butter, cream and cheese, though these may lend it greater elegance. The richer version does, however, work well when it is used in small quantities, almost like a sauce, to accompany a dish like a steak of Salers or Aubrac beef (Michel Bras, who has a world-famous restaurant near Laguiole, on the Aubrac plateau, uses it in this way). A less rich *aligot* is a good accompaniment for a very salty or piquant main dish such as *saucisses fraîches*, fried liver deglazed with a dash of vinegar, or crisp-fried bacon (always supposing you can lay your hands on bacon that fries crisp these days). *Aligot* can also be eaten on its own as a main course, like *truffade*. Amazingly, however, in view of the amount of garlic it contains, it does not have a great deal of character on its own.

One last word on the mystery that surrounds the etymology of the word *aligot*. Some claim that it derives from *ail* (garlic), but in several areas *aligot* is made without garlic. Others see a connection with the Latin *aliquid* (something). The most likely origin is, however, the Old French *harigoter* (to tear or cut in pieces), which also gives us *haricot de mouton* (mutton stew). Interestingly, the latest thinking on the etymology of the word *haricot* (haricot bean) is that it comes not from a Mexican Indian word, *ayacotl*, but from *haricot* meaning a *ragoût* or stew – a case of a dish giving its own name to one of its ingredients, just as *pistou*, in the Nice area, has come to mean not only a basil-flavoured sauce but basil itself, and *aligot* sometimes refers in the Auvergne to the cheese used in it, Tomme fraîche de Cantal.

Here are two versions of *aligot*, a rich and a less rich one. They are both made in the same way.

⊷ Aligot I ↠

[*For four*]
500g (1lb 2oz) floury potatoes
140g (5oz) double cream
50g (2oz) butter
2 large cloves garlic, very finely chopped
freshly ground pepper
280g (10oz) Tomme fraîche de Cantal cheese, cut into
   very thin slices
salt

⊷ Aligot II ↠

[*For four*]
700g (1lb 9oz) floury potatoes
100–150ml (3½–5½fl oz) milk
30g (1oz) unsalted butter
3 large cloves garlic, very finely chopped
freshly ground pepper

400g (14oz) Tomme fraîche de Cantal cheese, cut into
   very thin slices
salt

Wash and boil the potatoes. Peel while still hot and mash in a heavy
saucepan with the heated cream or milk, butter, garlic and pepper
until a smooth consistency is obtained. Place over a very low heat and
stir in the cheese. Beat vigorously with a strong wooden spoon until
the mixture becomes elastic, add plenty of salt to taste (the cheese is
unsalted) and continue stirring. As the mixture heats up, it becomes
slightly softer. If it remains too stiff add a little more hot milk. As soon
as it makes long bubblegum-like strands when lifted with a spoon,
serve on very hot plates. Guests and any accompanying meat must be
ready and waiting: there is nothing more sullen than an *aligot* that has
cooled off.

⤛ Truffade ⤜

This dish, like the previous one, used to be one of the dishes it was
convenient for Auvergnat cowherds to make when they spent the
summer months up in the mountains, milking their cows and making
Cantal cheese. The ingredients that go into the two dishes are very
similar, yet, thanks to the versatility of potatoes, the result is not at all
the same.

When people see the word *truffade* for the first time on a restaurant
menu, they assume it must contain truffles (*truffes*). There is in fact a
connection even though the mushroom is not and never has been
used in the dish. When the potato was introduced from South America
into the Auvergne toward the end of the eighteenth century, the local
population nicknamed it *trufa* (truffle) in Occitan (p. xxi), or *langue
d'oc*, the language they then spoke almost exclusively. They probably
chose *trufa* because of the potato's shape, earthy origin and colour (the
first potatoes that came to France were fairly dark-skinned). Although
given the name of a much-prized delicacy, the potato initially aroused
much suspicion when it was introduced into the Auvergne (p. xv).

There are two schools of thought on how a genuine *truffade* should
be made in its true home, the Cantal *département*. In the course of

many conversations with local cooks, both amateur and professional, I found some people who swore that on no account must the potatoes or the cheese get a crust – though they did not object, curiously, to this happening if the dish was reheated. A more or less equal number of other people were equally vehement that a proper *truffade* should acquire a crisp golden crust and be turned out on to a plate. The same divergence is also found in books on Auvergne cookery.

When I recently had the nerve-racking experience of having to demonstrate the making of *truffade* on an Auvergne television channel that was interested in the fact that a Scot was writing a book on the food of the Auvergne, I opted to make the crisp, turned-out version. Fortunately for me, the *truffade* turned out fine (in both senses). After a shot of its crisp, browned surface, the ingredients and method were flashed up on screen. Some local viewers belonging to the non-crisp camp were apparently bemused by the fact that a Scot should re-commend the crisp version of *truffade*. Yet Suzanne Robaglia, in her 'bible' of traditional Auvergnat cuisine, *Margaridou* (first published in 1935), tells her readers to turn out the *truffade*, 'which should have the appearance of a golden cake'.

I give both versions here. One of the joys of Tomme fraîche de Cantal (p. 192) is the way it completely changes as it goes from a raw to a cooked state. Raw, it is fresh and creamy tasting, but has no particular character (it is unsalted) and is best eaten mozzarella-style with anchovies or anchovy paste. But once it melts, and more particu-larly once it and the potatoes acquire a scrunchy brownish-orange crust, it becomes a more moreish dish than any I know of.

⊷ Truffade I ⊶

This recipe, the uncrisp version, was given to me by Yvonne Puech, of the Hôtel Beauséjour in Calvinet (p. 108).

[*For four*]
60g (2oz) fat from raw ham (failing that, use green bacon fat)
800g (1lb 12oz) potatoes, washed, peeled and thinly sliced
salt
200g (7oz) Tomme fraîche de Cantal cheese, cut into thin slices

Chop the fat into small pieces and melt in a large non-stick sauté pan. Add the potatoes, mix well so that they are well coated with fat, cover and cook over an extremely low heat for at least 30 minutes. When the potatoes are soft, add salt to taste (the amount will depend on the saltiness of the fat used; the cheese is unsalted). Lay the cheese slices over the potatoes and cover. When the cheese has completely melted, stir it thoroughly into the potatoes and serve immediately. *Truffade* made this way goes well with a plain roast of pork, veal or beef, as it soaks up the meat juices.

⤙ Truffade II ⤚

This is the crisp version of *truffade*. Because it contains some Cantal as well as Tomme fraîche it has more character and is really at its best as a main course. The quantities are correspondingly larger than for the first version. You can increase them even further if you wish, as I have never known a *truffade* made this way not to be finished. The parsley is not a traditional addition, but I think it brightens up what can be a rather indigestible, if absolutely delicious, dish.

[*For four*]
1kg (2lb 4oz) potatoes
30g (1oz) unsalted butter
3 tablespoons frying oil
large pinch salt
freshly ground pepper
150g (5½oz) Tomme fraîche de Cantal cheese, cut into
  thin slices
150g (5½oz) young Cantal cheese, cut into thin slices
2 tablespoons parsley, finely chopped
3 large cloves garlic, finely chopped

Peel the potatoes and cut into very small dice. (Young potatoes, which are nicer with their skins left on, should be rinsed in running water after being diced and dried well before you fry them.) Heat the butter and oil in a large non-stick sauté pan (absolutely essential for this version of the dish), put in the potatoes and cook over a medium heat for about 15 minutes, turning them over frequently with a wooden spatula.

When the potatoes are nearly cooked and slightly browned, add salt and plenty of pepper. Lay the slices of cheese on top, cover, turn down the heat to low and cook for about 5 minutes, shaking the pan from time to time to make sure the melting cheese does not stick to the bottom.

When the cheese has completely melted and is bubbling merrily, strew the surface evenly with the parsley and garlic, mixed together. Turn up the heat to medium. Shake the pan from time to time, but do not stir its contents. Prise the edge of the *truffade* away from the side of the pan: if it is golden brown and a toasted-cheese smell is coming up from the dish, you can be sure that the bottom is well-browned and the *truffade* ready. Give the pan a good shake to make sure the *truffade* has come away from the bottom of the pan. Slide on to a large and hot serving dish or, better, turn it out on to the dish (wearing an apron to protect yourself from the eventuality of flying globules of melted cheese), so it can sport its appetizing crust. Serve immediately.

The reason for putting the parsley and garlic on top, *after* the cheese has melted, is to prevent any bits of garlic coming into contact with the hot pan, burning and giving the dish a bitter taste.

Be sure to use young Cantal, which has a thin rind and smells creamy, and not a mature Cantal with a strong tang to it, which is not appropriate for this dish.

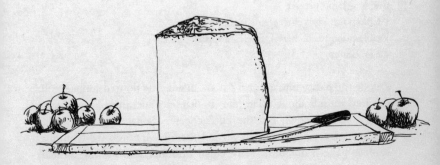

✦ Rissoles de Saint-Flour ✦

These *rissoles* are still sold on market days in Saint-Flour (Cantal). An ancient and once powerful seat of the Catholic church, Saint-Flour is perched on a rocky outcrop at an altitude of 881 metres. Icy winds from the nearby plateau sweep through its streets for much of the year, and the feeling of cold is, to me at least, accentuated by the dark and dour basalt from which its houses and cathedral are built. Its motto, referring to numerous unsuccessful attempts by the English to take the town during the Hundred Years War, is: 'Nul ne te prit jamais de force que le vent' ('No one except the wind ever took you by force'). No wonder people at market need these piping hot *rissoles* to resist the elements.

The French word *rissole* has nothing to do with the British rissole and all that it evokes. It is a pastry turnover identical to a *chausson*. The French word comes from the Latin *russeolus* (reddish-brown), no doubt because *rissoles* brown in the oven. The English rissole was sometimes spelled 'rishew' in Elizabethan times and, according to one theory, derives from the Norman French *réchauffées* (reheated meats).

[*For four*]
400g (14oz) chilled flaky pastry
170g (6oz) well-drained curd cheese
110g (4oz) young Cantal cheese, cut into slivers
3 egg yolks
pinch salt
pinch freshly grated nutmeg
freshly ground pepper
1 tablespoon fresh chives, finely chopped
1 tablespoon fresh chervil, finely chopped
1 egg, beaten

Divide the pastry into 4 equal parts. On a lightly floured surface, roll out into rounds about 15cm (6in) in diameter and 4mm (⅛in) thick. Into a mixing bowl, put the curd cheese, Cantal, egg yolks, salt, nutmeg, plenty of pepper, chives and chervil. Mix thoroughly until a smooth paste is obtained. Place equal amounts of this filling on half of each round of pastry 1cm (½in) from the edges. Moisten the edges with beaten egg and fold the pastry over the filling. Press the edges down well and crimp with a fork. Brush the whole surface of the *rissoles* with the rest of the beaten egg. Place on a lightly oiled baking sheet, and bake in a fairly hot oven (190°C/375°F/Gas mark 5) for about 45 minutes.

These *rissoles* can also be made with short pastry and deep-fried. They are correspondingly heavier. Some authorities swear that genuine Saint-Flour *rissoles* of the kind sold on market days in that town always used to be made that way. Possibly. But then, before the advent of microwaves, deep-frying was the most suitable cooking technique for an open-air market.

In another version a little diced ham is added to the cheese and egg filling.

Fish

In the devoutly Catholic Auvergne, fish was long prized as Friday's fare by those families who could afford to buy it, mostly in the form of *morue* (salt cod) or, in the northern Aveyron and southern Cantal, stockfish (wind-dried cod). Those of slenderer means either had to catch their own fish or fall back on *farinettes* (p. 23) and egg or cheese dishes. Today, partly as a result of Vatican II, the practice of not eating meat on Friday has fallen largely into disuse in the Auvergne, though fish is usually still available on that day in school and company canteens.

The countless streams, rivers and lakes of the Auvergne abound in fish of all kinds. They include trout, salmon, tench, gudgeon, roach, carp and char (though not herring, included in a list of freshwater fish by a well-known American book on Burgundian cuisine). But agricultural pollution has had a devastating effect on many streams and rivers, particularly affecting trout and crayfish, which are sensitive to even low levels of pollution. So that anglers can continue to practise their sport, rivers are often stocked with trout fry at the beginning of the year.

The Auvergnats mostly cook their fish in a classic, unfussy way – baked, *meunière* (fried in butter and garnished with chopped parsley and lemon juice), in a *court-bouillon* or, in the case of very small fish, deep-fried like whitebait (*friture*). But there are three specifically Auvergnat fish dishes which may be unfamiliar to many people: the sumptuous *tourte de saumon de Brioude* (p. 48), *truite au lard* (p. 43), and *estofinado* (p. 59), a dish made with stockfish, whose presence in the lower Massif Central is an enduring mystery.

⤙ Truite au lard ⤚

Go for a walk in the Auvergne and you will never be far from the sound of running water. Its mountains form a huge rainwater catchment area, with the result that springs seem to gush from every crevice. Farmers cunningly divert the water that tumbles down streams into *rigoles*, mini-canals no more than a foot or so wide which run almost horizontally along the top of steep fields and, through seepage, irrigate the pasture below before rejoining the stream farther down.

The streams, and even some of the larger *rigoles*, are an ideal habitat for trout, which are eagerly sought after by local anglers and highly prized as food. The day the fishing season opens, driving on small mountain roads becomes hazardous: they are thronged with over-excited anglers in search of an ideal *coin à truites*. They mostly use worms and grasshoppers as bait, though the occasional fly-fisherman is to be seen on larger rivers. Less orthodox – and illegal – methods include tickling, which requires great skill, and the much more expeditious discharging of a shotgun into the water – the trout are stunned and can be fished out with a net.

In recent years, anglers' hauls have become increasingly meagre, and local fishing associations have had to stock streams with trout fry. One does not have to look far to put one's finger on the reason for this state of affairs: pollution. While the air of the Auvergne is mostly as clean as any in France, except in the few areas where there is heavy industry, the quality of its water has been badly affected by farmers, who can increasingly afford, thanks to EU subsidies, to blanket their fields with nitrates, herbicides and pesticides. Because much farm terrain is steep, it takes no more than a heavy storm to wash the poison straight into the nearest stream. When quizzed about their responsibility, farmers – many of whom are keen anglers – whinge about the devastating effects of their wives' washing powder or the powerful detergents used by slaughterhouses or milk co-operatives to clean their plant. Although such pollutants do have a harmful effect, at least when the waste water does not go through a water treatment plant, it is the farmers themselves who are the main culprits. In this, they are as hypocritical as the message the nitrate fertilizer manufacturers blazon prominently on their sinister 100 kilo plastic bags of white powder: '*Respectez nos rivières, respectez la dose*'.

This does not mean that every stream is polluted at all times, or that the fish taken from them are unfit to eat. It is just that, like crayfish (p. 50), trout are extremely sensitive to low levels of pollution.

A common way of cooking trout in the Auvergne is with crisp-fried raw ham. The two flavours combine surprisingly well. Although some versions of the recipe call for the fat of green bacon, or even of smoked bacon, *truite au lard* properly uses the fat trimmed off raw ham. True Auvergnats insist that slightly stale fat produces a tastier result. I would agree, while insisting on the word 'slightly'.

There is an Auvergnat saying which goes: the trout should swim three times – in water, in the frying-pan and on the plate. The saying dates from poorer times, when fat was positively perceived as a cheap source of energy for people who needed to be able to perform what would today seem to be extraordinary feats of manual labour. In our more weight-conscious times, we mostly prefer our food not to be 'swimming' in fat.

[*For four*]

4 trout of about 250g (9oz) each

30g (1oz) plain flour

freshly ground pepper

salt

100g (3½oz) raw ham fat (if possible, cut from a thick
    slice) or, failing that, salt pork belly fat or unsmoked
    bacon fat, trimmed of rind

1 large clove garlic, finely chopped

2 tablespoons flat-leaf parsley, finely chopped

1 tablespoon best wine or cider vinegar

Clean the trout, flour lightly and season with pepper and a very little salt (to allow for the salt in the ham fat). Cut the fat into 5mm (¼in) squares or dice, and fry gently in a non-stick frying-pan large enough to accommodate the 4 trout in a single layer (if you do not have a large enough pan, cook the fish in 2 batches, keeping the first batch piping hot while cooking the second; alternatively, use 2 frying-pans). When the ham fat pieces are light brown and crisp, remove and set aside, leaving the rendered fat in the pan. Turn up the heat. When the fat is just on the point of smoking, add the trout and fry over a medium heat for about 6 minutes per side, or until the skin is crisp.

Transfer the trout to a very hot serving dish. Discard most of the fat from the pan. Reheat the ham fat pieces briefly in the pan and arrange over and around the fish. Put the garlic, parsley and vinegar into the pan, deglaze briskly and pour over the trout. Serve immediately. The trout may be served on their own as a first course, or with boiled new potatoes as a main course.

Gourmand de truite à la châtaigne en paupiette ◄◄ de chou vert et ventrèche croquante ►►

The Hôtel du Commerce in Saint-Constant, a village 10 kilometres from Mourjou, was for a long time a small country hotel-restaurant that enjoyed a solid reputation for traditional food. A Havas guide to the Auvergne (1948) mentions as one of its specialities *faude*, another word for *falette* (p. 136). When I moved to the Châtaigneraie twenty years ago, it continued to offer good basic Auvergnat cuisine at very Auvergnat prices (i.e. low).

In 1994, it was taken over by a young couple, Pierre and Sylvie Ratier, who changed its name to Auberge des Feuillardiers (*feuillardiers* are people who make barrel hoops from chestnut branches split down the middle). They also proceeded to transform the place into one of the best restaurants for kilometres around.

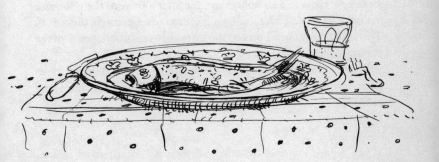

Pierre's parents had tried their chance in Paris, like so many other Auvergnats, but came back to their native Cantal after a twelve-year stint because they were 'homesick'. Pierre attended Toulouse's prestigious catering school, the Ecole Hôtelière, then moved to Paris, where he gained precious experience working at the Jockey Club and the Ritz. At the Ritz he rose to the position of '*demi-chef de partie (entremets)*' – the *entremets* being, curiously, vegetables, soups and hot *entrées* such as *soufflés*. The legendary chef of the Ritz at the time, Guy Legay, was a hard taskmaster. The highest praise Pierre could get out of him was: 'Maybe we'll make something of you.' Pierre emerged with a cast-iron culinary technique. As he was not interested in making a career in the world of prestigious restaurants owned by banks or business groups – he had always wanted to be his own boss – he left the glitz of the Ritz for the remote and peaceful environment of Saint-Constant.

He was determined to stay in what he rather alarmingly calls '*gastro*' (*cuisine gastronomique*), rather than carry on with the rustic style of cooking practised by his predecessors. It was no easy task persuading the culinarily conservative locals to accept his imaginative cuisine, even though it was often firmly rooted in the Auvergnat tradition (to wit the present recipe). They might, for example, ask testily: 'Why is there no *pounti* on the menu?' Many were flummoxed by the occasional presence of ingredients as 'exotic' as mace, cardamom and dill – though I did see one local customer hold up a sprig of dill, ask the rest of the table what they thought it was (no one hazarded a guess), put it gingerly into his mouth, masticate and, in the end, approve (it probably reminded him of the taste of the Ricard he had just had as an apéritif). Gradually, though, Pierre managed to persuade his customers to try some new tastes and combinations, and after four years the restaurant has built up quite a local following on top of its clientele of tourists. This is due in no small part to the extremely reasonable prices of the Ratiers' four set-price menus.

Pierre's way of doing trout subtly combines the different types of sweetness contained in the trout flesh, chestnuts, cream and cabbage.

[*For four*]

4 trout weighing about 250g (9oz) each
2 tablespoons olive oil
1 carrot, finely sliced
1 leek, finely sliced
1 branch celery, finely sliced
1 bay leaf
1 sprig fresh sage
3 cloves garlic, halved
200ml (7fl oz) good white wine
500ml (18fl oz) water
200ml (7fl oz) double cream
200g (7oz) cooked fresh or frozen chestnuts, or
  unsweetened tinned chestnuts
salt
freshly ground pepper
1 cabbage weighing 500g (1lb 2oz)
4 thin slices salt pork belly or green streaky bacon
200g (7oz) unsalted butter, cut into small dice

Fillet (or get your fishmonger to fillet) the trout, leaving the skin on. Pull out any remaining tiny bones with tweezers. Set aside the bones, large and small, for the *fumet*.

Heat 1 tablespoon of olive oil in a medium-sized saucepan and fry the carrot, leek, celery, herbs and garlic for a few minutes. Add the trout trimmings and bones and the white wine, reduce over a high heat for 2 minutes, add water to cover the ingredients, and simmer for 30–35 minutes. Put through a fine strainer or *chinois* and reduce the liquid until only about 250ml (9fl oz) of *fumet* is left.

Put the cream in a small saucepan over a medium heat and reduce by two-thirds. Away from the heat, add the cooked (for procedure, see p. 186) or tinned chestnuts, and mash coarsely to produce a thick purée. Heat 1 tablespoon of olive oil in a non-stick sauté pan. Fry the fillets over a high heat, skin side down, for 2 minutes, season with salt and pepper on the flesh side, and set aside. Pull the leaves off the cabbage, wash thoroughly, and blanch in plenty of fiercely boiling salted water for 5 minutes. Drain the cabbage leaves, refresh them under cold running water and remove their ribs. On a flat surface, lay out 2 cabbage leaves so they overlap slightly and place a trout fillet in the middle across the overlap. Spread a quarter of the purée on to the fillet, cover with a second fillet, and fold over the cabbage leaves to form a *paupiette*. Repeat the operation with the other trout fillets. Place the *paupiettes*, fold side down, in a lightly oiled baking dish into which they fit tightly. Bake in a moderate oven (180°C/350°F/Gas mark 4) for 10–12 minutes. Keep warm.

While the *paupiettes* are cooking, fry 4 thin slices of salt pork belly or green streaky bacon (*ventrèche*) in a non-stick sauté pan, without any fat, until crisp. Dab with kitchen roll. Reheat the *fumet*. When the *fumet* comes to the boil, whisk the diced and softened butter vigorously into it, piece by piece. Pour the sauce over the *paupiettes*, top with slices of *ventrèche* and serve immediately.

(Auberge des Feuillardiers, Route de Saint-Santin, 15600 Saint-Constant. Tel. 04 71 49 10 06.)

❧ Tourte de saumon de Brioude ❧

Salmon once teemed in all the larger rivers of the Auvergne. In the early nineteenth century wealthy British anglers found it worth their while to travel all the way to the river Truyère, which flows into the Lot at Entraygues, in search of good salmon fishing. Salmon disappeared from the upper Lot in about 1860, when weirs were built on the river. The only Auvergne river where the fish is found today is the Allier.

Our attitudes to salmon have changed down the years. It has a lot to do with availability and its converse, rarity. When salmon was extremely common in the Auvergne, it loomed very large in people's diets and was consequently looked down on: in the nineteenth century, monks at the monastery of Lavoûte-Chilhac, near Brioude, became so sick of eating salmon that they begged their abbot not to serve it more than three days a week. The fish was held in such contempt it was even served to prisoners.

Things had changed by Escoffier's time, towards the end of the century. By then, salmon had become scarcer and was deemed worthy of appearing on the finest tables. Escoffier argued, rightly to my mind, that if cod, then common, was as scarce as salmon it would have been just as highly prized. Today, with the advent of fish farms, salmon, both fresh and smoked, has once again become widely available and affordable, while cod supplies are under threat from over-fishing. Maybe the scales are about to be tipped back the other way, and cod will gain the upper hand in the appreciation stakes.

Those who still love salmon – and I include myself – will find that this salmon pie, with its delicate accompanying flavours of cream, mushrooms and herbs, gets the very best out of the fish.

[*For six*]

2kg (4lb 7oz) salmon or 1kg (2lb 4oz) salmon fillets
200ml (7fl oz) double cream
300g (10½ oz) unsalted butter
200g (7oz) fairy ring mushrooms or cèpes, finely
    chopped
large pinch nutmeg
salt
freshly ground pepper
700g (1lb 9oz) short pastry
1 egg, beaten
2 tablespoons chervil, finely chopped
3 tablespoons tarragon, finely chopped
juice ½ lemon

Fillet (or get your fishmonger to fillet) the raw salmon, and remove the skin and bones. Pull out any remaining tiny bones with tweezers. Slice half the salmon into thin escalopes. Blend the rest with the cream and 100g (3½oz) of the butter. Incorporate the chopped mushrooms, nutmeg, and salt and pepper to taste.

Divide the pastry into 2 pieces, one slightly larger than the other. On a lightly floured surface, roll out the larger piece to a circle about 6mm (¼in) thick and 30cm (12in) in diameter, and place on a lightly oiled baking sheet. Put the blended mixture neatly and compactly on to the centre of the pastry, leaving a 4cm (1½in) margin free at the edge. Arrange the salmon slices on top so they overlap slightly. Season with salt and pepper. Roll out the other piece of dough to the same thickness and place it over the filling; it should be large enough to cover it completely. Fold the edge of the bottom round of pastry back over the edge of the top round, fold again so the border rests against the enclosed filling and seal well by crimping with the thumb and fingers. Brush the surface with beaten egg, and cut one or two slits in it with a sharp knife. Bake in a fairly hot oven (190°C/375°F/Gas mark 5) for 45–60 minutes or until the pastry begins to turn golden brown. Cover with aluminium foil towards the end of cooking if the pastry seems to be about to burn.

After putting the pie into the oven, melt the rest of the butter gently and add the chervil, tarragon and lemon juice. Leave to infuse in a warm place. When the pie is nearly cooked, reheat the butter mixture, add salt and pepper to taste and beat vigorously. Serve the pie immediately on hot plates, with the sauce spooned over it.

⤙ Ecrevisses ⤚

Poaching – in the sense of shooting or fishing out of season rather than on somebody else's property – is second nature to many Auvergnats, particularly those of the male gender. Or perhaps it would be more accurate to say 'was': that most highly prized quarry of poachers, crayfish, has almost completely vanished from Auvergne streams and rivers in the past ten years. Local farmers claim they have been wiped out by an American-imported disease. But it is more likely that their environment has quite simply become too polluted for them to survive (it takes very little pollution to kill crayfish). When I first moved to the Châtaigneraie (p. viii) there were still just enough crayfish for the authorities to allow them to be fished two or three days a year; nowadays, the official season usually lasts only one day, but is sometimes completely cancelled.

The ingenuity of Auvergnats when it came to catching crayfish knew no bounds (the activity has become so rare that the past tense is perhaps more appropriate). Some of the techniques they employed were legal. Most people used a *balance*, a metal ring with a loose wire net dangling from it which collapses flat on the river bed, but whose sides rise and imprison the crayfish when it is raised from the water; they would bait it with bits of high meat or dead frogs (crayfish are scavengers), sometimes dipped in Pernod, an apparently irresistible flavour for the crayfish, and lower it into one of those deeper, still parts of a stream or river where the crayfish lurk among tree roots.

Others used a more rudimentary method: they would allow a sheep's head to rot, tie a piece of string to it, drop it into the water, wait for the crayfish to burrow into it, then yank it out of the water. Illegal at any time were such techniques as going out at night with a powerful lamp to attract the creatures, or pouring bleach or quicklime into the river, which stunned or killed the crayfish and any other fish that happened to be in that stretch of water. People in my village chuckle when they recall the case of a local man whose method was rather too drastic: he lobbed a homemade bomb full of oxyacetylene into a river pool, and it blew all the water – and fish – into the surrounding woods.

The gendarmes, who have very little to do in the virtually crime-free Châtaigneraie, used rather to enjoy dressing up in camouflage leotards and hiding in the woods near streams in the hope of catching a poacher and giving him – or, much more rarely, her – a hefty fine.

Auvergnats over a certain age mourn the passing of the golden age when crayfish were plentiful. Their eyes glint as they describe, with broad gestures of the hands, the width and the height of the sacks full of crayfish they used to bring back from the river. Many fondly remember catching and consuming their first crayfish as children.

Live crayfish are, however, still available in the Auvergne – from fishmongers, who fly them in from Yugoslavia or Poland. An enterprising fishmonger in Aurillac has a fleet of fish vans that travel the length and breadth of the surrounding countryside bringing fresh fish to people's doorsteps. Every Wednesday, at 4 p.m. sharp, the fish man announces his arrival in the village square in front of my house by hooting insistently. One day, he opened up his van to reveal a large basket of live and rather active crayfish. A friend who was staying with me insisted we should buy some. I agreed, on condition it was he who cooked them. This he did when the time came, dropping the crayfish from their plastic bag into a saucepan full of boiling water, hastily clamping down the saucepan lid and thrusting the bag into the rubbish bin as though exorcizing his 'murder'. The crayfish were excellent. But later during the meal we saw to our horror that a live crayfish was hobbling across the floor: my friend had not emptied the bag properly. We could not bring ourselves to boil up some more water specially to cook the brave survivor, so I scooped it up and drove it down to a nearby stream where, in the light of a torch, I saw it scamper vigorously away. But I could not help wondering how long it would survive the polluted water.

We ate the crayfish in the simplest Auvergnat way: plain, after being cooked in a carefully flavoured *court-bouillon*. Freshly-made mayonnaise goes well with crayfish done in this way, but I feel that they are even better tasted on their own, when they can be appreciated for 'the rich delicacy of their unassisted flavour' – an inspired phrase (quoted by Alan Davidson in his *A Kipper for My Tea*) applied to puffballs by the extraordinary Reverend Charles David Badham, MD, author of *A Treatise on the Esculent Funguses of England* (1847), and coiner of the verifiably true apophthegm: 'In France, the dinner is the thought of the morning, and sometimes the business of the day.'

[*For six*]
1 litre (35fl oz) good white wine
1 litre (35fl oz) water
1 carrot, sliced
1 small onion, sliced
1 large shallot, sliced
20 crushed peppercorns
1 clove
10 grains aniseed
1 sprig thyme
1 sprig tarragon
1 bay leaf
25g (1oz) salt
zest of ¼ lemon
48 live crayfish

Put the wine and water into a large saucepan. Add all the solid ingredients except the crayfish and bring to the boil. Simmer for 30 minutes. Bring to a fast boil, empty the crayfish into the liquid (making sure none are left clinging to the inside of the bag), cover and simmer for 10 minutes. Strain, keeping the *court-bouillon* for a soup or the basis of a sauce. Serve immediately. Crayfish cooked in this way are, in my opinion, even better cold.

Farçous de légumes et châtaignes,
↞ nage d'huîtres de Marennes ↠

Louis-Bernard Puech, known to friends and relations as Loulou, is nothing if not persistent. When he was studying at the Toulouse Ecole Hôtelière in the early seventies, he decided that he wanted to work with the great Lucien Vanel, then owner-chef of the city's most highly regarded restaurant. So one day the young Loulou dropped in on Vanel and asked him if by any chance he needed anyone to help him out in the kitchen. Vanel, in the best boorish tradition of top chefs, threw him out on his ear. A few months later Loulou tried again – with the same result. At his third attempt, he managed to elicit something more than abuse: by that time Vanel was more than a little intrigued by the lad's doggedness, and asked him where he came from. When Loulou said, 'Calvinet, Cantal,' Vanel, who (as Loulou knew) was born in Lacapelle-Marival, a village 60 kilometres from Calvinet, gave him a job.

After working with Vanel, then with Claude Peyrot at Le Vivarois in Paris (three Michelin rosettes), Loulou returned to Calvinet, which is 5 kilometres from Mourjou, to take over the Hôtel Beauséjour, his parents' hotel-restaurant. His no-nonsense father, Marcel, greeted him with the words: 'You've been on holiday long enough.' There he showed equal persistence in his quest for perfection (the establishment already had a red R in the Michelin guide). With firm encouragement from his wife, Isabelle, who has a pharmacy in the same village, he battled hard to improve his already considerable culinary skills by going on training courses with leading restaurants (L'Ambroisie in Paris, Le Jardin des Sens in Montpellier, La Côte d'Or in Saulieu). His efforts paid off: in 1996 he was awarded a Michelin rosette.

Another lasting influence on Loulou's culinary style has been his mother, Yvonne (p. 108). She remembers how, as a boy, he would come and sniff what was cooking on the stove as soon as he got back from school. He still uses her recipes for vol-au-vent cases and for a succulent, slowly braised ham dish where the sauce is given consistency by generous quantities of pork rind (which is removed after cooking).

Loulou is a stickler for top-quality *produits du terroir* (products firmly rooted in the local rural tradition) and mostly uses local suppliers. He gets his meat from Raymond Vigier (p. 126) in the same village of Calvinet, his fruit and vegetables from the itinerant Daniel Ville (p. 143), and his *foie gras* from Delclaux (p. 102).

Although his cuisine has a strong element of what he calls '*terroir réinterprété*', Loulou is perhaps most at home with fish and regularly drives 40 kilometres to Aurillac's fish market to pick up the best of what is on offer that day. The recipe he has given me combines products of the *terroir* and of the sea. Originally, the dish consisted of the *farçous* on their own, without an oyster sauce. They were a variant of the traditional *farçous* (p. 19), which he served as *amuse-gueule* or *mise-en-bouche* (posh parlance for appetizers), topped with a very thin slice of raw ham fat, the size of a large postage stamp, fried to crackling crispness. The combination of Swiss chard top, chestnut, celeriac and ham fat was a real winner. I remember an official reception in Aurillac where several platters of *amuse-gueule* – which takes no '*s*' in the plural – provided by local chefs, including Loulou, were being handed round with drinks. Loulou's offerings disappeared in a trice, with some guests even lunging immediately for a second *farçou* after tasting the first, while the unimaginative little squares of bread topped with smoked salmon, *rillettes* or lump eggs that the other chefs had brought were eaten at a more decorous pace.

Loulou then did a bit of daring lateral thinking and added the oyster sauce to the *farçous*. The combination may sound outlandish, but works very well: tasting is believing.

[*For six*]

2 sticks celery

100g (3½oz) celeriac

150g (5½oz) Swiss chard stalks

150g (5½oz) fresh or frozen chestnuts, peeled (for procedure, see p. 186)

30g (1oz) lard

salt

freshly ground pepper

150g (5½oz) Swiss chard tops

piece of pig's caul measuring 20 × 30cm (8 × 12in)

6 *fines de claires* oysters

juice ½ lemon
50ml (2fl oz) double cream
40g (1½oz) unsalted butter

Chop the celery, celeriac and Swiss chard stalks very finely (to the size of garden peas). Boil in salted water for 10 minutes and set aside. Chop the chestnuts very finely and fry gently in the lard until slightly browned. Put the diced vegetables and chestnuts into a mixing bowl, add salt and pepper to taste, and mix thoroughly. Blanch the Swiss chard tops for 1 minute in salted boiling water. Remove and cut into 6 squares measuring 10 × 10cm (4 × 4in). Spread out the pig's caul and cut into 6 squares of the same size. Spoon a dollop of the filling on to each square of Swiss chard top and roll up to form a *paupiette*. Wrap up in the pig's caul. Bake in a hot oven (200°C/400°F/Gas mark 6) for 15 minutes.

Open the oysters and put them and their water into a blender. Add the lemon juice and blend thoroughly. Put through a fine drum sieve or *chinois*. Bring the resulting sauce to the boil in a small saucepan and add the cream. Put the *farçous* on to very hot plates. Whisk the softened butter vigorously into the sauce, pour round the *farçous* and serve immediately.

⤙ Morue à l'auvergnate ⤚

After I had been living in Mourjou for some years, Louis-Bernard Puech of the Hôtel Beauséjour (see previous recipe) told me that a Mourjou man, Roger Lacipière, was making a name for himself as owner-chef of a bistro in the Sorbonne area of Paris. Mimi Cantarel, a Mourjou woman who had been to school with Lacipière, ate at his restaurant every time she visited her fireman son in the capital. 'It's a very good place,' she told me. 'And you get plenty to eat, unlike some restaurants in Paris.' Slightly apprehensive as to the implications of that last remark – Auvergnats tend to prize quantity above quality in restaurants – I decided to try out his bistro, Les Fontaines, one day during a Paris trip when I happened to be in the area. I almost missed it as I walked up the Rue Soufflot towards the Panthéon: Les Fontaines looks more like an ordinary bustling Paris café, with a glass-walled terrace projecting on to the pavement, than a restaurant. It was 12.15 and I got the last available table. The menu, handwritten and roneoed every day, offered a tempting range of classical and more unusual dishes at prices which by Paris standards were more than reasonable. I chose a *salade d'épinards crus aux joues de raie* as a starter (not cheeks of skate, in fact, but pieces cut from the tail, which are known as 'skate nobs' in English). There was such a hefty layer of steamed skate on the spinach that almost no green was to be seen. The salad was perfectly dressed and the fish ultra-fresh, but so generously served I felt it should have been classified as a fish course rather than a starter.

My next dish was a *ragoût d'agneau de lait à la provençale*. It came in a little copper casserole, with boiled potatoes on the side. I lifted the lid: inside there were thirteen (admittedly small) pieces of lamb in a deliciously garlicky and tomatoey sauce. The last time I had been defeated by quantity in a restaurant was when I was served half a large breaded chicken at a Weinstub in Vienna – but on that occasion a doggie bag was provided. With great reluctance and embarrassment – '*Monsieur a fini?*' the waiter asked quizzically – I had to leave several pieces of lamb in the casserole. But my fears about quantity elbowing out quality had been completely allayed: this was *cuisine bourgeoise* of the highest order.

When I got to know Roger, I naturally wanted to know what prompted such extraordinary generosity. The secret emerged gradually as he told me the story of his career in the restaurant business. Like many an Auvergnat (p. xv), he went up to Paris as a young man to work in the catering trade, after his elder brother had got the family farm. He found a job easily thanks to the Auvergnat network in the capital, first as a waiter, then as manager of the Restaurant Santer. Very early on he got into the habit of going to Les Halles, Paris's central food market, in the early hours of the morning to buy food for the next day's meals. Being a gregarious sort of fellow, he became friends with many suppliers.

But soon Roger began to tire of choosing produce for others to cook. He had always adored good food: his earliest culinary memory is of catching a whiff, from outside his grandmother's house, of the *civet de lapin* she was cooking gently on the edge of the kitchen range. 'She always used mature rabbits – they taste better. She killed the animal by putting a funnel into its mouth and pouring *gnole* [homemade brandy] into it. That way she got rid of the rabbit-hutch smell.' It was she who told Roger he should become a cook. And from the age of twelve on, he did indeed cook for the family when his parents were away.

But he never went on to have any formal training. While managing the Restaurant Santer, he picked up the basics of classic cuisine from Jeannette, a bad-tempered and often drunken chef, one of whose many idiosyncrasies was that she would change her chef's outfit every time it got spattered with food (which was of course often). Later, Roger learnt some more sophisticated culinary skills from Henri, a man who had worked at the world-famous Grand Véfour restaurant in Paris for sixteen years.

Shortly after taking over Les Fontaines in 1985, Roger felt confident enough to take command of the '*piano*', as French chefs call the kitchen range. Although he spent most of the day and evening cooking, he still somehow found time to go to the food market, which by this time had moved out to the suburb of Rungis. He would turn up at about 5 a.m. every morning except Sunday and pick up spectacular bargains, partly because it was the end of proceedings and the market was about to pack up, and partly because he had long been friends with many of his suppliers and they would knock a bit extra off for him. The luck of the draw explained the presence on his menu, all at unbeatable prices, of, say, a *ragoût de cuisses de sarcelle* (teal legs), a classic *homard à l'américaine*, or stuffed pheasant breasts (when I saw '*suprêmes de faisan farcis*' on the menu, I thought the plural was a mistake; but no, this being Les Fontaines, two stuffed breasts were served on a large oval plate).

'It's just that if I get a knock-down price I like to pass it on to the customer,' Roger says. 'And I think it's a good way of doing business. As we say in the Auvergne, you can't catch flies with vinegar.' Among the flies he caught at Les Fontaines were local publishers, politicians (Lionel Jospin, Jack Lang, Jacques Delors, Laurent Fabius) and film stars (Marlène Jobert, Jean Yanne), as well as many of his supplier chums and a host of other anonymous fans of his cooking. I use the past tense because, unfortunately for his customers, Roger decided to retire in 1997 and put Les Fontaines in the hands of a manager, while keeping a supervisory status for himself. At the time of writing, he was fairly convinced his successor in the kitchen was doing a reasonable job, but seemed to be suffering from withdrawal symptoms and did not rule out the possibility that he might take over at the helm again. He misses the buzz he used to get out of the tension which builds up in any bistro that is packed out – the fear that a sauce might go wrong, that a customer's order might get forgotten, that all the diners at a large table would order different *hors-d'oeuvre* and different main courses (a situation known in the restaurant trade as '*l'épicerie*'). On one occasion when he had got a little behind and waiters reported that customers were beginning to get restive, he took the heat out of the situation by emerging from the basement of Les Fontaines, where the kitchen is located, and announcing in a loud voice: 'I hope you'll bear with me, but I'm having a few problems because my microwave has broken down.'

One of the dishes that regularly featured on Roger's menu was this *morue à l'auvergnate*, which is a surprisingly subtle way of dealing with salt cod. It is a recipe he got from Jeannette of the spotless apron.

[*For four*]
800g (1lb 12oz) salt cod
1.5kg (3lb 4oz) salad potatoes
50ml (2fl oz) oil (peanut or sunflower)
2 large cloves garlic, finely chopped
2 sprigs flat-leaf parsley, finely chopped
3 egg yolks
150ml (5½fl oz) cream
freshly ground pepper
Salt

Put the salt cod in a large receptacle (enamel, glass or china) and cover with plenty of water. Leave for 36 hours, changing the water at least 3 times. Wash the potatoes and boil in their skins in unsalted water. Leave to cool, if possible overnight.

Remove skin and bones from the salt cod, and cut into little strips. Peel the potatoes and slice not too finely. Heat the oil in a non-stick sauté pan over a medium heat and fry the potatoes until they begin to crisp. Add the salt cod and continue cooking, allowing the fish to brown slightly. Turn down the heat to low, stir in the garlic and parsley, and leave to cook for a minute or two.

Beat the egg yolks into the cream. Increase the heat under the pan to high for a few seconds, adding plenty of pepper. Away from the heat, but while the pan is still very hot, quickly stir in the egg yolk and cream mixture, which should thicken very slightly. Add a little salt if necessary, and serve immediately.

↤ Estofinado ↦

My first encounter with stockfish (unsalted wind-dried cod) came in the mid-seventies, when I tasted that delicious Niçois speciality, *estocaficada*. It is a dish where the startlingly gamey flavour of stockfish is accentuated by garlic, tomatoes and black olives. Later I came to translate Jacques Médecin's *La Cuisine du Comté de Nice* (*Cuisine Niçoise*, Penguin, 1983), which naturally contains a recipe for *estocaficada*, and began to look more closely at this Ur-food extraordinary. A highly valuable bundle of calories, vitamins and minerals – stockfish was used as legal tender in Iceland until the turn of the century – wind-dried cod from Scandinavia was much appreciated as a preserve in southern Europe from very early times. The French manuscript of 1392–3 which has been published as *Le Mesnagier de Paris* says it could be kept for as long as twelve years: '*Item, quant icelle morue est prise es marces de la mer et l'en veult icelle garder .x. ou .xii. ans, l'en l'effondre et luy oste l'en la teste, et est seichee a l'air et au soleil, et non mye au feu ou a la fumee. Et ce fait, elle est nommee stofix.*'★ The reference books I consulted at the time I translated Médecin said that nowadays stockfish is eaten in Portugal, Spain, the Côte d'Azur and Italy (especially Venice), as well as parts of Africa.

A few years later I moved house to the Châtaigneraie, which is a good 150 kilometres from the Mediterranean as the crow flies. I assumed that the only fish traditionally eaten there, apart from the produce of its lakes and rivers, was, as in the rest of the Auvergne, salt cod (*morue*). Then one November day I went into the *superette* in my nearest market town, Maurs. As I stood in front of the fruit and

---

★ *Le Mesnagier de Paris*, Livre de Poche, 1994, II, v, p. 194. (*Item*, when this cod is caught in coastal regions and you wish to keep it for ten or twelve years, you gut it and cut off its head; it is dried in the air and in the sun, and not exposed to fire or smoke. When this has been done, it is called *stockfish*.)

vegetable counter, my nostrils were engaged by a curiously insistent and not very pleasant smell which reminded me of the fish food which, as a boy, I used to give our goldfish. There, next to bags of potatoes, was a cluster of stockfish standing upright in a tub like *baguettes* at the baker's. Just as when I had last encountered them, in a Nice grocery, I caught a split-second image of agonizing pain: this optical illusion was caused by the way the gill-bones of the dried and headless fish formed what looked like a screaming mouth. What on earth, I wondered, was the creature doing in the Massif Central?

Friends in Mourjou told me that *estofinado* was a favourite local stockfish dish, eaten from All Saints' Day to Easter (the reasons for this 'season' became clear later). Local restaurants apparently vied with each other to produce the best version. I telephoned a warmly recommended restaurant in the village of Almon-les-Junies, near Decazeville, to book a table for the following Sunday, but it was booked out. Eventually I and some friends managed to get a table two Sundays later. When we arrived in Almon, it struck us as odd that such a small village should have a spacious car-park, much of which was occupied by large coaches. It turned out that the village had three competing *estofinado* restaurants, and had had to build facilities to cope with the coachloads of old-age pensioners, Algerian war veterans and hunters' associations whose winter gastronomic outings centred on stockfish.

Our meal began, naturally, with vegetable soup, followed by a platter of raw ham and *saucisson sec*. Next came a *bouchée à la reine* (vol-au-vent with a mushroom and sweetbread filling), a pause, then the *estofinado*. It looked like a steaming bowl of mashed potatoes. But when sampled it revealed its other ingredients: cream, eggs, garlic, parsley and what looked like little wood chips – the stockfish. The flavour was indescribable. Behind the familiar tastes there lurked a flavour that was neither fishy nor meaty nor cheesy, but had overtones of all three – and was excellent. When asked if we wanted a second helping (a tradition with *estofinado* in restaurants), we rashly beamed and nodded, and another steaming bowl appeared. Little did we realize that the *estofinado* was not the *plat de résistance*. It was followed by roast chicken, cheese and *îles flottantes* with *fouace* (p. 175).

Later, after seeking the advice of Jeanne Chabut (p. 7), I tried making *estofinado* myself. She had warned me it was time-consuming and complicated, so, to make it worthwhile, I waited till I had a houseful of guests before attempting the dish. The stockfish I bought was extremely hard and plank-like. As a joke I laid its tail on one chair and its 'mouth' on another, and took a photograph of my ten-year-old god-daughter sitting on its middle (with a piece of newspaper to protect her clothes from the smell). The stockfish's woodlike qualities persisted during the first stage of making the dish, which requires it to be sawn up into sections and soaked in water: as I sawed away, a gentle rain of stockfish dust fell to the floor.

Soaking stockfish is no simple operation like desalting salt cod. It takes anything from six to ten days for the dried fish to reconstitute itself, and it needs to be soaked in running water (or under a dripping tap). If this is impossible, the water it soaks in has to be changed very frequently. This is because stockfish is not salted at all and can go off very quickly. Hence its consumption during the winter months only. In 1988 the Rodez Chamber of Commerce rashly organized a mammoth *estofinado* banquet in mid-August as part of a campaign to promote local tourism; 1,500 portions were served, but most were left untouched as the stockfish had gone off in the heat.

People in Mourjou, who tend to make *estofinado* less often now that transport to local restaurants has become easier, used to tie their sawn-up stockfish to a rock (it remained in one piece because they left a sliver of skin connecting the sections) and put it for a week in an outside cattle trough with spring water trickling into it. The rock was to stop it floating to the surface and thus risk being stolen by dogs or foxes. If they did not have the right kind of cattle trough they might leave the stockfish in a small stream or *rigole* (irrigation channel), after first taking the precaution of tying it up in a bundle of twigs to keep scavengers away. Paul Ramadier, prime minister of France in 1947, who hailed from Decazeville, the small industrial town in the heart of *estofinado* country, reportedly reproduced the cattle trough technique when he lived in Paris by putting his stockfish in the lavatory cistern of the prime minister's residence, Hôtel Matignon (to the great alarm of the staff), thus ensuring that the water it was soaking in got changed several times a day.

My stockfish had swollen considerably after six days of soaking under a trickling tap from a rainwater tank. There was scum on the water – and a stink that defied description (according to people in Mourjou you can always tell when *estofinado* is being made in someone's house because the smell seeps out; nowadays many shops sell pre-soaked stockfish for that reason). When the stockfish was cooked (a 45-minute simmer), I embarked on the lengthy task of picking the flesh off the bone. I had nearly finished – neat piles of skin, bones and flesh littered the kitchen table – when my guests returned from a walk. The smell that greeted them as they came in from the bracing Auvergne air prompted various reactions, the mildest of which was 'I'm not eating any of that stuff!' The fact that those same people later ate their words, and indeed clamoured for second and third helpings of *estofinado*, was not so much a tribute to my cooking as evidence of the extraordinary way the aggressive flavour of stockfish transmogrifies itself, when combined with potatoes, cream, eggs, garlic and parsley, into something delicate and gently aromatic.

I was naturally interested in finding out how stockfish had become a traditional dish in the Châtaigneraie. Its presence on the Côte d'Azur was easily explained: for centuries Norwegian sailors had exchanged it for fresh fruit and vegetables. But this far inland? The books I consulted were of little help, apart from revealing that the area of the southern Massif Central where *estofinado* was eaten was larger than I had imagined, stretching as far as Figeac (Lot) to the west and Villefranche-de-Rouergue (Aveyron) to the south. The fact that this area is bisected by the river Lot, which was for a long time navigable from Bordeaux as far as Vieillevie, just before Entraygues, seemed an important clue.

Authors offered various theories about the presence of stockfish in the area, some of them plausible enough, but none supported by hard evidence. It had been brought there, they variously alleged, by North European pilgrims on their way to Santiago de Compostela, by Norwegian merchants who had come to buy wool in Villefranche and

Figeac in the late Middle Ages, or by local soldiers who had fought in Louis XIV's campaigns in the Low Countries and picked up the habit of eating stockfish there (it was not explained why they should have brought it back with them).

An enthusiastic local historian (a retired civil servant) told me he had evidence of stockfish being introduced to the area in the mid-fourteenth century by a British soldier whose name he pronounced as Robert Kenolisse, and who at the head of an army of 30,000 troops spent five years unsuccessfully laying siege to the small town of Montsalvy, in the hills above Vieillevie. This sounded a promising line of inquiry: such a large number of soldiers tied down for so many years would have had a far greater chance of establishing stockfish in the local diet than the occasional pilgrim or wool merchant.

In a chapter entitled 'Un Ilot insolite de consommation du stock-fisch: les confins Rouergue-Quercy', in *Alimentation et régions* (Presses Universitaires de Nancy, 1989), Guy Mergoil contributed by far the most thorough examination so far of the *estofinado* phenomenon in the southern Massif Central. Mergoil quotes yet other 'explanations' for the presence of stockfish, but concludes that it is well-nigh impossible to distinguish myth from reality. However, he goes on to say that since stockfish could be kept for a very long time and has a high nutrition/ volume ratio its consumption could easily have been introduced by troops in the Middle Ages, become more widespread with the development of river traffic and trade with northern Europe, and then been boosted in the nineteenth century as a result of the industrial revolution in and around Decazeville and the arrival there of many Spanish immigrant workers. He charts *estofinado*'s gradual transformation from poor peasant fare into a rather expensive dish for special occasions. He supplies no direct evidence that the English introduced stockfish into the area, but simply quotes a cookery writer (Henri Philippon in *Cuisine du Quercy et du Périgord*) who surmises that this was so.

Could my retired civil servant, I wondered, come up with chapter and verse? Unfortunately, when pressed, he was unable to give me the exact reference for what he had jotted down. After I had spent a fruitless day in the Archives Départementales du Cantal trying to track down his quote, the trail went dead. All I managed to establish was that the Englishman who allegedly fed his troops on stockfish was in fact Sir Robert Knolles or Knollys, that he was one of the Black Prince's captains, and that he had indeed spent some time in south-west France during the Hundred Years War (he was known to the French at the time as Canolles).

A visit to the Bibliothèque Nationale in Paris provided me with no evidence that Knolles was ever tied down for years trying to take Montsalvy. But a book by Abbé J. Rouquette, called *Le Rouergue sous les Anglais* (Imprimerie Artières et J. Maury, 1887), showed that English troops were almost constantly present in the Rouergue after 1360, when the treaty of Brétigny gave Edward III the whole of south-west France. Some of them formed uncontrolled armed bands of *routiers* that looted villages, extorted money and held people to ransom.

According to Rouquette, groups of English *routiers* holed up for several years in what is now the Châtaigneraie, making sorties from time to time when they ran short of supplies. One group, who had built a small fortress called Castel d'Alzo, made an expedition to Millau on 19 November 1379, captured fourteen inhabitants of the town as well as a large number of cattle, and took them back to their hideout. The hostages were released when an envoy from Millau, Guilhem Pellegry, paid a ransom which included money, a dagger and a chest, as well as ten partridges. All that remains of Castel d'Alzo, or Castel d'Auze as it is now called, are some ruins tucked away in the steep-sided valley of the Auze river, 8 kilometres as the crow flies from Mourjou. In the commune of Mourjou, there are similar ruins at a completely inaccessible site called Méallet, which is known locally as '*le village des Anglais*'. It is not impossible that Méallet was also a base used by another group of *routiers*.

All this shows that the English were well established in the area for a number of years, and certainly long enough to have introduced stockfish. That stockfish formed part of the victuals of Edward III's troops in France seems well established. H. J. Hewitt, in *The Organization of War under Edward III* (Manchester University Press, 1966), says that victuals obtained in England for foreign campaigns included 'fish: commonly stockfish or herrings or "dried fish", bought in hundreds or thousands, and chiefly for Gascony'.

One or two other mysteries remain. We do not know what form *estofinado* took before the potato's arrival in the area towards the end of the eighteenth century. But on the analogy of the bread-and-cheese dish *patranque* (p. 30), which preceded the potato-and-cheese *truffade* (p. 36), it is likely that stockfish was mixed with bread, or at least eaten with bread.

Why is *estofinado* consumed only in an area surrounding one stretch of the upper Lot and not farther down the river? Mergoil suggests that it is because peasants farther downstream had more abundant resources and therefore did not need to rely on dried fish. He also points out that they had much less running water at their disposal for the soaking process. But there is much evidence that when running water was lacking another technique was used – both in France and in Italy – to make the woodlike stockfish fit for human consumption. According to *Le Mesnagier de Paris*, if the *stofix* were first beaten with a mallet for an hour it then needed to be soaked in warm water for only twelve hours or so, rather than for several days ('*Et quant l'en l'a tant gardee et l'en la veult mengier, il la couvient batre d'un maillet de boiz bien une heures et puis mectre tremper en eaue tiede bien .xii. heures ou plus*'★).

Why stockfish is so called also remains a mystery. Both the Old English '*stocc*' and the Old High German '*stock*' mean 'a stick'. But to what does the stick refer? Most plausibly, in my view, it describes the phenomenal stick-like hardness of the fish. Others argue that it got its name because it was habitually beaten with a mallet or stick (many of the examples given by the Oxford English Dictionary of the use of the word stockfish in early texts refer to its being beaten). Mergoil mentions yet another possible derivation: it was so called because the fish was dried on wooden poles.

As with many peasant dishes, there are several ways of making *estofinado*, but the basic ingredients vary little. Some say no *estofinado* is complete without walnut oil, either added smoking-hot and in large quantities at the last moment, or used to sauté the stockfish flakes in. Others (including myself) find that the pungency of walnut oil cancels out the subtle stockfish flavour. It also makes an already rich dish much richer. Another addition commonly found in restaurants – but frowned upon by the purists – is hard-boiled eggs. They have the effect of spinning out the dish. It is also rumoured that some less

---

★ *Le Mesnagier de Paris*, p. 194. (And when you have kept it for quite a long time and you wish to eat it, you must beat it for a good hour with a wooden mallet, then put it to soak in lukewarm water for twelve hours or more.)

scrupulous restaurateurs get round the problem of the price of stockfish (a high 180 francs a kilo) by adding a certain quantity of much cheaper salt cod to their *estofinado*.

Often walnut or another oil is used to 'lubricate' the dish. Mashed potatoes, in the orthodox version, can absorb a vast amount of oil. The following recipe, which was given to me by Eliette Pons, of l'Auberge de la Cascade near the charming little *bastide* of Villecomtal (Aveyron), uses diced potatoes instead, which are less absorbent and thus obviate the need for oil on top of the eggs and lashings of cream. Of the many versions of *estofinado* I have tasted, this is the best.

[*For eight*]
650g (1lb 7oz) stockfish (unsoaked)
650g (1lb 7oz) potatoes, peeled and cut into very small
   dice
vegetable oil
800ml (28fl oz) single cream
2 large cloves garlic, finely chopped
freshly ground pepper
4 tablespoons flat-leaf parsley, finely chopped
4 eggs, beaten
salt

Saw the stockfish into 15cm (6in) lengths, place in a very large saucepan and soak for 6 days under a trickling tap (alternatively, change the water twice a day). Rinse, place in well-salted boiling water and simmer for 45 minutes, skimming from time to time.

Sauté the potatoes gently in oil in a non-stick sauté pan until cooked. Strain the stockfish. As soon as it is cool enough to handle, quickly separate the flesh from the skin and bones (if the stockfish is allowed to cool too much it becomes impossibly sticky). Cut a little of the skin (about 1 tablespoonful) into very thin strips and add to the fish flakes.

Put the potatoes into a large, deep fireproof dish or casserole, add the fish and mix together over a very low heat. When very hot but not sizzling, add the cream, garlic, pepper and parsley and continue stirring until hot. At the last moment mix in the eggs, stir a little longer (but do not allow the eggs to solidify), add salt to taste, and serve immediately.

As with *truffade* (p. 36), which uses the unsalted Tomme fraîche de Cantal, it is important to salt the *estofinado* properly, as stockfish is not salted. This is not always adequately stressed by cookery writers – indeed, the authors of no fewer than six books on the cuisine of the Massif Central in my possession imagine that stockfish is salted as well as dried and assume that *estofinado* needs no salt at all. This suggests that none of those authors ever actually bothered to make an *estofinado*.

(Auberge de la Cascade, Polissal, 12320 St-Félix-de-Lunel. Tel: 05 65 44 61 54.)

Pork

The pig is the animal that looms largest in the Auvergnat kitchen, and arguably in the Auvergnat psyche as well. According to Celtic legend – the Auvergnats have partly Celtic roots – the Great Pig in the sky possessed regenerative powers. During the rural community's long years of penury, the pig was a vital source of energy. Even today, almost every farming household lovingly rears one or more pigs for consumption by family, relatives and friends. The date of the pig's slaughter is a major event on the calendar, a day of festivities – for all but the pig – and magic, when a living animal is abruptly transformed into a wide variety of fresh and preserved products. Auvergnat *charcuterie* justly enjoys a high reputation. '*Charcuterie d'Auvergne*' is the proud message blazoned on Auvergnat-owned *charcuterie* shops' blinds and shutters in Paris and other cities.

In that context, it is easy to understand why alarm bells have begun

ringing in the Auvergne. It all has to do with Brittany, a region which, incidentally, shares Celtic roots with the Auvergne. Brittany produces 55 per cent of France's pork while accounting for only 7 per cent of its land area. Those figures alone tell the story: the region has become one huge concentration camp for pigs. It is dotted with hundreds of battery farms of up to 20,000 pigs each. Its water table and rivers are becoming increasingly polluted by slurry. One farmer was recently sent to prison for repeatedly preferring to pay fines rather than respect anti-pollution legislation that restricts the dumping of slurry. The reaction of Breton farmers to the fact that the building of new battery farms has been virtually put on hold in Brittany has been to cast their beady eyes on other regions of France – 'virgin lands' like the Loire Valley, Aquitaine and the Auvergne. The Auvergne already has some battery pig farms – there is one in my village, and it delivers an almighty pong when the wind is blowing in the wrong direction – but they are mostly tiddlers compared with their Breton counterparts. And the Auvergnats, both environmentalists and farmers, are in no mood to see any more such batteries built – environmentalists for the obvious reason that they oppose anything that might further pollute the Auvergne's rivers, and farmers because they want to preserve the up-market image of Auvergnat charcuterie and pork (any new battery farms would be entitled to slap the description 'Auvergnat' on their produce).

It is edifying to compare the conditions that industrially raised pigs have to suffer with the lifestyle of most of their Auvergnat counterparts. Pigs are intelligent animals and have great difficulty in coping mentally and physically with the inhumane and cramped conditions of the battery farm. They are accordingly stuffed with anti-stress drugs and antibiotics, which find their way into the end product sold to the public: pork. Many of them spend much of their lives standing on their back legs (the hams) with the front part of their bodies hoist into the air by a sling placed behind their front legs. The aim of the torture is to produce bigger hams.

Many pigs in the Auvergne, particularly those intended for family consumption, are still allowed to roam the woods, where they forage for chestnuts, beechmast, acorns, roots and grubs during the day, returning to their sty in the evening to enjoy a meal that may consist of anything from kitchen scraps, potato peelings and Jerusalem arti-chokes to cooked nettles, bran, whey, apples and chestnuts specially dried for them in *sécadous* (p. 9). Others are kept in fields with electric fences where they can still live a normal social life. Sows have little corrugated shelters reminiscent of Nissen huts, from where they can dozily watch over their litters of piglets as they career playfully around the field. Just occasionally, a wild boar will barge through the fence surrounding the field and get to a sow on heat. The result is a litter of slightly darker piglets with a hint of the stripes that are the distinctive livery of baby boars. Cowherds occupying the few remaining *burons* (p. 191) in operation in the mountains still use pigs symbiotically: the animals are partly fed on the whey that is left over from cheese-making, which would otherwise be thrown away.

There is evidence that pigs which enjoy a varied diet and congenial living conditions taste better. That was certainly the belief of a farmer in the tiny Cantal village of Le Trioulou – quoted by André Meynier, in his book *Ségalas, Lévézou, Châtaigneraie* (1931) – who in 1922 installed proper sanitation and sophisticated feeding troughs in his pigsties to that end. A German farmer went one better a few years ago: he devised a pig-raising unit which included an automatically flushing toilet area in one corner (the pigs, whose reputation for muckiness is quite unjustified, quickly learned to use it), a pig-operated shower (pigs adore being sprayed with water), cushions and a toothed metal scratching post. He swore that his pork was the best in Germany. One is tempted to believe him.

But all good things have to come to an end. Little does the family pig realize that a date in December, January or February has been marked down as the day of its slaughter. The chosen day will be during the week that precedes a new moon, otherwise the meat, it is believed, will not keep properly. It takes a lot of hands to cope with 100–200 kilos of flesh and bone, so friends and relatives are invited to help out. The day before the slaughter, all the implements, utensils and receptacles such as preserving jars that will be needed are washed and made ready. The pig gets nothing to eat during its last twenty-four hours in this world and, intelligent animal that it is, may at that point begin to get the jitters. All doubt is removed from its mind when men come to catch it in the morning, tying a rope round its muzzle, grabbing a fore and a hind leg and bringing it down sharply on to a bench in the cold winter air. It squeals like a baby, though far more deafeningly. Children, who sometimes will have treated the pig like a pet and given it a name, find the scene so difficult to take that they hide in their bedrooms with cottonwool in their ears or sit in front of the television set with the sound turned up as loud as possible.

At this point the professional slaughterer performs his task (European legislation still – but for how long? – allows people to slaughter their own pig as long as it is for their own consumption, and as long as the actual killing is performed by a slaughterer). He inserts one of his razor-sharp pointed knives into the animal's neck. Steaming blood spurts out and is caught in a large pot, where it has to be swirled around by hand to prevent it from coagulating. This task is usually entrusted to a *mangonièira* (an Occitan word of obscure origin). The *mangonièira* is a woman member of the family or a relation or friend who is in charge of supervising the cleaning and preparing of the meat that will be turned into charcuterie. She is usually someone who has passed the age of the menopause – as with the stirring of *aligot* (p. 32), there is a persistent belief, passed down from the darkness of time, that a woman with a period, like a full moon, will cause the meat to go off. When the blood has been drained and the pig is dead, its bristles are burnt off with a blowlamp (in the old days this was done by covering the animal with straw and setting light to it). The pig is hosed down until it is completely clean. Its head and trotters are cut off, and its hind legs hoisted on to hooks. It is then slit open, and out tumble its intestines and stomach, a rich medley of red, violet, blue and white.★

Work then starts on turning this huge slab of flesh and bones into a manageable source of food for a period of many months, if not a whole year. As a pig depicted on the tiled wall of a Paris charcuterie proclaims: '*Chez moi, de la tête à la queue, tout est délicieux.*' Nothing could be closer to the truth.

First, the *mangonièira* peels off the thick skin on the outside of the *petit boyau* (small intestines), making sure she does not pierce the thin inner skin, which will be used as casing for *saucisses* (both fresh and dried). The *gros boyau* (big intestine) serves to make the typically 'misshapen' Auvergnat *boudin* and *saucisson sec*. She washes out the *gros*

★ A favourite dish of the Romans was a whole roast sow stuffed with sausages, chickens and game birds. At the time of serving, the sow's belly was slit open to reveal the delights inside. The dish was wittily called *porcus troianus* (Trojan pig). The reason I mention this is that the French word for a sow is *truie*, which derives from *troia*, an abbreviated form of *porcus de Troia*, a late variant of *porcus troianus*.

boyau with a little dish-washing liquid, the *petit boyau* with vinegar and salt; both are then rinsed very thoroughly.

The head is split open. The tongue is put in preserving jars, with a little pork rind, so it is ready for sterilization. The rest of the head, including the ears and snout, is used to make *fromage de tête* (p. 79). The neck, or upper part of the hand, which is quite fatty, is minced for use in a *terrine*. The knuckles of both the fore and hind legs are given the same treatment as the tongue. The rest of the hand and other meaty odds and bobs are minced with a little fat and put into sausage casings. One person turns the mincing-machine handle while another pushes the casing, like some endless condom, over the spout where the coarsely minced pork comes out. Auvergnat *saucisses fraîches* are made of the same ingredients as *saucisses de Toulouse* (nothing but lean and fat pork, pepper and salt). A proportion of the *saucisses* are frozen, while others are hung up to dry on a horizontal rod suspended from the ceiling. Some of the *gros boyau*, after being filled with a mixture of cooked blood, cream and onions, becomes *boudins*; the rest is filled with sausagemeat and joins the *saucisses sèches* on the rod, eventually becoming *saucisson sec*. Much of the pig (chops, spare ribs, blade bone, belly) was in the old days put in salt to make *petit salé*. This method of preservation is still used, but it has largely been replaced by freezing. Remaining fatty bits (mesentery, the outer skin of the *boyaux*, kidney fat and so on) are melted down to make lard. Any solid residue from that becomes a crude but tasty pâté called *fritons* or *grattons*. The bladder may be used as a receptacle for lard, or else dried and turned into a tobacco pouch. In the old days a huge pocket in the *gros boyau* served as a casing for a speciality of ultimate frugality, *sac d'os* (literally 'bag of bones'), which contained chopped-up spare ribs, sternum bone, tail and rind, all previously salted. Families rarely make the knobbly *sac d'os* nowadays, though it can be found on sale at an enterprising Aurillac *charcuterie*, Roland Mas (Rue du Rieu). It is dried for several months, and eaten after being boiled up in soup, traditionally at Easter. Of similar shape to *sac d'os*, and also made by only a very few *charcutiers*, is a huge and bulbous *saucisson sec* weighing up to 1 kilo and called a *jésus* (apparently so called because the piece of casing used, the same as for *sac d'os*, shows a protuberance down one side, when filled with sausagemeat, that is thought to resemble the infant Jesus in swaddling clothes). Because of its great thickness, the *jésus* has less of a tendency to dry out than an ordinary *saucisson sec*.

After a hard morning's work, everyone sits down to lunch, which often consists of the parts of the pig that are better eaten fresh (heart, kidneys, liver). But there is no lingering over lunch, as plenty of work remains to be done. There are the hams to be dealt with, the sterilization of the preserving jars, and the clearing up, not to speak of the traditional distribution of the *parts* (shares). This involves taking gifts of fillet of pork and *boudin* round to the curate, the schoolteacher and various neighbours. According to the Auvergnat tradition of *donnant, donnant* (give and take), the neighbours will return the compliment when they come to slaughter their own pig.

Depending on its size, the killing and processing of a pig can take up to three days. The received wisdom is that the larger the pig, the better its taste. My local butcher, Raymond Vigier (p. 126), likes to buy a proper farmyard pig for his own family's consumption. He goes for monsters weighing 400 kilos, which produce hams that weigh up to 35 kilos each. He once gave me a slice of one of his hams: it measured 44 centimetres lengthwise, had a 5-centimetre layer of fat round the edge, and was extraordinarily tasty. But on most farms the family pig weighs 'only' 200 kilos. Its hams (or ham – sometimes one hind leg is cut up, frozen and eaten later on in the form of roast pork) weigh about 20 kilos each.

There are various ways of salting a ham. One way that produces very good results is to line a solid-sided plastic bottle crate with a very large clean cloth or folded sheet and place the ham, skin-side down, on it. Then 150 millilitres of marc or brandy is poured over the ham, followed by a large handful of coarse salt. These are then rubbed into the flesh. The cloth is folded over to enclose the ham, and any gaps

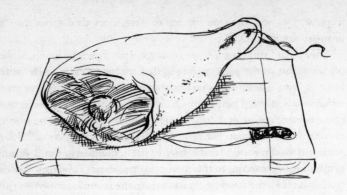

between the ham and the sides of the crate filled with cloth. Then handful upon handful of salt is sprinkled over the top. The saying goes that 'the ham will take up the salt it needs'. The crucial question is the length of time it is left in salt. A 20-kilo ham will be ready after about five weeks. It is then taken out, washed, dabbed dry and put in a special ham-drying bag with fine enough holes to let in air but not flies. The ham is dried either in the loft (if it does not get too hot) or in one corner of a large fireplace.

Legrand d'Aussy (p. xiv), in his fascinating account, *Voyage Fait en 1787 et 1788, dans la ci-devant Haute et Basse Auvergne*, reports that the Auvergnats kept their hams hanging up for years as a sign of wealth. When one of their offspring got married, they would take down the oldest and serve their honoured guests with what he describes as 'desiccated, rancid and half-rotten food'.

That is not a description would fit the hams you see hanging in farmhouses today, which are usually eaten not long after they have been cured. But, sadly, most commercially bought Auvergne ham, except for that available from careful *charcutiers* who use the old methods, is tough, oversalted and tasteless. This is because the hams are injected with a salt solution and then dried too quickly. A giveaway is their colour: if the ham is tawny brown, it will be tough and probably too salt; if it is mauvish-red, it will melt in the mouth and not leave you gasping for a glass of water.

⤚ Tourifas ⤛

An interesting and tasty combination of cheap ingredients, if rather time-consuming to make. It dates from the days when time was a cheap commodity when other things were scarce. Eugen Weber, in *Peasants into Frenchmen* (Chatto & Windus, 1977), quotes the case of a woman who 'would walk from her village to the market, 35 kilometres each way, to sell her dozen eggs at 14 sous rather than 12'. Something of the same attitude persists even today in France's infinitely more prosperous rural areas: I know of several people in Mourjou who will drive 15 kilometres to market to buy cheese or *charcuterie* at a franc or two less per kilo, blithely ignoring the money they spend on petrol, let alone the time they spend getting there and back. But then the function of the market has changed somewhat. On top of providing greater choice and an opportunity to compare prices, it has become a kind of social ritual, rather like mass, where you get a chance to meet friends and acquaintances and catch up on the latest news and gossip.

[*For four*]
50g (2oz) salt pork belly or green streaky bacon
100g (3½oz) lean raw ham
100g (3½oz) button or fairy ring mushrooms
3 sprigs flat-leaf parsley, finely chopped
75g (2½oz) spring or Welsh onion, finely chopped
1 teaspoon plain flour
200ml (7fl oz) vegetable or meat broth
freshly ground pepper
juice ½ lemon
salt
4 small slices brown bread (wholemeal or rye)
60g (2oz) unsalted butter or lard
2 eggs, beaten
100g (3½oz) breadcrumbs

Chop the fat into very small dice and blanch in boiling water for 5 minutes. Strain, put into a small non-stick sauté pan and heat gently until the fat becomes opaque, slightly browned and crisp. Dice the ham and mushrooms very finely and add to the fat. Add the finely chopped parsley and onion. Sprinkle the flour over the pan and stir well. Add the broth and plenty of pepper, and simmer for 15 minutes until most of the liquid has evaporated to form a fairly thick sauce. Sprinkle with lemon juice, stir, add a little salt if necessary and leave to cool. When cool, refrigerate for 1 hour.

Spread the mixture on the pieces of bread. Heat the butter or lard in a small non-stick sauté pan until very hot. Dip the pieces of bread first in beaten egg, then in breadcrumbs, and fry briskly until golden.

❖ Terrine de campagne ❖

Terrine de campagne is one of those dishes whose quality can vary from the sublime to the inedible. The stiff, raw-red, colourant-packed *terrine* found in many French and British supermarkets bears no relation to a properly made *terrine* of grey complexion – the natural colour of cooked liver and meat – with a coating of crumbly aspic.

This recipe was given to me by Yvonne Croutes, a farmer's wife who lives near me in Mourjou. We met under rather unusual circumstances, which I think are perhaps worth recounting because they turned out to be highly serendipitous. I was driving home slowly one night on roads that had received a dusting of snow. From time to time I tested my tyres' adhesiveness by braking sharply: there was not the hint of a skid. I joined a mainer road where the snowfall had been a bit heavier and the layer compacted. Driving even more slowly, I came down a slight slope to a bend and just touched the brakes. Instead of slowing down, my car slithered majestically straight on and through a barbed-wire fence, coming to rest with a clunk one metre from the road at the top of a steep field.

Although the car was festooned with barbed wire, I had done no more than break a couple of old wooden stakes. But naturally I felt I had to make amends to the owners of the fence. The garage hand who pulled my car back on to the road told me they would be happy with a bottle of wine or something of that kind. So next day I found out where they lived and dropped by with a bottle of Clairette de Die.

It was about 11.30 a.m. A stout, upright woman with sharp, intelligent eyes opened the door and let me into a vast kitchen whose walls were lined with highly polished copper pans, pewter plates and cattle competition diplomas. 'Madame Croutes? I've come to apologize for breaking your fence,' I said sheepishly. I explained what had happened. She accepted my apologies and bottle with a knowing chuckle. After we had talked about this and that for a few minutes, she poured me a glass of Salers, a local gentian-flavoured apéritif. 'The men should be back soon, but here's something to keep you going.'

She went over to a television monitor and turned it on. The inside of a cowshed appeared on the screen: this, she said, was her husband's newly installed video surveillance system for keeping an eye on the cows during calving. 'No one can say we're behind the times here in the Cantal,' Raymond Croutes said when he and his two grown-up sons, a joky, jolly trio, returned from the cowshed and I complimented them on their state-of-the-art farm equipment.

I apologized again for breaking their fence. 'Oh that's all right. There's a nasty hump on the road there, and as soon as there's any ice or snow, people miss the corner. Lucky you weren't going too fast – one car tumbled all the way down to the bottom of the field. It's so steep not even the tractor could get it out, so we had to hitch up a couple of oxen to do the job.'

It was by now nearly midday, when farmers round here have lunch. 'I must be going,' I mumbled. 'First you must see my cows,' Raymond said. He proudly showed me round his barn, which contained twenty Holstein and twenty Salers cows. Each stall bore a name – Fanny, Brigitte, Ginette and so on – to which, he said, its occupant answered. At one end of the barn was a spacious pen with fifteen calves happily sitting munching or wandering around. 'No crates here, as you can see,' Raymond pointed out proudly.

When we got back to the farmhouse, the table had been laid. A mouth-watering smell issued from a large and already cut *terrine*. 'Of course you'll stay for lunch, won't you?' Yvonne said in a tone that was one of certainty rather than interrogation.

I protested feebly and sat down to a meal which consisted of the following: the *terrine* (which lived up to its olfactory promise), a huge cep omelette (with more mushrooms than egg), roast veal with *truffade* (p. 36), cheese (Cantal of course), orange salad and a home-made *quatre-quarts* (a rich Madeira cake) whose intense deep yellow colour told of the many farm eggs that had gone into its making.

Conversation during this semi-improvised feast ranged from the nearby annual Salers cattle fair, which is attended by Australian and Scots buyers, to rugby and water-divining, a gift Yvonne had discovered relatively recently that she possessed.

After a glass of homemade ratafia (a mixture of grape juice and fruit spirit) to round off the meal, I drove very slowly home, reflecting on the rare joy of having been able to make my excuses and stay. Now, when I drop in on the Croutes, who have become good friends, I am careful to do so in mid-morning or mid-afternoon, for I have discovered that if I nudge a mealtime Yvonne is bound to offer me a drink and say: 'Of course you'll stay for lunch/dinner, won't you?' – an invitation I find very, very difficult to refuse.

Yvonne, who has also given me a recipe for *chou farci* (p. 151), makes, as I discovered during that first meal, an excellent *terrine* that manages to retain a soft, moist texture while remaining fairly low in fat (after cooking it very slowly for twelve hours – in the old days the *terrine* used to be put among the embers of the fire – she drains off the excess fat).

[*For twelve*]
500g (1lb 2oz) salt pork belly or green streaky bacon
500g (1lb 2oz) lean pork (fillet or hand)
500g (1lb 2oz) pig's liver
1 large onion, finely chopped
28g (1oz) salt
½ teaspoon freshly ground pepper
large pinch freshly grated nutmeg
large piece pig's caul fat
6 shallots, sliced
1 bay leaf
1 sprig thyme

Mince the meat and liver, and mix well with the onion, salt, pepper and nutmeg. Line a medium-sized casserole with the caul and add the *terrine* mixture, pressing it down well. Put the shallots, bay leaf and thyme into a small muslin bag and bury in the mixture. Add 200ml

(7fl oz) of water to the casserole. Put the casserole on an electric plate set at a very low marking or into a very cool oven (150°C/300°F/Gas mark 2). Cook for 12 hours. Drain off as much fat as possible, remove the muslin bag, and allow to cool slightly. Turn the *pâté* out on to a fine sieve and allow more fat to drain off. Remove the caul and press the *pâté* through the sieve into a *terrine* dish of suitable size. Press down to make it compact, leave to cool completely and refrigerate. The *terrine* is best eaten 2 or 3 days later.

This 'slim-line' *terrine* makes a change from the over-richness which is the *péché mignon* of French *pâté* cooks. The reason for enveloping the *pâté* with caul fat during the slow cooking process is to enable it to be turned out cleanly.

✦ Fromage de tête ✦

The recipe for this most economical of dishes was given to me by Louise Aymar of Mourjou, who, when she still raised a pig each year for family consumption, made the finest home-cured raw ham I have ever tasted. Lovingly manufactured from a mature pig of 250–300 kilos, it came in huge slices too long to fit on to a dinner plate, so each slice had to be cut up into sections. Even when thickly cut (in the Auvergnat tradition), it was as soft and as tender as Parma ham, and had a subtly aromatic taste reminiscent of its Italian cousin, though it showed greater marbling and was very different in colour – mauvish-red rather than tawny-red. As in any self-respecting Auvergnat household, the Aymars used every part of the pig when it was slaughtered. The head would be turned into *fromage de tête*, also known as *pâté de tête de porc*. It is a very different preparation from *terrine* or *fritons*, containing as it does a higher proportion of aspic to fat than they do, as well as uncooked parsley and garlic, which give it a refreshingly pungent note.

[*For ten*]
1 pig's head (with brain, tongue and eyes removed)
300g (10½oz) pork rind, trimmed of fat

bouquet garni
2 onions
4 cloves
3 cloves garlic, finely chopped
4 sprigs flat-leaf parsley, finely chopped
salt
freshly ground pepper

Get your butcher to cut the head up into 3 or 4 pieces. Pack them and the pork rind tightly into a large pan, add the *bouquet garni* and onions studded with cloves, and cover with water. Cover and weigh down the lid to ensure all the meat is covered with water. Simmer over a very low heat for 4–5 hours. Drain off the liquid and reserve. Remove the meat, rind and ears from the bones, trim them of any excess fat and chop quite finely (do not blend). Put into a bowl and add the garlic and parsley, salt and pepper – about 18g (¾oz) of salt and 1g (15 grains) of pepper per kilo of the mixture – and enough of the cooking liquid to produce a fairly mushy, but not too liquid, mixture. Mix thoroughly and press down into *pâté* moulds or loaf tins. Refrigerate. This dish is better eaten 2 or 3 days later. If you wish to keep it longer, it is best frozen rather than sterilized, as high temperatures blunt the garlic and parsley seasoning.

You may be wondering what the term *fromage de tête* has to do with cheese. It is a throwback to the origin of the word *fromage* itself, which derives from the vulgar Latin *formaticum*, something that is pressed into a form or mould. The North American term for brawn, headcheese, is simply a translation of *fromage de tête*.

↞ Oreilles de porc au fromage ↠

It is a mystery to me why the English expression 'to make a pig's ear of' means 'to mess up'. I have always found the elegantly curved and pointed auricles of the pig a rather endearing part of its anatomy, whether they hang down, blinker-like, over the animal's eyes or, as in some breeds, stand erect and to attention. They taste good, too, though they could hardly be described as having a lot of character.

Here they are given extra flavour by an aromatic broth and a cheese sauce.

[*For four*]
4 pig's ears
salt
green leaves of 1 leek
4 flat-leaf parsley sprigs or 8 stalks
1 sprig thyme
1 bay leaf
1 large onion
2 cloves
5 peppercorns
2 cloves garlic
30g (1oz) unsalted butter
300ml (10½fl oz) milk
30g (1oz) plain flour
100ml (3½fl oz) double cream
70g (2½oz) young Cantal cheese
pinch freshly ground white pepper
pinch freshly grated nutmeg

Put the pig's ears in plenty of well-salted cold water in a large saucepan and bring to the boil. After 1–2 minutes of vigorous boiling, move the pan partly off the heat and skim. Wash the leek leaves and use the largest of them as an envelope to enclose the parsley, thyme and bay leaf. Secure with string. Put the envelope, the other leek leaves, the onion studded with cloves, the peppercorns and the garlic into the pan with the ears. Lower the heat, cover and simmer for 1½–2 hours, skimming from time to time.

Towards the end of the cooking time, make a Mornay sauce as follows. Melt the butter gently in a heavy saucepan. Heat the milk in another pan with 80ml (3fl oz) of the ears' cooking liquid. Stir the flour into the butter and cook slowly, stirring all the time with a wooden spoon, for 2–3 minutes without browning. When the milk has almost reached boiling point, pour it over the butter and flour mixture, away from the heat, and whisk until absolutely smooth.

★

Return the pan to a low heat, bring to a simmer and cook gently for about 1 minute, stirring. Add the cream gradually. Bring back to boiling point. Remove from the heat and stir in the cheese, cut into very fine slivers, until it has melted completely. Add pepper, nutmeg and salt to taste.

Butter a gratin dish. Remove the ears from their cooking liquid, cut into thin strips, arrange in the dish and cover with Mornay sauce. Bake in a fairly hot oven (200°C/400°F/Gas mark 6) for 20 minutes or until the surface begins to turn golden brown.

⤛ Boudin aux châtaignes ⤜

I include a recipe for *boudin aux châtaignes* just on the off-chance that you have an opportunity to obtain some pig's blood. But if you cannot, or would rather not, make your own *boudin*, lightly sautéed chestnuts can make an excellent accompaniment to a bought *boudin*.

Boudin aux châtaignes is mainly a speciality of the Limousin, though it is also occasionally made by *charcutiers* in the Auvergne. My first acquaintance with the dish was the result of chance – or rather stupidity. I was living at the time in the Sologne, a region of lakes and large shooting estates just south of Orléans. One evening, returning by rail from Paris to Orléans, I did not look carefully enough at the list of stations served by the train I boarded: as the train approached Orléans I got up, picked up my luggage and went to the end of the carriage. To my horror the train swept through the station and on all the way to Limoges without stopping. I felt an absolute fool as I sheepishly returned to my compartment, where I was greeted with compassion untinged, I felt, by any *Schadenfreude*. The train arrived in Limoges at 8 p.m., and the next train back to Orléans would have arrived in the early hours of the morning. I had never been to Limoges, so I decided to stay the night and go back next morning. Next to Limoges's marvellous Belle Epoque station, which straddles the railway lines, there was a hotel with an interesting menu, which included *boudin aux châtaignes*, something I had never heard of, let alone tasted. They turned out to be delicious, small *boudins* the size of British bangers. Some *boudins* have large dice of pork fat in their filling to keep it moist and not too crumbly. In the Limoges *boudins* the fat was replaced by small fragments of chestnut, which served the same purpose and whose sweetness combined magically with the cooked pig's blood, just as in the classic *boudin*-and-apples combination. This recipe will make larger, misshapen *boudins* of the more typically Auvergnat kind.

[*For eight*]
600g (1lb 5oz) fresh or frozen chestnuts, peeled (p. 186)
225g (8oz) back fat
225g (8oz) flair fat
600g (1lb 5oz) onions, finely chopped
2 litres (70fl oz) pig's blood
500ml (18fl oz) milk
65g (2½oz) salt
freshly ground pepper
boudin casings (*gros boyau*)

Boil the chestnuts in a little water for 20 minutes or until soft. Chop to the size of garden peas. Mince the fat, put in a saucepan and melt gently. Add the onions and cook over a low heat until completely soft. Put into a mixing-bowl, add the blood, milk, chestnuts, salt and pepper, and mix well. Knot each casing at one end. Take one casing and fit the unknotted end over the edge of a plastic funnel, taking care not to split it. Ladle the mixture into the funnel and fill the casing to nearly full, allowing enough casing at the end to be knotted. Proceed in the same way with the other casings. Put the *boudins* into a wire chip-basket or old-fashioned wire lettuce-shaker. Bring a large pan of water to a simmer, remove from heat and lower the *boudins* into the water. Return to a very low heat and simmer for about 30 minutes. Prick gently with a needle. If blood seeps out, they will need a little more cooking. When cooked, the *boudins* should be transferred carefully to a bowl of cold water for 2 minutes, then laid out to dry on a flat surface.

Tarte au boudin de cochon et aux
⊰⊱ herbes vertes, beurre fondu aillé ⊱⊰

When Jean Puech was France's agriculture minister in the Balladur government (1993–5), he wanted to show off some of the attractions of the area around the village of Rignac (Aveyron), of which he was mayor, to his fellow European agriculture ministers. One such attraction is the tiny village of Belcastel, which is overlooked by a medieval castle and has a high-arched 600-year-old bridge over the Aveyron river, down which the occasional kingfisher streaks. The village has been tastefully spruced up without becoming too bijou. It has only one tiny car-park, one general store, two restaurants and no silk-screen print vendors or souvenir shops. There has been a total freeze on all new building or new commercial premises.

What Puech chiefly wanted to show off in Belcastel was one of its two restaurants, Le Vieux Pont, which is run by Nicole Fagegaltier (in the kitchen) and her sister Michèle (front of house). The sisters' main memory of the ministers' visit was that they were forced by their tight schedule to gallop through a gourmet meal in 45 minutes, while riot police whose job it was to protect them from a possible demonstration by angry French farmers sat starving in their wire-meshed coaches outside.

I can sympathize with the riot police: to be cheated of Nicole's sublime cuisine while glimpsing others enjoying it inside a restaurant would to me be the most refined form of torture imaginable.

Nicole, sometimes inaccurately described as self-taught by food writers and guide books, started her training at the catering school of Souillac at the age of fifteen and went on to study at its more famous Toulouse equivalent. In 1983, at the age of twenty, she took over operations at Le Vieux Pont, which her parents, and her grandparents before them, had run as a straightforward country restaurant. She soon attracted attention, winning an Electricité de France sponsored cookery competition for 'most creative cook in the Midi-Pyrénées region' in 1985. This earned her a trip for two to the Balearic Islands and her own weight in prunes. In 1988 she was crowned 'French gastronomy's most promising cook'.

Instead of taking off into the culinary stratosphere as she could have done, Nicole decided that her roots were in the Aveyron and that she would prefer to stay put in Belcastel. She had learnt much about cooking from her grandmother and mother, and was steeped in local culinary tradition. Some of her earliest memories of the kitchen are of the *pascades* (p. 25) they made with onions, dandelions or apples, and of a very thick *soupe au fromage* (p. 6), the eating of which would always generate an atmosphere of great conviviality. She also has fond memories of Elie Pons, a retired miner from nearby Carmaux (Jean Jaurès's stronghold), who boarded at Le Vieux Pont first for a month, then for six months, and eventually stayed for fifteen years. He was known as '*le roi du gougeon*' ('the gudgeon king'): he would spend the whole day catching whitebait in the Aveyron that ended up on customers' plates (that would not be allowed under today's draconian fishing regulations).

Nicole is an extraordinarily gifted and imaginative chef. Her cuisine draws extensively on fine local produce (raw ham, venison, veal, beef, walnuts, walnut oil, cep mushrooms, lamb sweetbreads and Laguiole cheese, to name but a few), but also brings into play vegetables, herbs and spices less frequently used by French restaurant chefs (purslane, fresh sage, coriander, juniper berries, saffron, mace). She finds in-spiration in old recipe books, culinary memories or simply what she finds at market. To her, the work of the chef is like that of a painter, with flavours balancing each other like colours.

Nicole is helped by her very able husband, Bruno Rouquier, in the kitchen, and by her sister, Michèle, who twelve years ago left an office job to join her in the restaurant, and whose welcoming smile is a delightful bonus. Le Vieux Pont earns one rosette in the Michelin guide, and a high 15 out of 20 (two chef's hats) in the Gault-Millau

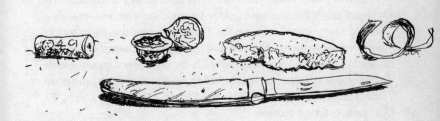

guide. It is not expensive for all that: in 1994 Le Vieux Pont won the Gault-Millau award for the restaurant offering the best value in the whole of France.

In this *tarte au boudin de cochon et aux herbes vertes, beurre fondu aillé*, Nicole strikes a characteristically fine balance between the very carefully proportioned ingredients of the tart filling and the punch of the garlic butter.

[*For four*]
150g (5½oz) puff pastry
1 small shallot, finely chopped
80g (3oz) unsalted butter
30g (1oz) bread, soaked in a little cream
1 egg
60g (2oz) ground almonds
30g (1oz) raw ham
20ml (¾fl oz) double cream
20g (¾oz) spinach
20g (¾oz) Swiss chard tops
40g (1½oz) flat-leaf parsley
400g (14oz) *boudin*
2 cloves garlic
16 small salad leaves (rocket or dandelion), lightly dressed

On a lightly floured surface, roll out the pastry to a thickness of about 6mm (¼in), cut 4 discs measuring 11cm (4½in) in diameter, prick with a fork and leave to rest.

Fry the shallot gently until translucent in 20g (¾oz) of butter. Put into a blender with the bread, egg, ground almonds, ham, cream, spinach, Swiss chard tops and half the parsley, and blend.

Bake the pastry rounds in a hot oven (220°C/425°F/Gas mark 7) for about 10 minutes or until golden brown. Remove and set aside.

Using a very sharp knife, cut the *boudin* into very thin slices (or get your *charcutier* to do so). Butter 4 *quiche* moulds (non-stick if possible) measuring 11cm (4½in) in diameter. Line with overlapping *boudin* slices to form a rosette, spread the filling evenly over them, and place a round of puff pastry on top. Bake in a fairly hot oven (190°C/375°F/Gas mark 5) for 15 minutes.

Melt the rest of the butter. Crush the garlic and add to the butter immediately. Chop the remaining parsley finely, add and mix well. Unmould the tarts on to hot plates, with the *boudin* slices uppermost, top with the salad leaves and pour the garlic and parsley butter around each tart.

(Le Vieux Pont, 12390 Belcastel. The hotel annexe, in an imaginatively converted barn across the bridge, has seven rooms. Tel: 05 65 64 52 29.)

⤙ Petit salé aux lentilles ⤚

Petit salé aux lentilles (salt pork with lentils) is a classic Auvergnat dish that has become one of the mainstays of *cuisine bourgeoise*. Like *blanquette de veau*, *boeuf bourguignon* and *navarin d'agneau*, it often features as a *plat du jour* scrawled in whitewash on the windows of cafés in Paris and other French cities that cater for lunching office workers.

To those who had to put up with the kind of tasteless overcooked yellowish-red lentils served up at school meals, the word lentil may have a sinister ring. But there are lentils and lentils (and cooking and cooking – yellow lentils can be very tasty when cooked properly and given the right accompaniment). Neither the yellowish-red Egyptian lentil nor the large brown German lentil can compare with the lentil used in this dish: *la lentille verte du Puy*. Its official denomination as the green lentil from the town of Le Puy-en-Velay (Haute-Loire) is not the work of some over-enthusiastic chamber of commerce – though local enthusiasm there is: a Le Puy politician, Paul Girollet (1859–1948), wrote a 'Hymne à la Lentille' which praised the pulse's qualities in rhapsodic style. In 1930 the Russian botanist Helena Barulina wrote a 300-page book on lentils in which she classified fifty-nine cultivated varieties. Among them was one she named *Lens esculenta dupuyensis*. Because of concern that people might wrongly conclude that someone called Dupuy had developed the variety, its name was later changed to *Lens esculenta puyensis*.

What is so special about *Lens esculenta puyensis* grown in the region of Le Puy compared with those of the same variety grown, as they are, in Germany, Algeria or the United States? Major factors are thought to be the climate (the area around Le Puy is the driest in the Massif Central) and, above all, a volcanic soil, which gives it a high iron, magnesium and polyunsaturated fatty acid content.

Because of those qualities, the Le Puy lentil has always sold at a premium. At the turn of the century, when it commanded a price on average 30 per cent higher than lentils from elsewhere, the Société Agricole et Scientifique de la Haute-Loire warned consumers against common yellow lentils from the Cantal and elsewhere that were being dyed green and sold as Le Puy lentils. Later, genuine green lentils – but from Russia, Germany and North Africa – were mixed half and half with the Le Puy product. This led growers to push for their own lentil to be recognized with an *appellation d'origine*. It was only some sixty years later, in 1996, that it was granted an *appellation d'origine contrôlée* (AOC), thus becoming the first dried vegetable to get AOC protection in France. Sadly, the price differential between Le Puy lentils and green lentils imported from elsewhere (which is currently about 100 per cent) has hit the industry hard, and sales of Le Puy lentils are steadily declining. In 1997 the lentil crop also had the misfortune to be ravaged by a gall-fly of the Cecidomyidae family.

As anyone who has run their fingers through raw Le Puy lentils will know, they have a peculiar tactile attraction, a heaviness in relation to size that is more commonly found in the mineral world than the vegetable. They also have a marvellous mottled blue-green colour reminiscent of some wild bird's eggs. Christian Maillebouis tells us, in his valuable little monograph on the subject, *La Lentille verte du Puy* (Ostal del Libre, 1995), that their colour comes from a blue pigment called anthocyanin ('blue flower' in Greek), also found in bilberries and cornflowers. The pigment is located at various depths in the lentil's tegument, or outer covering, which is yellow. It is the irregular distribution of the blue pigment that produces a mottled effect, and the combination of the two colours, blue and yellow, that produces the lentil's distinctive shade. It is almost a disappointment when Le Puy lentils turn brown during cooking, even if it is a nice warm earthy brown. This colour change during cooking is virtually unique among vegetables, and surely adds to the magic of the lentil.

Now for the more down-to-earth problem of cooking *petit salé aux lentilles*. In France, *petit salé* (salt pork) is available from any good *charcuterie*, often in both its raw and cooked versions. Elsewhere unsmoked gammon will fill the bill perfectly well.

[*For six*]

2kg (4lb 6oz) uncooked *petit salé* consisting of *palette*
   (blade bone), spare ribs and lean belly
3 medium onions
6 cloves
4 cloves garlic, peeled
bouquet garni consisting of 4 sprigs flat-leaf parsley or
   8 parsley stalks, 1 sprig thyme and 1 bay leaf
freshly ground pepper
500g (1lb 2oz) Le Puy green lentils
salt

Soak the salt pork for at least 12 hours in plenty of water. Remove, rinse and put into a large pot with just enough water to cover. Bring slowly to the boil, skimming if necessary. After 10 minutes' boiling, taste the water. If it is not at all salty, or only slightly salty, proceed to the next step. If it tastes fairly salty, pour off the water, rinse the pork, cover with fresh water and bring to the boil again. Stud each onion with 2 cloves and add to the pork along with the garlic, the *bouquet garni*, and plenty of pepper. Bring back to the boil and simmer for 1½ to 2 hours, or until the meat can be pierced easily with a fork. Remove from the heat, allow to rest and remove as much fat as possible with a bulb baster or by gently pressing a small ladle down into the liquid so the fat dribbles over the edge into it. An even better technique is to allow the pork to cool in its cooking broth, place it in the refrigerator or very cool place for several hours or overnight, and then peel off the soft layer of fat that will have formed on its surface.

Rinse the lentils, add to the pork and bring back to a simmer. As the lentils begin to swell (after about 20 minutes), add a little water from time to time to ensure they remain immersed. Simmer until cooked (this takes about 45 minutes, depending on how fresh they are; they should remain firm but not *al dente*). Check seasoning and add salt if necessary. Strain off most of the liquid and set aside for a soup. Remove the *bouquet garni*. At this point you can, if you wish, discard the onions, as they will have contributed almost all their taste and become rather insipid. If you want to serve them, lift them out gingerly, so they do not disintegrate, and arrange on a large, warmed serving dish. Add the pork pieces and pour the lentils around them. Dijon mustard goes very well with *petit salé*.

Although not a traditional Auvergnat dish, a salad of lentils left over from a *petit salé aux lentilles* can be delicious, carrying a hint of salt pork through to another meal. Make a dressing of Dijon mustard, grapeseed oil, lemon juice, parsley and plenty of spring onion (or mild white onion), both finely chopped, and mix thoroughly with the lentils. If you want to have enough leftover lentils to make a substantial lentil salad, it is as well to cook two 500g (1lb 2oz) packets of lentils with the *petit salé*. Don't worry if there seems to be too much lentil salad – its flavour changes for the better with age (as long as it is well refrigerated). This would seem to be the effect of the chopped onion macerating in the dressing, which has an equally beneficial effect on a potato salad after 24 hours. Before Dr Richard Lacey and his brigade of food-safety ayatollahs slap a fatwa on me for encouraging slovenly food conservation habits, I should say I have more than once eaten lentil salad that was four days old without any ill effects – except the shock of seeing a guest who had been enthusing over the salad drop his fork with horror when told its age.

When intending to make a salad, it is best to use the technique, suggested above, of allowing the *petit salé* to cool in its cooking liquid, so that virtually all the fat can be removed. If too much fat is left in the lentils you will be left with a sludgy salad.

Recipes sometimes suggest adding the lentils to the *petit salé* when it is half cooked rather than fully cooked. This can be dangerous if using bought *petit salé*, which can be treacherously salty. In France any butcher's assurance that his *petit salé* has been '*au sel*' for only a couple of days and is therefore not very salty should be taken with a pinch of you know what. Despite the soaking process, unexpected quantities of salt lurking deep in the meat and bones can leach into the dish, making it inedible.

✦ Potée ✦

Various versions of *potée* are found all over agricultural France. It is an archetypal peasant dish, drawing on the produce of the kitchen garden and the store cupboard. Like its cousins, *pot-au-feu* (boiled beef and vegetables) and the Auvergnat *mourtayrol* (boiled mixed meats and vegetables – p. 139), it is traditionally served in two stages. The broth, in which the flavours of salt pork and various vegetables intermingle, is followed by the strained meat and vegetables. The broth that is left over from a *potée* is served on its own the following day (or days), when it is known as *soupe aux choux* (p. 10).

To make a successful *potée*, you need to have high-quality produce and to respect scrupulously the cooking times of the various ingredients. If the cabbage is overcooked, for example, it will take on the consistency of jellyfish familiar to those unfortunate enough, like me, to have experienced the horrors of school cabbage.

Auvergne's most famous poet, Arsène Vermenouze, wrote a whole recipe for *potée* in verse (he calls it *soupe aux choux*, but actually the result is closer to a saffron-less *mourtayrol* in that it includes pork, a hen and beef).

Potée is a hearty, filling dish at its best on chilly autumn or winter days. In the Auvergne, however, the notion of what constitutes a filling dish is sometimes a little hazy, as was shown by the experience a few years ago of some particularly gluttonous friends who were staying with me. They made a day trip to the remote village of Vezels-Roussy (Cantal), whose only café-restaurant, La Bergerie, was famous for the gargantuan meals it served (I would have joined them, but three restaurant meals in three days would have been too much for me). They reported that after devouring the traditional first two courses of soup and locally made *charcuterie* (raw ham, *saucisson sec* and *pâté*) they were served what looked like a *potée* (a mountain of cabbage, swedes, sausages and salt pork) instead of the roast chicken they had ordered. When they told the waitress they thought there must be some mistake, she replied with a sweet smile that it was only a 'side dish' and that she would be bringing the chicken in a minute.

[*For eight*]

1 salt blade of pork

750g (1lb 10oz) salt spare ribs

500g (1lb 2oz) salt breast of pork (as lean as possible)

2 large onions, peeled

4 cloves

freshly ground pepper

1 small Savoy cabbage

500g (1lb 2oz) carrots, halved and cut into even lengths

500g (1lb 2oz) turnips or swedes, quartered

6 potatoes, quartered

8 *saucisses fraîches* (p. 72)

salt if necessary

Soak all the salt pork for at least 12 hours in plenty of water. Remove, rinse and put into a large pot with 5 litres of water. Bring slowly to the boil, skimming if necessary. After 10 minutes' boiling, taste the water. If it is not at all salty, or only slightly salty, proceed to the next step. If it tastes fairly salty, pour off the water, rinse the pork, cover with the same amount of fresh water and bring to the boil. Stud each onion with 2 cloves and add to the pork with plenty of pepper. Bring back to the boil and simmer for 1½ hours. Remove from the heat and allow to rest. Quarter the cabbage, wash thoroughly in between the leaves and blanch in plenty of fiercely boiling water for 5 minutes. Drain and refresh under cold running water.

Remove as much fat as possible from the salt pork liquid with a bulb baster or by gently pressing a small ladle down into the liquid so the fat dribbles over the edge of the ladle. Add a little pepper and bring back to a gentle boil. Add the carrots. After 10 minutes, add the turnips or swedes, potatoes and sausages. After another 10 minutes add the cabbage and boil for a further 10 minutes or until the vegetables are cooked (but not overcooked). Lift the meat and vegetables out of the broth with a slotted spoon, place in a large dish, cover with foil and keep warm in a very low oven until needed. Check the broth for salt and correct if necessary. Serve it as a first course – the authentic Auvergnat fashion is to place slices of half-rye bread in each soup bowl before ladling the soup over them.

★

The left-over broth should be kept for *soupe aux choux* the next day. But if you wish to consume it more than 24 hours later make sure it is kept in a cool place or in the refrigerator – many Auvergnats have unpleasant memories of eating *potée* broth that has gone sour (a reaction due to the presence of cabbage).

Game

Eating anything that moves is claimed to be a character trait that the French inherited from their ancestors, the Gauls. However that may be, it is a fact that they pioneered the consumption of snails and frogs (I use the word 'pioneered' advisedly, since more frogs and snails in garlic butter are now consumed, proportionately, by tourists visiting France than by the French themselves). In the days before shooting regulations came in, the French shot at any furry or feathered creature that came into their sights. Birds, particularly thrushes and blackbirds, were encouraged to do precisely that by the berry-laden holly or wild service trees that were planted near farmhouses. In winter Rémy Chabut (p. 7) used to station himself inside what used to be my barn (it is currently being converted into one section of Mourjou's 'eco-museum', the Maison de la Châtaigne), swivel aside the piece of wood that covered a small square aperture he had made in one of the doors, push his gun through and pick off birds alighting on the huge holly tree standing next to the barn. Many years later, his wife Jeanne remembered without a shred of nostalgia how she and a woman friend had once achieved the mammoth task of plucking ninety-five blackbirds he had shot for a banquet.

Rémy Chabut was of course flouting the rules that forbid hunters to use a gun within 200 metres of human habitation. Even today, scant attention is paid to such 'annoying' regulations. One day my local butcher, Raymond Vigier (p. 126), found a partridge in the courtyard behind his shop. It was a farm-raised bird that had been released just before the shooting season, and, although timid, was not frightened enough to take to the air. Raymond rushed inside to get his gun and finally managed to persuade the partridge to fly up to the top of the roof. He then shot it. 'My neighbours heard the bang and opened their windows expectantly,' he remembers with a chuckle. 'They thought I'd at last shot my wife!'

Pheasant, partridge and boar are nowadays quite often bought from specialized farms and released at the beginning of the shooting season when there is a shortage of wild game. When times were leaner and the hunting committees could not afford to buy in game, people cast their net wider to include more or less any bird that did not taste nasty. Even today, France is the European Union country that allows the biggest number of bird species (sixty-five) to be shot by hunters. Almost everyone over the age of forty that I have talked to in Mourjou remembers, for example, eating crow (or rook); some even admit to having eaten sparrows (I knew that *uccelletti* were an Italian speciality, but was unaware the French shared their taste for tiny birds).

Crow is apparently quite tasty *en civet*. Before the last war, there was a diabolical product on sale called Corbeau-dort (Sleep-crow), which took the form of grains of corn that had been soaked in a soporific drug. Scattered on the fields during sowing time along with untreated grain, it would be eaten by crows. They promptly fell asleep and could easily be gathered up and prepared for a *civet*. Since young birds were preferred, another method of hunting was to pick them straight out of their nests when they were nearly fledged.

Each spring Henri Lavigne, a carpenter friend of mine, used to take a nearly-fledged jay, magpie or crow out of its nest – not to eat but to tame. He then let the bird free, but it would come when called and land on his arm or head in the hope of getting a morsel of food. Henri's wife, Jeanne-Marie, was less keen on the birds because they liked flying around and exploring the house, ruining her efforts to keep the furniture polished. One year, she discovered that one of the two crows in residence (to which her young daughter had become greatly attached) had unpicked a sampler she had been working on for weeks. She had never liked the bird. What particularly irked her was that it would get into the hen coop, eat any egg in sight and, worse even in her eyes, pretend it was a chicken by giving a rather convincing imitation of clucking. In a fit of rage, Yvonne grabbed the offending crow, wrung its neck, caught its innocent companion and did the same to it, then plucked and drew the two birds and served them up for dinner *en civet*. Understandably, her husband and daughter felt a little off their food that evening.

The game most commonly shot and eaten in the Auvergne is boar, hare, rabbit, roe deer, red deer, woodcock, woodpigeon, partridge and pheasant. As in the rest of France, they are usually cooked in a straightforward, classical fashion – roast or *en civet* (the recipe for hare *civet* given on p. 100 works equally well for boar, venison or rabbit).

↞ Cassolette de cèpes, escargots et noix ↠

Mauricette Cayron might still be working as an accountant in a Paris insurance company had she not met her future husband, Jean, at a Club Med camp in Greece. Jean was a waiter at L'Escargot de Montlhéry, a Paris restaurant, and persuaded her to take up a job behind the cash desk at the same establishment. Although Jean was born in Bordeaux, his parents came from the Aveyron and used to holiday in the Châtaigneraie. When Mauricette and Jean were tipped off that the Hôtel du Nord in Montsalvy (Cantal) was up for sale, they took the plunge and in 1970 turned it into one of the most welcoming and reliable hostelries in the area. The hotel has had the much-coveted red R in the Michelin guide (for 'good food at moderate prices') since 1979.

Good food was in Mauricette's family – her great-aunt had worked as a cook for the singer Fréhel before the war. She had always liked cooking, but had had no formal training. For the first three years she employed professional chefs and trained 'on the job'. Later she went on cookery training courses. Now a fully-fledged chef, she favours

dishes which treat good local produce simply, such as rabbit stuffed with a mixture of raw ham, mushrooms and shallots, *civet* of piglet in Auvergne wine, *ris de veau aux cèpes*, and this tasty autumnal entrée, a *cassolette de cèpes, escargots et noix*.

[*For four*]
200g (7oz) cep mushrooms
80g (3oz) unsalted butter
20g (¾oz) shallots, finely chopped
120ml (4fl oz) white Côtes d'Auvergne, or similar dry
  white wine
4 dozen snails, without their shells
1 teaspoon Ricard or other aniseed-flavoured *apéritif*
120ml (4fl oz) double cream
⅓ nutmeg, freshly grated
salt
freshly ground pepper
40g (1½oz) freshly shelled walnuts, chopped
1 tablespoon parsley, finely chopped

Chop the mushrooms fairly finely, put them in a non-stick sauté pan on a medium heat, and get them to render any water they contain. Add the butter and shallot, and sauté gently until the mushrooms turn golden. Add the white wine, turn up heat and reduce by half. Reduce the heat and add the snails, Ricard, cream, nutmeg, a large pinch of salt and plenty of pepper. Add the walnuts and continue to cook just long enough for them to heat through, but no longer, otherwise they will colour the dish purplish-brown. Check seasoning. Transfer to very hot *cassolettes* and serve.

(Hôtel du Nord, 15120 Montsalvy. Tel. 04 71 49 20 03.)

⊀ Civet de coeur et de mou de chevreuil ⊁

In the not so distant days when most people in the Auvergne could not afford to eat much meat, they were happy to supplement their often monotonous diet with the occasional rabbit, hare, pigeon, partridge, deer or wild boar. Today, now that they are better fed, they still enjoy a spot of shooting. The game is provided by Mother Nature or, in leaner years, by specialized farms and aviaries. It is easy to distinguish between the two types of game animals. The pheasant that continues to forage unconcernedly in the ditch like a chicken when you stop your car has come from an aviary, as has the partridge you almost trip over on a path by a cornfield. Boar, being more intelligent, should perhaps know better than to trust two-legged creatures. Yet it quite often happens that when they are released from the van that has brought them from the boar farm they refuse to do what they are supposed to do: flee the assembled hunters. Only after they have been much shouted at by men and barked at by dogs do they realize the hand which once fed them is about to shoot them. They rarely manage to dash more than a few yards before crumpling in a hail of lead.

But boar are canny and prolific animals, and any that survive in the wild are quick to found large families, particularly in areas like the Châtaigneraie, whose steep wooded valleys afford plenty of thick cover. When this happens, they become a serious pest, guzzling whole swathes of maize crops (this is not in fact as big a problem for farmers as it might seem, since they get EU compensation for damage by boar; and I know of at least one case of a less scrupulous farmer letting his own cows loose in a maize field and then claiming the crop had been eaten by boar).

When there is a plethora of boar, the local hunting federation gives permission for unlimited culling. In the 1995–6 shooting season, the forty hunters in my village shot forty-three boar (that figure does not take account of the many animals which were shot and wounded, but not killed, and which would probably have died later after days of suffering). Two tonnes of boar meat were crammed into deep-freezes, and for many months afterwards families were eating the stuff until it was coming out of their ears.

Roe deer are not classified as pests, like boar, though they too can damage crops and saplings. The number that each commune may shoot is strictly regulated each year by a *plan de chasse* drawn up by the local branch of the Fédération Nationale de la Chasse, which takes into account the number of deer observed in the wild.

Hunters regularly get together for an almost ritual feast, at which they partake of the lights and heart of deer or boar cooked in a *civet* which is thickened with the blood of the animal. This is an almost exclusively male occasion: there may be the occasional wife or girlfriend present, but most spouses, as one of them told me, prefer to avoid 'having to talk about past hunting exploits the whole evening'. The cooking of the *civet* is an ordeal for the cook, whether he or she is professional or not, as the hunters are extremely fussy about how their fetishistic repast is prepared.

The stew may sound repellent, but I can assure you that it is an excellent, intensely flavoured dish when made with good wine and good vinegar (the vinegar provides an essential astringent note). The following recipe was given to me by Fernande Faven (p. 173). It works equally well with boar's or even pig's heart and lights.

[*For four*]
50ml (2fl oz) good cider vinegar or 30ml (1fl oz) sherry
  vinegar
150ml (5½fl oz) roe deer blood, or the blood of another
  animal
250g (9oz) roe deer heart
250g (9oz) roe deer lights
30g (1oz) roe deer liver
30g (1oz) oil
2 shallots, finely chopped
1 clove garlic, finely chopped
1 bay leaf
2 sprigs thyme
2 sprigs wild thyme
salt
freshly ground pepper
750ml (26fl oz) good full-bodied red wine
30g (1oz) dark bitter chocolate

Mix the vinegar with the roe deer's blood (this stops it curdling). Carefully trim the heart, lights and liver of all gristle, windpipe, arteries, fat and so on. Cut up the heart and lights into small pieces, and dab dry with kitchen paper. Chop the liver very finely. Heat the oil in a non-stick sauté pan and brown the pieces of heart, lights and liver. Add the shallots, garlic, bay leaf, thyme, wild thyme, a large pinch of salt, plenty of pepper and the wine. Bring to the boil, cover and simmer very gently for 2 hours, checking from time to time that the wine is not drying up and adding a little water if necessary. Away from the heat, add the chocolate and the blood and stir well. Return to a low heat, and when the sauce is thick enough to coat the back of a spoon transfer the *civet* to a very hot serving dish. Serve with boiled potatoes and, if you wish, fried *croûtons* as well.

⤙ Civet de lièvre ⤚

The terrain of the Auvergne, much of which consists of grass-covered hills and mountains, is highly suited to the lifestyle of the hare. It is also reputed to produce animals with a particularly fine flavour. The wild hare population has been maintained at a reasonable level, particularly in the last twenty years or so, during which the once plethoric rabbit population has been severely hit by myxomatosis. But every now and then each commune's hunting committee tops up hare numbers with a few specimens bought from specialized hare farms. These quite often start behaving like wild animals, surviving for a year or two and growing to a respectable size.

[*For six*]
30ml (1fl oz) good cider vinegar, or 20ml (¾fl oz) sherry
    vinegar
1 hare of about 2kg (4lb 6oz), with its blood and liver
2 onions, finely sliced
1 sprig thyme
2 bay leaves
6 juniper berries
1 tablespoon oil
40ml (1½fl oz) cognac
salt
freshly ground pepper
30g (1oz) lard
200g (7oz) lean salt pork belly or green bacon
20 pickling onions
1 tablespoon flour

1 clove garlic, finely chopped
750ml (26fl oz) good red wine
60ml (2fl oz) double cream

Mix the vinegar with the hare's blood (this stops it curdling). Remove the gall bladder from the liver, and wash out the hare's stomach cavity to remove any traces of gall. Cut the hare into about 10 pieces. Put half the sliced onion, the thyme, bay leaves, juniper berries, oil, cognac, a little salt and plenty of pepper into a china bowl and mix well. Pack the hare pieces tightly into the bowl, coating them on all sides with the marinade. Leave for several hours or overnight in a cool place, turning over the pieces at least once.

Heat the lard in a large non-stick sauté pan and fry the salt pork or bacon and pickling onions until brown. Remove and set aside. Put the remaining sliced onion into the sauté pan, sprinkle with flour and fry gently until the flour has caramelized (i.e. turned light brown). Add the hare pieces in 2 batches and brown on all sides. Transfer to a casserole, add the marinade and its contents, the garlic and enough red wine to cover. Cook in a medium oven (180°C/350°F/Gas mark 4) for 2 hours.

Add the salt pork or bacon, the pickling onions and the liver, cut into thin slices, to the stew and continue cooking very gently on top of the stove for 5 minutes. Remove from the heat and strain the sauce into a saucepan. Put all the ingredients except the thyme and bay leaves into a large serving dish and keep warm.

Allow the sauce to settle for a minute or two, then remove as much fat as possible with a bulb baster or by gently pressing a small ladle down into the liquid so the fat dribbles over the edge of the ladle. Bring the sauce slowly to a simmer. Mix the cream with the blood thoroughly in another saucepan. Away from the heat, ladle a little of the hot sauce into the blood and cream mixture, and mix well. Pour in the rest of the sauce, whisking vigorously. The sauce should become thick enough to coat the back of a spoon. If this is not the case, return to a very gentle heat and continue whisking for a minute or two until it reaches the coating stage. On no account allow the sauce to boil.

Check seasoning, allowing for the saltiness of the salt pork or bacon. Pour the sauce over the hare pieces and serve immediately.

Poultry

As I already pointed out in the introduction to the Eggs chapter, most Auvergne farms still have their little cohort of egg-producing hens, with a cock or two to fertilize them, wandering round the farmyard and the surrounding fields. There are usually a few ducks too, and, on the bigger farms, some geese and turkeys. Some farmers raise flocks of guinea fowl, the source of perhaps the most subtle-tasting of all domesticated poultry.

Until relatively recently, most poultry raised on farms was kept for market or reserved for special occasions such as birthdays, anniversaries or religious holidays. Only the work-weary egg-laying hen would regularly find its way to the farmers' table (in boiled form) once its useful life had come to an end. But now that the Auvergnats are more prosperous, thanks largely to EU hill-farming subsidies (which account for more than half their income), they are able to indulge themselves more often.

⊰ Rillettes de canard au foie gras mi-cuit ⊱

If one gets to market early in the large village of Maurs, 15 kilometres from Mourjou, the poultry van marked 'Delclaux – *spécialités quercy-noises*' that sets up near the west end of the church seems to be spilling over with rather untidy heaps of poultry and rabbits. The overcrowding is simply to allow for demand – by the end of the morning, the van will have been virtually cleaned out. Customers, who include myself, buy their poultry from Delclaux because they know they are getting genuine, strong-legged farm (as opposed to farmed) poultry, and good value for money as well – the chickens come straight from farms to

Delclaux without going through any middleman, and the Delclaux family rear their own ducks.

The business, which Yvon and Colette Delclaux started up in the village of Cuzac (Lot) in 1953, is two-pronged. At their newly modernized little processing plant – 'Those EU norms that require tiling everywhere are ridiculous – they're going to kill off a lot of people who are smaller than us,' Yvon grumbles – there is a mouth-watering boutique lined with a bewildering variety of tins and jars: duck and goose *foie gras*, *galantine de dinde* with *foie gras*, *magret de canard* stuffed with *foie gras*, *confits* of duck's *magret*, gizzards and wings, rabbit *terrine*, *pâté quercynois* with duck *foie gras* and green peppercorns, duck *fritons*, boned quails stuffed with duck *foie gras*, smoked *magret de canard*, and *rillettes de canard au foie gras mi-cuit*. When *foie gras* is present in any speciality, it accounts for 20 to 30 per cent of the whole.

The van, which sells mainly fresh produce, navigates during the week from one market to another within a radius of about 35 kilometres from Cuzac. In addition to the heaps of ducks, guinea fowl, chickens, pigeons and the occasional *coq*, there are trays of raw *foie gras*, vacuum-sealed duck *magrets*, both fresh and smoked, raw duck's carcasses (stripped of most of their meat) for soup, stuffed duck's necks, and both raw and preserved duck's gizzards, wings, hearts and necks, and a great slab of *rillettes de canard au foie gras mi-cuit*.

Now I do not normally go for *rillettes*, usually a mushy, mashed-up *pâté* of lengthily cooked meat mixed with fat. They can be made from pork, goose or duck. In most cases, the proportion of (expensive) meat to (cheaper) fat tilts heavily in favour of the latter, so quite apart from dietary considerations *rillettes* tend to cloy. But there are *rillettes* and *rillettes*, as I discovered one cold morning at Maurs market when Yvon Delclaux had left his tray of *rillettes de canard* out on display instead of keeping it, as he usually does, tucked out of sight in the van's refrigerated compartment. What is this? I asked myself, with a tingle of expectancy. Here were *rillettes* with hardly any visible fat: they were the right colour – grey-brown, instead of the usual colourant-charged reddish-brown; and they were studded with large nuggets of pinky-buff *foie gras*. I could not wait to get home and taste them. They were breathtakingly good, combining the flavour of lean duck meat, duck-skin crackling, duck fat and *foie gras mi-cuit*.

Here is the Delclaux's recipe for *rillettes de canard au foie gras mi-cuit*. It was given to me by their daughter, Nicole, who now runs the business with her husband Jean–Marc Saldana.

[*To make 1.5kg (3lb 5oz) of rillettes*]
300g (10½oz) duck fat
1.8kg (4lb) duck, jointed but not boned
25g (1oz) salt
5g (¼oz) freshly ground pepper
300g raw duck *foie gras*

Melt the duck fat over a low heat in a thick casserole. Add the duck pieces, the seasonings and a little water, cover and cook as slowly as possible, either on an electric hotplate with a very low setting or in a cool oven (150°C/300°F/Gas mark 2) for 8 hours. Check from time to time that the mixture is bubbling gently, but not burning.

While it is cooking, prepare the *foie gras*. Using a very sharp knife, meticulously shave off any green patches on the *foie gras* (they denote the presence of bile, and will make the dish irremediably bitter if not removed). Soak the *foie gras* in plenty of tepid water for 30 minutes. Remove and dab dry. Pull the *foie gras* apart and ease out the network of cartilage and veins with your fingers. Cut the *foie gras* into pieces about the size of a walnut.

Drain most of the fat off the duck pieces and reserve. Allow the duck to cool until lukewarm, then remove all bones (but not the skin). Blend briefly, so that one or two chunks remain whole. Add the fat and mix well. Check seasoning (remembering that it should taste very well salted, as the perceptible degree of saltiness diminishes when a dish is eaten cold). Pour into a rectangular bread tin (or similar mould) large enough to accommodate the *rillettes* and *foie gras*. Distribute the *foie gras* pieces evenly over the surface of the mixture and press down into it. Put the tin into a moderate oven (180°C/350°F/Gas mark 4) in a *bain-marie* and cook for 1 hour. Remove, leave to cool and refrigerate for at least 12 hours. Like *foie gras* on its own, the *rillettes* are best eaten 4 or 5 days after being made.

The temperature at which these *rillettes* are served is very important. One does not need to go to such extreme lengths as Pierre Wynants, of Comme Chez Soi in Brussels (three rosettes in the Michelin guide), whose sublime *mousse de bécasse* (woodcock mousse) is brought to the table in two successive servings (the perfectionist Wynants reckons that if served in one dollop the mousse warms up too much by the time the final mouthfuls are eaten). Even so, these *rillettes* are decidedly less appealing if soft and sweaty, so make sure they are properly chilled before serving. The best accompaniment is toasted half-rye bread (p. 179).

If you have difficulty in finding duck fat, a simple way of procuring it is to buy fresh *magrets de canard*, make a fine criss-cross grid of deep cuts on its fatty skin side, and begin by frying the *magrets* on their skin side: gigantic quantities of good-quality fat will be rendered, which can be poured off into a jar leaving studs of crispy brown skin.

(Produits Régionaux Delclaux, 46270 Cuzac. Tel: 05 65 34 27 13.)

⤙ Terrine de foie gras mi-cuit ⤚

Purists may wonder what a recipe for *foie gras* is doing in a book on the food of the Auvergne. Yet although *foie gras* is closely identified with south-west France, ducks and geese are also force-fed on the southern and south-western confines of the Auvergne, and their raw livers are on sale at many markets. It is equally true that *foie gras* is not a common dish throughout the Auvergne, and that it is a fairly recent import in those areas where it is eaten, filtering down from bourgeois tables over the past few decades.

Anyone who has tasted home- or restaurant-made *foie gras mi-cuit* will automatically prefer it to bought *foie gras*, whether it comes in a tin or a sterilized jar. There are two reasons for this. First, there is its price. Many people imagine all *foie gras* to be prohibitively expensive. This is true only of tinned *foie gras*: a tiny 50-gram tin can cost up to 90 francs (or 1,800 francs per kilo!) in some shops – and is certainly not worth the price. But raw *foie gras*, if bought direct from a farmer or a dealer like Delclaux (see previous recipe), costs a 'mere' 190–220 francs per kilo – a bit more than Parmesan, or one and a half times the price of the best fillet steak. Slightly more expensive, vacuum-packed raw *foie gras* from Gascony is now available in French hypermarkets. But when it is remembered that an average-sized duck liver of 600 grams will provide six people with generous helpings costing about 21 francs each, it can hardly be described as a great luxury.

The second point in favour of *foie gras mi-cuit* is its incomparably more complex, aromatic taste, which makes it as superior to the tinned version as caviar is to lump eggs. While the *mi-cuit* is semi-soft and sweet, and has a nose as overpowering as a Meursault's, tinned *foie gras*, which has necessarily cooked for too long and at too high a temperature, has the consistency of butter straight out of the fridge and only a hint of the *mi-cuit*'s fragrance. I can speak with some authority on the matter, as I was recently careless enough to overcook a *terrine de foie gras* for friends who were staying with me. Every mouthful of my botched dish tasted like a sullen reproach, while my friends' sudden rush of politeness ('No, Peter, it's delicious – really!') was deeply suspect. I made sure I got it right next time. By the way, the term *mi-cuit* (half-cooked) is misleading, because the *foie gras*, although pinkish-buff in the centre, is certainly much more cooked than it is raw. As for the relative merits of goose *foie gras* and duck *foie gras*, they are a bit like those of Bordeaux and Burgundy or Wagner and Brahms – a matter of taste. The two types of *foie gras* are cooked the same way, though the proportions given here are for duck liver.

[*For six*]

1 raw duck *foie gras* weighing about 600g (1lb 5oz)

30ml (1fl oz) good port or *vin de noix*

15ml (½fl oz) Armagnac

pinch nutmeg

8g (¼oz) salt

freshly ground white pepper

Meticulously shave off any green patches on the *foie gras*, however tiny, with a very sharp knife (they denote the presence of bile, and will make the dish irremediably bitter if not removed). Soak the *foie gras* in plenty of tepid water for 30 minutes. Remove and dab dry. Pull the larger lobe away from the smaller one. Open each lobe with a small, not too sharp knife, and ease out the network of cartilage and veins with your fingers while trying to break up the *foie gras* as little as possible.

Put the port or *vin de noix*, Armagnac, nutmeg, salt and pepper into a medium-sized china bowl and stir until almost all the salt has dissolved. Add the *foie gras* pieces and spoon the marinade over them, turning them over so every surface is moistened. Cover the bowl with clingfilm and place in the top of the refrigerator for 4 hours. Spoon the marinade once again over the pieces and refrigerate for at least another 8 hours.

Remove from the refrigerator. Take a *bain-marie* dish large enough to accommodate the *terrine*, fill with water 3cm (1½in) deep and place in a cool oven (150°C/300°F/Gas mark 2). Press the *foie gras* pieces down into an ovenproof earthenware or china *terrine*, oval in shape and at least 7cm (3in) high and with a capacity of 600ml (21fl oz). Slot the pieces in as tightly as possible in such a way that almost no air pockets are left. Add a tablespoonful of water to any marinade remaining in the bowl (most of it will have been absorbed by the *foie gras*), stir well and pour over the *terrine*.

Place the *terrine* in the bain-marie and cook uncovered for about 45 minutes or until the sides of the *foie gras* are separated from the sides of the *terrine* by a very thin layer of transparent melted fat. *Do not overcook*. Remove the *terrine* from the oven and from the *bain-marie*, put on its lid and allow to cool at room temperature for 3 hours. Refrigerate overnight. The *foie gras* will improve if kept refrigerated for 4 or 5 days before being eaten. You can keep it for up to a month in the refrigerator by pouring enough just-melted lard or, better, duck fat on top of it to seal the surface completely.

Foie gras is often served with toasted brioche or *pain de mie* (sandwich bread). But to my mind it is far more at home with thin slices of toasted wholemeal or half-rye (p. 179) bread.

⤛ Salmis de canard ⤜

This recipe was given to me by Yvonne Puech, of the Hôtel Beauséjour in Calvinet, 5 kilometres from Mourjou, an establishment that has sported the Michelin guide's red R (good food at moderate prices) for a good thirty years. An experienced cook with a thorough knowledge of local culinary traditions, she handed over to her son, Louis-Bernard (p. 53), fifteen years ago. He has since notched up a Michelin rosette while keeping the red R.

Yvonne and her husband Marcel built the hotel in 1938 with the help of loans from farmers (local banks had not yet moved into the lucrative business of lending money to restaurateurs). There was hot and cold water in every room, something of a rarity in those days for a simple country hotel. And the two lavatories on each floor were such an innovation that, just after the hotel was built, the local primary schoolteacher brought her pupils along to look at the flushing cisterns, which most of them had never seen before.

In 1939, Marcel was mobilized and taken prisoner by the Germans. At the age of nineteen, Yvonne was left to fend for herself and run the hotel with her even younger sister-in-law. She proved quite resourceful: as they were non-smokers, they were able to exchange their tobacco ration coupons for produce from farms; they provided lunches for schoolchildren and got eggs and chickens in return; they sent potatoes and swedes to acquaintances in the Hérault *département*, who sent them back bottles of an *apéritif* called Athéna. There was no oil, so Yvonne made salad dressings with goose fat.

The Germans showed their faces only once in Calvinet. As they drove through the village in convoy, Yvonne remembers frightened schoolchildren scattering in every direction. The Germans shouted '*Petits Français, courir vite!*' but did not stop. *Maquisards* were more of a problem. In the Châtaigneraie, where the Resistance was more loosely organized than in the mountain fastness of the Margeride, the *maquisards* are chiefly remembered as people who tended to throw their weight about and requisition more or less any food they wanted. They therefore had a rather poor image in the eyes of the local population. When they took a whole ham from Yvonne, she asked for an IOU. They duly gave her one. It read: 'Your repayment will be Victory.' One local man, looking back on the period, summed up a widespread view of the Resistants among the rural community: 'Not all the *maquisards* were yobs, but every yob had gone into the *maquis*.'

So much food continued to be produced locally during the war that there were few privations. This is attested by the menu of Yvonne's brother and sister-in-law's wedding feast in 1942, even allowing for the fact that the diet on most days would of course have been incomparably more frugal and humdrum. It included, among other things, cooked ham (a luxury at the time), *foie gras maison*, more ham (this time *en papillote* with a cream sauce), a *salmis* of guinea fowl, *galantine de volaille truffée*, turkey with wild watercress, cheese, *vacherin chantilly*, chocolate cake, apple tart and almond frangipane.

For centuries Calvinet was celebrated for its livestock fair, which was instituted by a charter of 1266. The charter stipulated that it could sell partridge, hares, wild rabbit and otter pelts (which were more highly taxed than fox pelts). After the Second World War, its fair started up again and continued to be held eight times a year until the early sixties. Farmers from as far afield as the Pyrenees and Lorraine drove there to buy piglets. Yvonne would open her restaurant at 5 a.m. to cater for them – they were ravenous after driving through the night, and started the day with a hearty cheese soup. They paid for their livestock in banknotes, which they brought in shoe-boxes. They did not like to have too much cash with them on the market-place, so during the day they left their shoe-boxes in Yvonne's safe keeping under the kitchen table.

If the buyers were wary, the vendors were wily: she remembers local farmers bringing cauldrons of pigswill with them to the fair, so they could feed their pigs just before they were put on to the public weighbridge. As there was only one weighbridge, transactions went on the whole day. Yvonne's establishment was full at lunchtime and again for supper, which was usually followed by a dance.

Yvonne remains very active at seventy-eight. She can sometimes be found in her son's kitchen, amidst a gaggle of young *commis*, quietly making a *galantine* or a *poule farcie* (p. 116). More often she is in the laundry room, ironing towels, tablecloths and napkins, an activity she claims to enjoy.

As a tribute to his mother's cooking, Louis-Bernard Puech still occasionally features her recipe for *salmis de canard* on his menu. The dish, whose dark colour somehow contributes to its remarkable intensity of flavour, is certainly not out of keeping in a one-rosette restaurant.

[*For four*]
120ml (4fl oz) fresh duck's blood
1 tablespoon good vinegar
50g (2oz) salt pork belly or green streaky bacon, cut into
    very small dice
1 duck, cut into pieces
600ml (21fl oz) good red wine
salt
freshly ground pepper
40g (1½oz) unsalted butter
1 onion, finely chopped
bouquet garni
2 lumps sugar
100ml (3½fl oz) Madeira

Mix the duck's blood with the vinegar to prevent it from curdling. Put the salt pork or bacon in a casserole and heat until it browns slightly and becomes semi-transparent. Add the duck pieces and cook over a medium heat. When they are browned, turn down the heat to low, add two-thirds of the wine, a little water, a large pinch of salt and plenty of pepper, and cover. Cook gently for 90 minutes on top of the stove or in the oven.

Chop the duck's liver coarsely. Heat the butter in a thick-bottomed saucepan. Brown the onion lightly over a medium heat, then add the *bouquet garni*, the liver, a good pinch of salt, plenty of pepper, the sugar, the rest of the wine and the Madeira. Cover and simmer for about 90 minutes. Remove the *bouquet garni* and put the sauce through a fine drum sieve or *chinois*. Pour a little of the sauce into a smaller saucepan containing the duck's blood, stir well, then gradually add the rest of the sauce. Place over a low heat and stir until the sauce thickens slightly. Correct the seasoning if necessary.

Transfer the duck pieces to a very hot serving dish, pour the sauce over them and serve immediately.

Plain boiled potatoes, pasta, or steamed turnips are a good accompaniment to this dish.

⤙ Tourte de canard aux châtaignes et aux pommes ⤚

For many French, the summer holidays are synonymous with the seaside. That is why its coastline, although 3,120 kilometres long, is in many places as jammed with roasting human flesh as Blackpool or the Costa Brava. In recent years, however, there has been a big shift away from the seaside to what the French call '*tourisme vert*' – holidays inland, which offer anything from fishing and yachting on lakes to gentle hikes in rolling countryside, serious mountain walking or just *far niente* in an unspoilt, unpolluted rural environment. Hence the development of *gîtes* (rented country cottages with self-catering facilities), *tables d'hôte* and *chambres à la ferme* (where guests eat at the same table) and *fermes auberges* (p. 22). In the Châtaigneraie, many farmers have made *gîtes* out of abandoned cottages, outbuildings – not too close to the pigsties – and even *sécadous*, huts in which chestnuts used to be dried for the winter, sometimes next to the farm, sometimes in the depths of chestnut woods.

This shift has been accompanied by efforts to provide *touristes verts* with things to do or go and see – riding, tennis (courts are now found in almost every village), eco-museums that show what country life was like in the past, and weekend fairs with folk music, dances and buffets. In the Châtaigneraie there is a dynamic association called Les Relais du Heurtoir. It includes *fermes auberges*, producers of honey, cheese, *pâtés* and poultry preserves, and patchwork and flower arrangement studios.

Les Relais du Heurtoir was the brainchild of Yvonne Croutes and her sister-in-law Claudine Croutes, of La Ferme du Sériès, who make succulent preserves of the ducks and chickens they rear themselves.

They also do the catering at events such as Mourjou's Foire de la Châtaigne (Chestnut Fair – p. 166), and present their products at local markets in Aurillac and Lafeuillade-en-Vézie. One of the dishes to be found at such markets is this unusual duck, chestnut and apple pie, which they devised for the Mourjou fair. In it, the richness of the duck is beautifully set off by the sweetness of the chestnuts and tartness of the apples.

[For four]

100g (3½oz) fresh or deep-frozen chestnuts, peeled, or
   tinned chestnuts
600g (1lb 5oz) chilled short pastry
1 egg yolk, beaten
200g (7oz) raw duck meat
salt
freshly ground pepper
ground allspice
100g (3½oz) Bramleys or similarly tart apples, peeled and
   sliced

Cook the chestnuts (for procedure, see p. 186) if fresh or deep-frozen. On a lightly floured surface, roll out two-thirds of the pastry to a circle about 6mm (¼in) thick. Line a 23-cm/9-in pie tin with it. Brush the edge with egg yolk. Chop the duck meat coarsely and put it in a layer on the pastry. Season with a large pinch of salt, plenty of pepper and a tiny pinch of allspice. Crumble the chestnuts and strew over the meat. Cover with the sliced apple. Roll out the other piece of pastry to the same thickness and place on top of the pie. Press down so it sticks to the glazed pastry. Make a small gash in the middle of the pie and insert a rolled piece of foil to make a chimney.

Bake the pie in a fairly hot oven (200°C/400°F/Gas mark 6) for 20 minutes, then turn down the heat to moderate (180°C/350°F/Gas mark 4) and bake for a further 40 minutes, covering with foil if the top looks in danger of burning.

This recipe can also be made with cooked duck leftovers, but it will not be as succulent. If using cooked duck, add 3 tablespoons of duck stock to the filling, otherwise it will turn out too dry.

⤚ Pintade farcie ⤛

Walking through the woods and fields of the Châtaigneraie you are quite likely to encounter a freely roaming flock of guinea fowl foraging for insects and grain in the leafmould and hedgerows. When they are surprised, their defence mechanism is to form a solid undulating and ululating mass which, as it careers this way and that, looks like some large and alarming creature. Or at least that is what they think. Wily Reynard is not fooled, of course, and people who have flocks of guinea fowl regularly curse foxes for the havoc they cause.

Because of their intense gregariousness, guinea fowl are occasionally at threat from another creature – a two-legged one. It is not unknown for two flocks of guinea fowl belonging to neighbouring farms to team up during the day and then go home for the night to only one of the two coops. There is no problem if the two farmers are on good terms. But if, as is sometimes the case in small hamlets of two or three farms, grudges built up over generations have matured into solid mutual loathing, the happy recipient of the extra fowl may decide to claim that they are rightfully his. And it is very difficult to prove the opposite.

Although they have been domesticated since antiquity, guinea fowl like their liberty and do not thrive unless allowed to roam. They are reluctant to lay eggs in the coop, preferring to construct large, ramshackle nests on the ground in undergrowth, where both eggs (ten or more) and nestlings are highly vulnerable.

This recipe for *pintade farcie* (the word *pintade* derives from the Portuguese *pintada*, or 'painted bird') was given to me by Juliette Vigier, who rears excellent guinea fowl in Mourjou. Her stuffing is distinctive in that it contains, on top of the traditional Auvergnat stuffing ingredients, a strong whack of juniper berries. She does not have to go far to get them: the neighbouring woods are dotted with prickly juniper trees. A classic seasoning for game, juniper berries go particularly well with guinea fowl, whose flavour is half-way between chicken and pheasant.

[*For four*]

60g (2oz) Swiss chard tops (or whole young leaves)

1 guinea fowl of about 1.8kg (4lb), with its liver

1 small chicken liver

50g (2oz) lard

150g (5½oz) sausagemeat

10 juniper berries

25g (1oz) flat-leaf parsley

1 small onion

3 cloves garlic

3 eggs

120g (4oz) plain flour

11g (½oz) baking powder

salt

freshly ground pepper

Put the Swiss chard tops (whole if the leaves are young and the size of sorrel leaves; only the green parts of the tops if they are large) in a blender with the guinea fowl's liver, chicken liver, lard, sausagemeat, juniper berries, parsley, onion, garlic, eggs, flour, baking powder, a large pinch of salt and plenty of pepper. Blend until fairly smooth. Check seasoning. Wash out the guinea fowl's stomach cavity and season it with a little salt. Loosely pack the stuffing into the bird, leaving about 3cm (1in) of unfilled space at the vent (the baking powder will cause the stuffing to expand slightly). Sew or skewer the vent, truss the guinea fowl and sprinkle with salt and pepper. Put the bird, breast up, in an oiled roasting pan, and place in a hot oven (220°C/425°F/Gas mark 7), with the fan on if you have one, for 20 minutes. Pour 200ml (7fl oz) of water into the pan and turn the oven down to 190°C/375°F/Gas mark 5. Roast for about 80 minutes more, basting from time to time and adding a little more water if it looks like drying up. Remove the bird from the oven to a hot serving dish, and place in the turned-off oven with the door half open. Deglaze the roasting pan, adding a little more water if necessary. Transfer the liquid to a saucepan and boil down quickly until about 250ml (9fl oz) is left. Check seasoning (it should be well salted). Transfer to a sauce boat, preferably of the '*gras-maigre*' type, and serve with the guinea fowl, whose flesh will have settled by this time, and its stuffing.

Some authorities claim that guinea fowl has rather dry flesh. I have not found this when using the old roasting technique of putting water in the roasting pan. Paradoxically, the humidity that results in the flesh remaining moist and tender does not prevent even a guinea fowl's skin from turning crisp.

If you find that you cannot get all the stuffing into the stomach cavity, roll the surplus up in a blanched cabbage leaf, tie up with string and place alongside the bird in the roasting pan. If you have no cabbage leaf, put the stuffing in a papillote of aluminium foil.

⊷ Sanguette ⊷

My first experience of *sanguette* (also spelled *sanguète*) was unnerving. Jeanne Chabut (p. 7) popped out of her front door as I was walking past and said: 'I've got something for you.' She popped back in again, and re-emerged with a soup plate filled with a mysterious coagulated substance of the most violent carmine-red I had ever seen outside a painting. She explained that it was the blood of a chicken she had just killed, mixed with chopped onions. 'It'll make you a nice little supper,' she said. My initial revulsion had to do with the colour more than anything. I love black pudding, which is also made from blood, but is cooked when you buy it, a process that turns the red blood to a less alarming deep brown colour. How was I to cook it? Just fry it, she said, then flip it over and fry it on the other side, making the kind of gesture she made when expertly tossing one of her huge *farinettes* (p. 23). I did indeed eat it for supper (though I did not risk tossing it over). It was very tasty, and had a curious almost rubbery texture reminiscent of overcooked *crème caramel*.

There are four ways of cooking *sanguette*. You can cook it the way Jeanne suggested; you can cut up the coagulated blood-and-onion mixture into dice before frying; you can press the mixture into egg and breadcrumbs, and deep fry; or you can add a little vinegar to the blood while it is still warm – this prevents it from coagulating – and then cook it in a frying-pan, where it turns to a thick paste that can be spread on bread or toast. My own preference is for Jeanne's method.

[*For two*]
1 small onion, very finely chopped
50ml (2fl oz) cream
blood of 1 chicken
30g (1oz) lard or unsalted butter
1 tablespoon good wine vinegar

Put the onion and cream in a large soup plate. Pour the blood over it, mix well and leave to coagulate. When it is firm, heat some lard or butter in a frying-pan until it sizzles and slide the mixture into it. Fry until crisp, then turn over and fry on the other side. Transfer to a hot dish, deglaze the pan with the vinegar and dribble evenly over the *sanguette*. Serve immediately.

One version of *sanguette* calls for the addition of a few raisins to the mixture.

← Poule farcie →

Many years ago, when I was in my culinary infancy, we decided to have roast chicken for supper. I phoned a neighbouring farm and mistakenly ordered *une poule* (a boiling hen). The farmer's wife suspected as much: when I went round to get the chicken, she asked me whether I was quite sure I wanted *une poule* and not *un poulet*. I persisted in my mistake, bought the bird, prepared it for roasting and stuck it in the oven. Three hours later, the hen's flesh was still bullet-hard even though it was almost burnt to a cinder. I had not realized that the only way you can deal with a boiling hen is, of course, to boil it.

Such a misadventure need not necessarily result from ignorance. At an Auvergnat *ferme auberge* that shall remain nameless, I and my parents were once served a *poule farcie* which, despite its sojourn in boiling water, was, if not bullet-hard, at least as tough as old boots (though quite tasty). I put this down to a miscalculation of the required cooking time on the part of the farmer's wife-cum-chef. But cannier customers of the *ferme auberge* later told me it was probably also the result of our being served a very old hen, which would have required three or four hours of boiling to become easily negotiable by my teeth, let alone those of my elderly parents.

When a proper boiling fowl is used, *poule farcie* has a beautifully moist texture and a taste that is subtly different from roast chicken – by the time it is cooked, its flesh is delicately imbued with an aromatic stuffing of raw ham, parsley, Swiss chard tops and garlic. The stuffing is so good on its own anyway, and the stomach cavity of the bird so relatively small, that an extra portion of it is often cooked in a blanched cabbage leaf (as in *pintade farcie*) and served on the side. (The extra stuffing at the nameless *ferme auberge* was the only part of the dish my parents managed to eat.)

[*For four*]
50g (2oz) white bread, trimmed of its crust
100ml (3½fl oz) milk
2 eggs
200g (7oz) raw ham
1 large boiling hen of about 2kg (4lb 6oz), including its
    heart and liver
5 tablespoons flat-leaf parsley, finely chopped
2 large cloves garlic, finely chopped
freshly ground pepper
salt
1 onion
2 cloves
5 whole peppercorns
bouquet garni
4 large carrots, sliced
1 stalk celery
4 small turnips or 1 swede, sliced
3 leeks, trimmed and sliced

Soak the bread in the milk. Break the eggs into a mixing bowl and beat well. Chop the ham and the chicken's heart and liver very finely. Add them to the eggs along with the parsley, garlic and soaked bread. Season with plenty of pepper and a little salt (allow for the presence of the ham). Amalgamate well. Trim as much fat as possible from under the chicken's skin and from the stomach vent. Wash out the stomach cavity and fill it with stuffing, but not too compactly. Sew or skewer the vent and truss the chicken.

Put the chicken, onion studded with cloves, peppercorns and *bouquet garni* into a large pot containing 4 litres (140fl oz) of water. Bring to the boil, skim and simmer for 90 minutes. Check the seasoning of the water (it should be moderately salty). Add the carrots, celery, turnips (or swede) and leeks, and simmer for a further 30 minutes or until the bird is tender, making sure there is always enough broth to cover the meat and vegetables.

Transfer the bird and vegetables to a large serving dish. Strain the broth into a soup tureen, removing the *bouquet garni* and peppercorns. Serve the carved chicken and vegetables in large soup plates, with plenty of broth ladled over them.

◄◄ Poulet au fromage ►►

This straightforward dish is also known as *poulet bourbonnais*. It is a speciality of the Bourbonnais region, the northernmost part of the Auvergne, which includes the fertile Limagne plain.

[*For four*]
90g (3oz) unsalted butter
1 small onion, sliced
1 small chicken of about 1.2kg (2lb 10oz)
salt
freshly ground pepper
120ml (4fl oz) dry white wine
300ml (10½fl oz) milk
20g (¾oz) plain flour
2 egg yolks
100ml (3½fl oz) double cream
25g (1oz) freshly grated Parmesan
125g (4½oz) freshly grated Gruyère
pinch freshly ground white pepper
pinch freshly grated nutmeg

Heat 50g (2oz) of butter in a heavy casserole and cook the onion gently until it just begins to turn brown. Trim the chicken's stomach cavity of all excess fat and wash it out. Sprinkle the bird inside and outside with salt and plenty of pepper. Put it on its side in the casserole, cover and cook over a low heat for 45–60 minutes, turning it over once.

When the chicken is just cooked (you should be able to prise a leg away from the body easily, but the thigh socket should still be slightly pink), take it out and place on a board. There will normally be a certain amount of juice in the casserole. If there seems to be a lot of fat, tilt the casserole and remove as much as possible with a bulb baster or ladle. Pour in the wine (and about the same quantity of water if there is very little chicken juice) and, over a high heat, deglaze the bottom of the casserole with a wooden spoon. Reduce the liquid until there is about 100ml (3½fl oz) left. Put this liquid through a fine strainer, check its seasoning (it should be quite salty) and set aside.

Cut the chicken into 4 pieces (2 breast pieces and 2 legs), arrange neatly in one layer in a large buttered gratin dish, and keep warm.

Make a Mornay sauce as follows. Melt 20g (¾oz) of butter gently in a heavy saucepan. Heat the milk in another pan with the reduced chicken juice. Blend the flour with the butter and cook slowly, stirring all the time with a wooden spoon, for 2–3 minutes without browning. When the milk almost reaches boiling point, pour it over the butter and flour mixture, away from the heat, and whisk until absolutely smooth. Return the pan to a low heat, bring to a simmer and cook gently for about 1 minute, stirring. Remove from the heat. Blend the egg yolks and cream in a mixing bowl. Add about half the hot sauce to this mixture, very gradually at first, beating all the time. Pour the mixture back into the saucepan and continue beating until smooth. Put back on a gentle heat and stir for about a minute. Remove from the heat and stir in the Parmesan and 25g (1oz) of the Gruyère until they have completely melted. Add the white pepper, nutmeg and salt to taste. Pour the sauce over the chicken pieces, sprinkle with the remaining Gruyère, and bake in a fairly hot oven (200°C/400°F/Gas mark 6) for 15–20 minutes, or until the surface begins to turn golden brown.

★

If you want to be really authentic, use white Saint-Pourçain, a homely wine from the Bourbonnais, for the deglazing, and serve the same *appellation* at table (either a chilled white or a cool red).

⊰ Coq au vin ⊱

In his no-nonsense book *Real Good Food* (Fourth Estate, 1995), the cookery writer Nigel Slater puts in a plea for 'the return of some of the great restaurant clichés of the past'. His list of highly unfashionable dishes rarely found on the menus of Britain's trend-crazed superchefs (my phrase) includes duck à l'orange, chicken tarragon, beef Stroganoff and *coq au vin*. Few things, he argues, are as good as 'a properly made *coq au vin*'. I could not agree more. But there is a problem in deciding what exactly 'properly made' means in rural France, where chefs' minds are exercised less by the notion of fashionableness than by pressure to defend their regional culinary colours.

Coq au vin is a dish, like *potée*, which is found in slightly differing versions all over France. There is even a slender tome called *Coq au Vin*, which contains sixty-one slightly differing recipes for the dish. Needless to say, there are various schools of thought, even within the Auvergne, about what should go into the dish and how it should be cooked. Should it include the fowl's blood as well as wine? Should the *lardons* be smoked or unsmoked? Should the sauce be thickened with *beurre manié* and/or the mashed-up liver? Should the bird have marinated for a day in wine before cooking? Indeed, should the bird be a strapping two-year-old *coq* or just an ordinary (free-range) chicken? (I use the word *coq* because it is a way of avoiding the problem, in English, of the word 'cock'. Elizabeth David gets round that by referring to the bird as a 'cockerel', which the OED defines as a 'young cock'. So that won't really do for an adult bird. Other English-speaking cookery writers tend to say 'chicken', which is not specific enough. There *is* a problem, though. One does not want to fall into the trap of a Paris chef, whose menu posted outside his restaurant obligingly gave a literal English translation of '*le coq au vin spécial de notre chef*'. So, at the risk of seeming to chicken out, I have preferred to keep the French word *coq*.)

Coq au vin is also problematic because several regions – and none

more vociferously than the Auvergne – claim paternity for the dish. A chef by the name of Valentin (quoted in Roger Lallemand's *La Vraie Cuisine de l'Auvergne et du Limousin*, Quartier Latin, 1973) claimed many decades ago that *coq au vin* came to the Auvergne in the following way. When Caesar was besieging the Gauls, who had taken refuge on the Puy de Dôme mountain, the leader of the Gauls, Vercingetorix, sent him a scrawny old *coq* as a gesture of defiance. Caesar decided to get his own back. He agreed to a truce and invited his enemy to banquet with him the following day. One of the dishes served up at the banquet had a dark reddish sauce which the leader of the Gauls found very tasty. He asked what it was. Caesar said it was the *coq* he had been sent, transformed into a gastronomic delight by the art of his cook. He wanted to prove to the Gauls that the skills and experience of the Romans could only be beneficial to Gaul and its inhabitants. He therefore invited them to surrender – which they did not. In the real, as opposed to the apocryphal, world it took Caesar many a long battle to get the better of Vercingetorix.

Arguments over which region is the true home of *coq au vin* can never be solved to the satisfaction of all parties; nor is there any point in trying to do so, for *coq au vin* tastes different from one part of the country to another. Contrary to a widespread notion, the type of wine used in cooking changes the end product considerably (that is why the use of so-called 'cooking wine' can result in a wretched dish). I was once fortunate enough to be invited to dinner by a French couple who had prepared a *coq au vin* with a twelve-year-old Pommard. The same wine was served with the dish. It was an unforgettable experience. The *coq au vin* I ate that day would have tasted very different if a Bordeaux of equivalent calibre had been used. Or a Chanturgue (p. 209), generally deemed to be the only wine that should go into a genuine Auvergnat *coq au vin*. The wine may be unfamiliar to you – which is not surprising since it is little known even in France. It became very scarce until recently, when it made something of a comeback thanks to the efforts of a handful of determined wine-growers. It is a dark, earthy wine made on the hills overlooking Clermont-Ferrand.

The other problem with *coq au vin* is getting hold of your *coq*. Here in the Châtaigneraie, as in other rural areas of France, butchers and poulterers who get a proportion of their supplies directly from farms will supply one if you order it in advance. Otherwise, you will have to buy it directly from a farm. The farm I always go to for poultry is an organic one, though the farmer and his wife, Jean and Nicole Loubières, would never dream of calling it by that name. They have not a great deal of land and no great ambition to produce high yields, unlike some of their colleagues in the area. They have not listened to the siren voices of the Crédit Agricole, France's biggest bank, which encourages farmers to buy expensive machinery on the never-never. They are not interested in spending money on pesticides or herbicides. Their fields in early spring stand out from their neighbours' because they are completely covered with a dense carpet of golden dandelions. The only fertilizer they use is muck. They have ducks whose diet of maize is supplemented with what they can find in a reedy pond a stone's throw from the farmhouse. Their chickens forage in the hedgerows.

Buying a *coq* from that farm is not an exercise I particularly relish. I turn up and, after a few preliminaries about the weather and beef prices over a glass of wine, we get round to the question of whether they could sell me a *coq*. Nicole ponders for a moment: does she still need the bird to fertilize her hen's eggs? She decides she does not, and takes me into the farmyard, where a *coq* and a bevy of hens are happily scratching about on a dungheap. 'When do you want it?' I now have to pass a death sentence on the proudly strutting bird: do I allow it a stay of execution of a day or two, I wonder, or is it to be tomorrow at dawn?

When I turn up to collect the bird, Nicole takes it lovingly out of the refrigerator and shows it to me. The only feature of the slab of pale flesh that recalls the living creature seen earlier is its intact, and apparently sleeping, head. She has meticulously plucked and drawn the bird. But it is only after much insistence from me that she agrees to include the time she spent doing that in the price she charges.

[*For six*]

1 *coq*, at least 2 years old, and if possible from a farm; failing that, a very large free-range chicken of the highest quality will do – it should weigh at least 2kg (4lb 6oz)

50g (2oz) lard

15 pickling onions

100g (3½oz) salt pork belly or green streaky bacon, cut into strips

150g button mushrooms or, better, chanterelles, or 15g dried ceps (broken into small pieces and soaked for an hour in a little water)

For the marinade:

1 bottle Chanturgue or any good dark full-bodied red wine (such as Cahors or Corbières)

bouquet garni consisting of 2 sprigs thyme, 2 sprigs flat-leaf parsley or parsley stalks, 2 sprigs winter savory, 1 bay leaf

2 carrots, quartered

2 large cloves garlic

2 cloves

large pinch salt

plenty of freshly ground pepper

Cut the *coq* into pieces. Remove the skin from all pieces except the legs and wings. A properly fed *coq*, even a farm bird, will have a great deal of fat on it, especially in the stomach cavity. Remove as much of this as possible. Put the *coq* pieces in an enamelled or china receptacle, packing them tightly. Add the marinade and swirl over the pieces. Cover with a tight-fitting lid and leave in a cool place for 24 hours, tilting the receptacle once or twice to make the marinade moisten the uncovered pieces.

Next day, drain the *coq* pieces well. Heat the lard in a large casserole until sizzling. Dab dry with kitchen paper those *coq* pieces that have skin on them, and put in the casserole. Sauté gently until the skin is well-browned, turn over and brown on the other side. Remove the pieces and set aside. Put the onions and the salt pork or bacon in the casserole, cover and sauté over a low heat until the onions begin to turn golden. Return all the *coq* pieces to the casserole, pack tightly, add the mushrooms (if using dried ceps, do not add yet) and the marinade, including its solid ingredients, and bring gently to a simmer. Put the casserole in a medium oven (180°C/350°F/Gas mark 4) and cook for about 2 hours, or until the *coq* is tender but not falling off the bone. If using dried ceps, add them and their water half an hour before the estimated end of the cooking time.

While the *coq* is cooking, chop the liver as finely as possible, removing any gristle-like connecting tissue. Take the casserole out of the oven. Strain off the liquid into a small saucepan, and put the casserole back into the oven (turned off). Leave the liquid for 5 minutes, so the fat rises to the surface. Remove as much fat as possible with a bulb baster or by gently pressing a small ladle down into the liquid so the fat dribbles over the edge into the ladle. Put the liquid into a liquidizer with the chopped liver and blend thoroughly. Return to the pan and bring very slowly to a simmer, whisking all the time.

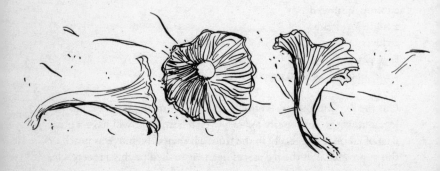

Take the casserole out of the oven. When the sauce has thickened slightly, pour it over the contents of the casserole and serve immediately.

The traditional accompaniment to *coq au vin* is boiled potatoes, which, when squashed with one's fork (yes, I know it is non-U), are an ideal vehicle for the sauce. But any other vegetable, or pasta, will also do.

If you have time, it is best to make the *coq au vin* the day before it is to be consumed. This enables you to remove almost all the fat from the sauce. After the stage where you pour the liquid off into a bowl, wait for it and the meat in the casserole to cool, then transfer both receptacles to the refrigerator. Next morning, put the casserole in a very low oven (150°C/300°F/Gas mark 2). Peel off the layer of fat that will have formed in the bowl (the liquid will have turned to jelly), heat the jelly until it becomes liquid again and finish the sauce as described above.

The liquidized liver produces a sauce that is very slightly grainy. But it is more subtly tasty than the smooth, glossy sauce you can obtain using the *beurre manié* technique (which involves whisking tiny knobs of butter and flour, mashed together in equal quantities, into the sauce and bringing to a simmer).

Many French restaurants tart up *coq au vin* by sticking triangular deep-fried *croûtons* on to the dish. This is not only an un-Auvergnat practice, but contributes plenty of calories without enhancing the taste in any way. Some recipes call for smoked *lardons*. To my mind, this is a great mistake, as the smoky taste, while not unpleasant *per se*, is an intrusive guest at this refined marriage of *coq* and wine.

Other Meat Dishes

The Auvergnats attach great importance to the quality of their meat, as indeed they do to that of most of their food. Just as they prefer vegetables from their own kitchen garden, because they know how they were grown and what fertilized them (manure in most cases), they like to establish where their veal, beef and lamb come from. And whenever possible they rear their own poultry and family pig (and sometimes even when this is not permitted: some families in the town of Aurillac (Cantal) keep farmyard animals in their gardens, a practice that is frowned on but not penalized by the authorities).

This insistence on quality means that butchers in the Auvergne tend to be key figures in the community. My local butcher, Raymond Vigier, in the neighbouring village of Calvinet, is certainly that. His wares include beef, veal, pork, lamb, poultry, game (in season), farm eggs, *charcuterie* and various specialities cooked by his wife Josette – *pâté, boudin, fritons, galantine, poitrine de veau farcie* and so on. Such is the excellence of his meat that Loulou Puech, of the one-rosette Hôtel Beauséjour in the same village (p. 53), prefers to buy from him rather than from a cheaper wholesaler. Raymond has also appeared on several television programmes about 'real beef' in the wake of the mad cow scare.

Raymond's establishment must be unique in France: it is a *boucherie-charcuterie*, café and sitting-room rolled into one. As you would expect of a butcher, he spends most of his time cutting up and selling meat. But just occasionally he slips through an opening in the wall of his tiny shop and emerges behind the bar in the next room, where a selection of his mates (mostly farmers) are to be found drinking at virtually any time of day. One half of the room is taken up by the bar counter and some spartan café tables and chairs, while the other, beyond a kind of proscenium arch, is a private space containing a large sofa, armchairs, a writing desk, a dresser, a fireplace and, sometimes, some ironing. When there is an important rugby match on television, Raymond's close friends are allowed to step through the looking-glass, so to speak, from the café into the plush comfort of the sitting-room, where they can see his huge television set, which is wheeled into the doorway of the adjoining kitchen.

The openness of this arrangement – Raymond and Josette removed the sitting-room wall because they found the café too cramped – is a reflection of the butcher himself, an ebullient and convivial, if occasionally choleric man. He goes about his business with a match stuck in his mouth. It serves partly as an ersatz cigarette, but also, he says, as something he can grind instead of his teeth if over-fussy customers or pernickety hygiene inspectors get on his nerves.

Raymond is himself fussy when it comes to dealing with his suppliers (one of whom also provides the top French chef, Joël Robuchon, with beef and veal). He buys all his meat, apart from poultry and game, on the hoof. His idea of relaxation on his day off (Monday) is to go to a farm and see how 'his' animals – by which he means animals he will soon be buying – are coming along. He has a particularly high opinion of meat from Salers cattle, a hardy mountain breed which produces relatively little meat or milk – both of them, however, of superlative quality. *Pace* the witless restaurant critic for the *Observer* newspaper – she once agreed with her ignorant dining partner that the mention 'short-horn' was irrelevant to the quality of their sirloin steak ('extraneous pretentious detail' is how she described it) – Salers beef has unique culinary qualities: a heavy marbling of the flesh and an intense 'beefiness' of taste. And no words can describe the deliciousness of its dripping (the consumption of dripping on toast with coarse salt sprinkled on top is one tiny corner of the gastronomic experience that seems to have eluded the French).

Salers cattle crossed with the meatier Charolais or Limousin breeds also produce excellent beef and veal. Many Salers-Charolais calves used to be exported to Italy and 'finished' in the Po Valley, but the mad cow scare, by sharply diminishing Italian demand for beef and veal, virtually put an end to that trade.

Mad cow has not affected Raymond's sales, because, as he says, 'customers know where my meat comes from'. The head of the meat counter in the Aurillac hypermarket, Géant, says his business would have suffered terribly had he not had the idea of opening a special Salers section: it was taken by storm by customers who rightly perceived the breed as being BSE-free.

What was particularly striking when the BSE crisis broke was the lack of anti-British feeling among Auvergnat farmers I spoke to. Although some of them have lost up to £12,000 in annual turnover as a result of flagging sales, they have a healthily cynical attitude that prevents them from pointing the finger of blame solely at the British. 'Do you think we're any better in France?' said one. 'I can assure you that the stocks of British beef held in store by French supermarkets are not going to end up on the rubbish dump. There have already been cases of "British beef" stamps being removed from carcasses.'

When I told Auvergnat farmers of my fury at the practices of those robber barons of British agribusiness (aka the animal-feed manufacturers), who had put not only rendered sheep in their rations for ruminants, but feather meal, clay and sawdust (which they were able to do because of lax UK labelling regulations), their reaction was wry resignation, not shared anger: 'The animals can't have grown very fast on a diet of clay and sawdust – perhaps they were added as a condiment?' And when I waxed indignant at John Major's antics in 1996 (the setting up of a 'war cabinet' to deal with stroppy European colleagues, a policy of 'non-co-operation' and, in the end, a 'charm offensive'), they rightly pointed out, with just a touch of self-satisfaction, that he had got nowhere by adopting such tactics.

⤙ Tripoux ⤚

The first time I set eyes on *tripoux* was in a Paris *charcuterie* many years ago, before I moved to the Auvergne: a heap of little greyish bundles sat on a large dish with chunks of orange-brown aspic clinging to them. What were they? The *charcutier*, who had bought them directly from a small manufacturer in the Aveyron, told me they were made from strips of calf's and sheep's tripe and a little ham, all tied up into a packet and cooked for six or seven hours in a broth flavoured with onion, carrot, garlic, cloves and white wine. All I needed to do was heat them up gently in a thick saucepan and add some boiled potatoes: '*Vous allez vous régaler,*' he assured me. They were indeed very tasty in a subtle, mildly tripey way, though their texture was a little too gelatinous for my taste.

It was only later, after adopting the Auvergne as my home, that I started grappling with the vexed question of what should and should not go into the making of *tripoux* (or *tripous*, as they are often spelled), and indeed which *département*, the Cantal or the Aveyron, could lay claim to be the home of the 'genuine' product. As in all such gastronomic controversies (cf. *cassoulet*, whose birthplace is claimed by Toulouse, Castelnaudary and Castres), the question of 'correctness' is largely otiose – there is no reason why the various versions should not all be delicious in their own distinctive ways. As for the question of the geographical origin of *tripoux*, this has as much to do with the historical rivalry between the two *départements* concerned as with historical fact.

As with their relatives, *trenels*, *petites* (found in Laguiole) and *manouls*, what goes into *tripoux* depends largely on the pattern of livestock farming in a given area. Thus, a *charcutier* in Aurillac will swear that nothing but calf's mesentery should be used, whereas one from the Aveyron, where large numbers of sheep are reared, will tend to use sheep's stomach and boned trotters, either on their own or combined with calf's tripe.

The consumption of *tripoux* is surrounded by a certain amount of ritual. Colette Guillemard claims, in her *Ethnocuisine de l'Auvergne* (Civry, 1980), that you cannot have experienced the true flavour of *tripoux* unless you have tasted them 'on Sunday, at about 11 in the morning, in one of those little cafés in Saint-Flour where men get together to sample [*tripoux*], washing them down with plenty of white wine, while their womenfolk are at mass'. At the same time, *tripoux* were not felt to be out of place at grander tables which would never have served, say, *boudin* or *fritons*: in 1948, the Grand Hôtel St-Pierre, then Aurillac's top hotel, advertised *tripoux* as one of its specialities.

The early-morning consumption of *tripoux* is a tradition that has now become folkloric. At village fêtes or gastronomic fairs, they are often on offer at times which seem absurdly early, but correspond to the hour (8 or 8.30 a.m.) when the morning *casse-croûte* is eaten by farmers. I recently partook of a *tripoux* feast at the neighbouring village of Calvinet. It was an al fresco event, organized next to the village lake where a fishing competition was about to start, and mainly attended by middle-aged men. At 8.30 a.m. sharp, we 'breakfasters' each had to tuck into three *tripoux* and boiled potatoes, which were followed by cheese and washed down by red plonk. By the time we had finished an hour later, the trout with which the lake had been thoughtfully stocked were beginning to be flopped on to the bank. Delicious as the *tripoux* were, such an early onslaught put my appetite completely out of kilter for the day (I ate one or two grapes for lunch, then felt ravenous by suppertime).

Getting hold of *tripoux* ingredients is so complicated that many *charcutiers* in the Auvergne buy their bundles of uncooked tripe already trussed by specialized firms, and then cook them according to their own recipes. Tinned and bottled *tripoux* are widely available in Paris. They can also be found in some specialized stores in Britain. So rather than give instructions for the tricky operation of making *tripoux*, I have preferred to suggest a reheating technique and an accompaniment which, I think, work particularly well. As remarked earlier, the texture of *tripoux* is gelatinous. This drawback (for some) is circumvented in the following recipe.

[*For four*]
500g (1lb 2oz) Le Puy green lentils (p. 87)
12 bottled or tinned *tripoux*
30g (1oz) lard
2 sprigs flat-leaf parsley, finely chopped

Cook the lentils as described on page 89. Remove the *tripoux* from the tin or jar. Remove as much aspic from them as possible and set aside. Slice the *tripoux* in half crosswise. Melt a little lard in a non-stick pan, add the *tripoux* and sauté gently, cut side down, for at least 15 minutes or until the surface is nicely crisp (it will turn an orange-brown colour). Set aside and keep warm. When the lentils are cooked, strain them and return to a very low heat after adding the *tripoux* aspic. Stir well. When the lentils begin to bubble, remove from the heat, check the seasoning (probably no salt will be needed, as the aspic is heavily salted), and transfer to a hot dish. Arrange the *tripoux* on top of the lentils and sprinkle with chopped parsley.

Confit de lapin aux petits pois
◄◄ secs de Saint-Flour ►►

French country hotels in general, and more especially in the Auvergne, are very tolerant places. They do not just put up with small children, they welcome them, even when trendily lax parents allow them to shatter the eardrums of other diners or career about among the tables and waiting staff, sometimes causing dishes to fly. Special high chairs are produced for the toddlers, who in many cases are allowed to eat the same food as the adults. And if they do not, they can often enjoy a special '*menu enfants*'. There is none of the culinary ostracism of children to which British restaurants are prone. French guide books do not have to specify, like *The Good Food Guide*, 'children welcome'.

French hotels are also tolerant about dress. To the best of my knowledge, no provincial establishment, however posh, insists on a tie being worn for dinner. And further down the scale hotel owners do not bat an eyelid if you turn up looking like a vagrant. I and two friends once did precisely that at the Auberge du Barrez, in Mur-de-Barrez, a charming little medieval town south-east of Aurillac. We had been on an extended Grande Randonnée hike on a sweltering summer's day, and bitten off a little more than we could chew, not realizing the hike ended with a 10-kilometre uphill stretch of shadeless track covered with scorching chips of white rock. Fortunately an old lady in a tumbledown cottage at the top of the hill took pity on us and saved us from dying of thirst, but we still arrived at the Auberge du Barrez looking grimy, bedraggled with sweat and carrying nothing but small rucksacks (we had arranged to meet two other friends at the hotel, who were going to bring us a change of clothes). Despite our appearance, and even before we had identified ourselves as people who had booked rooms, we were immediately greeted with a warmly commiserating smile by Marie-Thérèse, the wife of the hotel owner and chef, Christian Gaudel.

I and my friends agreed we had rarely enjoyed dinner as much as we did that evening: we were able to appease huge appetites with excellent food, and at the same time experience that rare feeling of having thoroughly deserved a meal after a hard day's slog and a shower.

After soup, we were served marvellously fragrant cep tartlets which

Christian bases on a recipe devised by Michel Bras, whose celebrated restaurant in Laguiole has two Michelin rosettes: thin, delicately browned slices of the mushroom fan out round the surface of the tart, concealing a succulent mixture of ground walnuts and cream beneath. The main course was this very simple *confit de lapin aux petits pois secs de Saint-Flour* (preserve of rabbit with Saint-Flour dried peas). The sweetness of the dried peas makes an ideal marriage with the 'sweetness' of the rabbit. The peas, which are not split peas but tiny round whole peas, are now unfortunately very difficult to come by except in Saint-Flour and Aurillac.

Gaudel, a man whose dead-pan expression belies a keen sense of fun, was brought up in the catering trade. His parents ran a hotel in Entraygues, 30 kilometres from Mur-de-Barrez. He learned how to cook from his parents and an uncle who occasionally helped out, and who had cooked at the Hôtel George V in Paris. But he feels the greatest inspiration came from his grandmother, who made the hotel's *pâtisserie* at home. When he was small he would go and watch her at work. From 1974 to 1982 he worked with his brother at the family hotel, then started up on his own in the brand new Auberge du Barrez in 1984. The hotel earns a well-deserved red R for 'good food at moderate prices' in the Michelin guide.

[*For four*]
4 large hind legs of rabbit
250g (9oz) salt
500g (1lb 2oz) duck fat (p. 105)
bouquet garni
2 carrots, peeled and sliced
1 onion, peeled and finely chopped
100g (3½oz) salt pork belly or green streaky bacon, cut
   into narrow *lardons*
500g (1lb 2oz) dried Saint-Flour peas, washed
1 bay leaf
2 sprigs parsley, finely chopped

Rub the rabbit legs with salt and leave for 12 hours (if it is more convenient, you can use the 2 hind legs, the saddle and the forelegs of a single rabbit).

Wash the excess salt off the rabbit legs, dab dry with kitchen paper and brown in a little duck fat. Transfer the pieces to a non-stick sauté pan into which they fit neatly, add the *bouquet garni* and the rest of the duck fat, and simmer very gently for 1 hour. Strain off the fat and keep for another use.

Fry the carrots, onion and salt pork or bacon gently with a little duck fat in a large non-stick sauté pan for 10 minutes. Add the peas and bay leaf, cover with water, bring to a simmer and cook uncovered for 90 minutes, stirring from time to time and adding a little water if necessary. Dried peas turn from an undercooked state to a mush very quickly, so it is vital to check several times if they are cooked after 90 minutes.

Strain the peas and their garnish, and transfer to a hot serving dish. Place the rabbit pieces on top and sprinkle with parsley.

(Auberge du Barrez, Avenue du Carladez, 12600 Aveyron. Tel: 05 65 66 00 76.)

⤙ Blanquette de chevreau ⤚

On the steep banks of the river Lot in the southern Cantal, just 6 kilometres from Mourjou as the crow flies, and on the arid *causses* (calcareous plateaux) in the Aveyron and Lot *départements*, numerous flocks of goats supply milk for a local goat cheese called *Cabécou*, a little 30g disc of soft, barely salted cheese. Every spring the goat flocks are swollen by a cohort of surplus kids, which the cheese makers sell to butchers in April and May, thus usefully supplementing their income.

Chevreau à l'oseille is without any doubt the most seasonally circum-scribed of dishes, as it is virtually impossible to find kid in butcher's shops outside those months. In my case, the pleasure of eating kid is enhanced by the rarity of the event. I suspect that if it were available all year round we would not happily eat it as often as, say, a leg of lamb. Kid has a delicate flavour that verges on the insipid, and it needs to be jazzed up with something astringent, like the Italian *gremolata* (a sprinkling of finely chopped lemon zest, parsley and garlic) or the sorrel used in this Auvergnat dish.

[*For six*]
1.5kg (3lb 5oz) kid, including a back leg and some saddle
50g (2oz) salt pork belly or green streaky bacon
3 cloves garlic
250ml (9fl oz) veal or chicken stock
salt
freshly ground pepper
500g (1lb 2oz) sorrel, stemmed, washed and shredded
3 egg yolks
200ml (7fl oz) cream
4 sprigs flat-leaf parsley, finely chopped

Get your butcher to chop up the kid into manageable chunks. Trim as much fat and membrane as possible from the pieces and put in a baking dish with the salt pork or bacon, cut into strips, 2 cloves of garlic, halved, and the stock. Place in a hot oven (220°C/425°F/Gas mark 7) for 10 minutes, baste, and lower the heat to fairly hot (190°C/375°F/Gas mark 5). Cook for a further 30 minutes, basting from time to time and adding a little water if necessary. Add salt to taste and plenty of pepper.

Cook the sorrel in a saucepan with very little water, stirring all the time until cooked. Beat the egg yolks and cream in a bowl with a large pinch of salt and plenty of pepper. Whisk into the mixture a little of the sorrel's cooking liquid and the remaining stock from the baking dish while still hot; they should together not exceed 300ml (10½fl oz). Pour the mixture into the saucepan with the sorrel and heat for a minute or two over a very low heat. Check seasoning. Pour the sauce over the kid, sprinkle with *persillade* (the parsley and remaining clove of garlic, finely chopped) and serve.

⤛ Gigot de sept heures ⤜

I live in an area whose narrow winding roads can ruin the travel calculations of those visiting me for the first time. A couple of friends driving from Saint-Etienne (Loire) said they would be with me in time for lunch. I foolishly decided to cook a roast leg of lamb. Allowing for my guests to be late, I put it in the oven at 12 p.m., so it would be ready for eating at about 1.30 p.m. When they had still not arrived at 1 p.m., I turned the oven very low. Still no sign at 2 p.m., so I turned the oven off. When they finally turned up at 4 p.m., a frantic twenty-minute blast of heat while we hungrily wolfed the first course failed to make the *gigot* more than lukewarm. But at least the meat had remained pink.

A year or two later, when some other friends said they would be staying overnight near Tours and asked if they could come to lunch, I decided to spare myself the tensions of a fine-tuned main course, since I knew they would be late (they had some 430 kilometres to drive in a morning – and were not early risers). So I opted for *gigot de sept heures*, which, as its name suggests, is a very slowly cooked dish that can be kept warm without suffering. It is found all over the Massif Central but is a particular favourite in the Bourbonnais (it even stretches up into the Berry, featuring in George Sand's recipe notebooks). *Gigot de sept heures* is also known as *gigot à la cuiller*, for reasons that are evident when you cook it – it is more easily served with a spoon than carved. What lends it its marvellously intense and complex flavour, as compared with the Greek lamb dish, *sofrito*, where the meat is also cooked until very soft, is the slow infusion of the lamb bone. For this reason, a boned leg of lamb will result in less intensity, though it may be more conveniently squeezed into the casserole. In this version of the recipe, no water at all is used: all the liquid that appears after seven hours' cooking will have seeped out of the meat and the vegetables.

[*For six*]
large leg of lamb weighing at least 2.7kg (6lb)
6 large cloves garlic, quartered
1 tablespoon vegetable oil
2 onions, finely sliced
400g (14oz) carrots, sliced
bouquet garni
salt
freshly ground pepper
700g (1lb 9oz) potatoes, very finely sliced

Measure the length of your casserole, so that when you buy the leg of lamb you can if necessary ask the butcher to saw off the end of the bone so it will fit into the receptacle. Trim as much fat as possible off the leg of lamb, and lard with the garlic. Place it in the casserole with the oil, and add the onions, carrots and *bouquet garni*, pushing them down the sides and under the leg of lamb to ensure as tight a fit as possible. Add plenty of salt and pepper, *but no water*. Cover and place in a very cool oven (150°C/300°F/Gas mark 2). After 90 minutes, check that some liquid has begun to seep out on to the bottom of the casserole. If it has not, add 20cl (7fl oz) water. After 4 hours, the level of the liquid should be about half-way up the sides of the casserole. Turn the leg over. After 5½ hours of cooking, add the potatoes in a layer on top of the meat, season with salt and pepper, and return to the oven for a further 90 minutes. After 7 hours the liquid should almost cover the joint. Serve from the casserole – with a spoon.

↤ Falette ↦

I first tasted *falette* (stuffed breast of veal), a stalwart of Auvergnat cooking, shortly after moving to the Châtaigneraie twenty years ago. One of the first things I did on my arrival was ask people in the village which their favourite restaurants were. One establishment which everyone agreed was exceptional was in the small village of Saint-Julien-de-Piganiol. Its special menus, as opposed to *menus ouvriers* (workmen's lunches), were served only at weekends. 'There's certainly plenty to eat – and it's not at all expensive,' said one neighbour admiringly. As I have already pointed out, quantity is sometimes a more highly regarded benchmark than quality in rural areas of France, so I asked if the food was good as well as copious. No problem, I was assured. But the place was always booked out for weeks in advance. I asked for the name of the restaurant so I could make a booking. 'Oh it doesn't have a name, it's just "chez Feyt".'

'Chez Feyt' turned out to be a long old building backing on to a farmyard. At one end there was a flight of steps leading up to the entrance. Apart from a Kronenbourg banner across the lintel and a faded menu in the window, which had no prices and simply said '*Entrée, plat du jour, fromage, dessert*', there was nothing to suggest that this was a restaurant. We were shown through a café area and past the open kitchen door into a huge back room packed tight with long tables and benches. The floor still had its original broad and deeply grooved chestnut planks.

Soon the room was full of people and resounding with an expectant hubbub. A huge hunk of rye bread (we were expected to cut our own slices) and a litre bottle of red wine were plonked on the table. There was no menu. The dishes just came, one after the other, unannounced and unexplained by the teenage waitress (a member of the extended Feyt family roped in to help out at weekends). An excellent soup was followed by a platter of *saucisson sec*, *fritons* and raw ham. One could tell from the vast dimensions of the ham slices, their mauvish-red colour and their slightly marbled texture that the ham had been home-cured. This was followed by crisp-skinned *truite au lard* (p. 43), whose accompanying dice of tasty fried fat almost certainly came from the same animal as the ham. I donated the tail of my trout to the Feyts' dog, a smart mongrel that went from diner to diner resting its chin on their thighs just long enough to find out whether it was going to get a morsel or a swipe.

Then came what we assumed to be the main course: a succulent *falette* (stuffed breast of veal). No sooner had we eaten that than a steaming *civet de lièvre* (p. 100) appeared on the table. After struggling through that richest of dishes, we were offered cheese. One glutton in our party still had room and took the home-made goat's-milk *fromage blanc* (a rarity) in preference to the Cantal. After all that, we longed for fresh fruit, if anything, but got *îles flottantes* with *fouace* (p. 175) instead. That was the work of the grandmother whom we had glimpsed, when passing the kitchen, busily stirring custard in a huge copper bowl over a low gas. As it turned out, the pudding's sweetness and featherlight texture formed such a contrast to what had gone before that we somehow drummed up enough appetite to eat it with enjoyment. The bill was microscopic – as was the dinner we ate that evening.

Falette, which is also known as *faude*, after *fauda* the Occitan (p. xxi) word, is one of those dishes that gets the best out of a cheap cut, in this case breast of veal (it is also sometimes made with breast of mutton or pork). In the old days, when farmers were still allowed to slaughter their own animals, they would sell the finer cuts of veal at market and keep the less-prized parts of the animal, such as breast of veal (brisket), for consumption by the family. There is not much meat and a fair quantity of gristle in brisket (a word which probably derives from the Old Norse *brjósk*, meaning cartilage).

What transforms this humble cut is the stuffing. In the Auvergne, the ingredients that go into it can vary widely – chestnuts and raisins are sometimes included. But the key flavours are always provided by a combination of Swiss chard tops, parsley and garlic, whose clean, fresh and pungent flavour permeates the veal meat. The stuffing is given an extra dimension by the presence of chopped ham. *Falette* is also excellent cold, accompanied by a green salad. Some people, including myself, even prefer it to the hot version. This recipe was given to me by Josette Vigier (p. 126).

[*For six*]

250g (9oz) Swiss chard tops (or whole young leaves)
80g (3oz) flat-leaf parsley
3 large cloves garlic
150g (5½oz) raw ham
100g (3½oz) salt pork belly or green streaky bacon
3 eggs
200g (7oz) plain flour
100g (3½oz) bread, without crust, soaked in milk and
   squeezed dry
2 onions
1 boned breast of veal, weighing 1.8kg (4lb)
50g (2oz) lard

4 carrots, finely sliced
bouquet garni
200ml (7fl oz) good white wine
200ml (7fl oz) water

Put the Swiss chard (whole if its leaves are young and the size of sorrel leaves; only the green parts of the tops if they are large) in a blender with the parsley, garlic, ham, salt pork or bacon, eggs, flour, bread and 1 onion. Blend until fairly smooth. Pack this stuffing not too tightly into the boned breast of veal (to be ordered in advance from your butcher), and sew it up all along the side to form a large sausage shape, keeping the stitches fairly close together. Put the lard into a large casserole over a high heat. Brown the *falette* well on all sides, then remove. Turn down the heat to low. Strew the bottom of the casserole with the carrots, the remaining onion, finely chopped, and the *bouquet garni*. Place the *falette* on top. Add the white wine and water, bring to the boil on top of the stove, cover, transfer to a fairly hot oven (190°C/375°F/Gas mark 5) and cook for 90 minutes.

⤙ Mourtayrol ⤚

Mourtayrol is a sumptuous saffron-flavoured concoction of several different boiled meats which, like *pot-au-feu* or *potée*, is served in two instalments, one liquid, the other solid. It is something of a mystery dish. It almost never appears on restaurant menus or family tables nowadays, not even at banquets. This is not easily explained. The reason can hardly be that saffron is no longer cultivated in the Rouergue, the home of the dish, as the spice is widely available today. There may of course have been a hiatus that caused it to fall out of use in local kitchens.

However that may be, *mourtayrol* (or *mourtaïrol* or *mortaïrol* or *mortayrol* – as often with regional dishes, there are several spellings) was once highly appreciated. In his *Dictionnaire des Institutions, Mœurs et Coutumes du Rouergue* (p. 33), Henri Affre writes: 'It enjoyed a very high reputation in monasteries, where it was all the more highly prized because it appeared on the table only every now and then and on certain feast days. In 1417 the monks of Saint-Amans-de-Rodez, when they made arrangements for a farming lease or revenues for their food allowance, made a point of expressly including in the deed "*los tres mortayrols*" [the three *mortayrols*] to which they were entitled each year.'

Amateur etymologists have speculated that *mourtayrol* may have got its name from the Occitan *mortero*, the meal served to relatives of a dead person after his or her funeral. But it in fact derives from the Latin *mortarium*, which, like the English 'mortar' and the French *mortier*, can mean both a kind of vessel and the substance mashed up in it. In the case of *mourtayrol*, the reference is to the substance: although it is today a stew consisting of solid chunks of meat, in its original form the various meats were mashed up before being served.

All the evidence – much of it kindly given to me by the food historians Philip and Mary Hyman – suggests that *mourtayrol* is a 'fossil' dish. It would seem to be the last surviving example of a multi-meat stew that was commonly eaten in several countries of Europe during the Middle Ages. The dish appears as *morterol* in *Libre de Sent Soví*, a fourteenth-century Catalan cookery manuscript. It turns up as *morterel* in the first printed version of the celebrated early fifteenth-century work, *Le Viandier de Taillevent*, though it is not found in any of the several manuscripts of the work (it is a so-called 'new' recipe, added later by the publisher or an unknown cook).

The dish also appears in other medieval European cookery manuscripts such as the French *Le Mesnagier de Paris* (as *mortereul*) and *Liber de coquina* (as *martoriolum*), the Savoyard *Du fait de cuisine* (as *morterieulx*), the Provençal *Modus viaticorum preparandorum et salsarum* (as *mortayrol*), the Tuscan *Libro della cocina* (as *mortarolo*), the English *Forme of Cury* (as 'mortrewes' – Chaucer calls the dish 'mortreux'), and the Dutch *Keukenboek* (as *mortroel*). All these recipes call for mixed meats (or fishes), and almost all for saffron. The dish subsequently disappeared from European cookbooks and, presumably, tables as the fashion for mashed-up meat dishes waned – though it survived, in its slightly different, more solid form, in the Rouergue. Curiously, none of the modern scholars who have edited the above-mentioned manuscripts seems aware that *mourtayrol* is just about alive and well and living on in the Massif Central.

The intermingling of different meat flavours (ham, chicken and beef) that is the distinctive characteristic of *mourtayrol*, in addition to the presence of saffron, is also found in two other slowly cooked

French dishes, the Toulouse version of *cassoulet*, which includes pork, lamb and goose, and the Alsatian pork, beef and lamb dish *baekeofa* (variant spellings include *baekaoffa*, *backenoff*, *baeckenoffe*, *beckenoffe*, *baeckeoffe* and *beekenohfe*).

[*For eight*]
400g (14oz) raw ham, if possible with bone
1kg (2lb 3oz) beef (*plat de côtes* or *culotte*)
1 boiling hen of about 1.8kg (4lb)
2 onions
4 cloves
bouquet garni
freshly ground pepper
salt
300g (10½oz) carrots
300g (10½oz) turnips
300g (10½oz) celeriac
300g (10½oz) leeks
2g (30 grains) saffron
8 slices slightly stale rye bread

Put the ham and beef in a very large saucepan and cover with water. Bring to the boil, then simmer, skimming from time to time. After 30 minutes add the hen, the onions studded with cloves, the *bouquet garni* and plenty of pepper. Bring back to a simmer and continue to cook for 2 hours. Check seasoning and add salt if necessary. Add the other vegetables, cut into not too small chunks, and simmer for a further 30 minutes. Five minutes before the end, add the saffron and stir well.

Put a slice of bread in each soup plate and fill the plate with the cooking liquid. Mash up and serve as a first course. Arrange the meats and vegetables on a large serving dish and serve with mustard and gherkins.

Vegetables

In the not so distant days when Auvergne farms were virtually self-sufficient, the kitchen garden lived up to its name, providing a wide variety of vegetables for the stewpot. Things have not changed much today: most gardens, both in the countryside and, more surprisingly, in towns, are given over almost entirely to the growing of vegetables and fruit. Often there is no flower garden as such, though the kitchen garden, where the really serious business of growing vegetables takes place, may be adorned with a few token flowers on its periphery. This arrangement will often of course be found in many other French rural communities as well. Where the Auvergnat kitchen garden differs is in the predominance of some vegetables and herbs and the rarity of others.

As the climate is often harsh because of the altitude, pride of place is given to hardy vegetables such as cabbage and Swiss chard, both of which occupy an important place in Auvergnat cuisine. Potatoes are also a staple. They are often imaginatively combined with cheese, as we have seen in the cheese chapter. This was not always so: potatoes were viewed with suspicion when first introduced towards the end of the eighteenth century (p. xv). Garlic, shallots and onions are all widely grown. Other common kitchen-garden vegetables are lettuce, carrots, turnips and French beans. There is a long tradition of growing pumpkins. Courgettes, which appeared in Auvergnat shops only some twenty years ago, have since caught on as garden vegetables. But Auvergnat cooks have not yet been able to bring themselves to commit 'infanticide' like their Provençal counterparts, and instead of picking courgettes when they are small and at their tastiest they often allow them to grow almost to the size of British marrows. Courgettes are the exception that proves the rule. Usually, Auvergnat culinary conservatism repels all intruders. Basil, for example, despite promotion on countless radio and television programmes and in magazine and newspaper recipes, has totally failed to gain a foothold in the Auvergnat kitchen garden, where the only herbs generally to be found are parsley, chives and, sometimes, tarragon.

With an ageing rural population and more and more working wives, kitchen gardens in the Auvergne have tended to shrink in the past few years. In my part of the Châtaigneraie, any shortfall in home-grown fruit and vegetables is made up for by Daniel Ville, an enterprising greengrocer whose lorry calls in on Mourjou and neighbouring villages twice a week. He has become something of an institution in his eight years of operation. He turns up in a huge lorry, which is decorated on the outside with a painting of a young lady in a bikini about to eat a banana and surrounded by kiwi fruit (Daniel has won several 'decorated lorry' competitions), and which has a horn as terrifying as that of the lorry in Steven Spielberg's film *Duel*. When his lorry draws up in the village square, I and my neighbours clamber up some metal steps into the vehicle. We exchange the latest news and gossip as we forage among the crates of produce. During the mushroom season, my neighbour the curate, Louis Bedel, likes to engage in some light badinage, claiming that he is afraid to go into the woods alone and would prefer to be accompanied and shown the best '*coins à cèpes*' by Daniel's sunny assistant, Sylvie Roualdes. When one village mayor said he would ban Daniel from doing business unless he erected trestles in front of the lorry and laid out all his produce on them, on the grounds that his steps were dangerous because they had no handrail, Daniel retorted that it was not worth his while setting up the display

because he spent only an hour in the village. The mayor sent along the local *gendarmes*, who were sheepishly forced to retreat by a bevy of customers, most of them nimble old ladies who felt insulted by the idea that they could not climb a few steps and threatened to organize a petition in Daniel's favour. Daniel not only offers an exceptional selection of ultra-fresh produce, but actively encourages certain growers to supply him with scarce items, such as scorzonera and what many people regard as France's best strawberry, Mara des bois, which is crossed with the wild strawberry.

The other source of vegetables here, apart from the kitchen garden and Daniel Ville's lorry, is of course the wild. The young shoots of bracken and black bryony are used as a salad vegetable. Many gather water blinks and watercress from pools where springs issue from the hillside. But, in Mourjou at least, people now tend to eat them cooked: an elderly couple of raw-watercress freaks recently went down with liver fluke, a particularly nasty and virtually incurable disease passed on from sheep to humans via the plant. In spring, dandelions are widely gathered. They are thought to be at their best when the nascent flowering bud is still tucked away in the core of the plant. Canny gatherers look out for fields with not-too-fresh molehills: any dandelions that the mole has smothered with earth will have become naturally blanched.

Mushrooms, although not strictly speaking vegetables, are convenient to discuss here since they are treated like vegetables in the Auvergnat kitchen. As so often when it comes to what they eat, the Auvergnats are fairly cautious about which mushrooms they are prepared to consume. Everyone picks ceps and field mushrooms, and most people eat parasol mushrooms, horse mushrooms, and horn of plenty (despite their off-putting French name, *trompettes de la mort*). But a fair number of mushroom hunters reject chanterelles, and almost no one of my acquaintance will touch hedgehog fungus, blewits, Caesar's mushroom or saffron milk-cap, which are all much sought after in other regions of France.

On the whole, owners of woods and fields do not mind other people coming to pick mushrooms on their land as long as they are for their own consumption. They do, on the other hand, object to those, especially from other *départements*, who turn up in vans, load up and sell their haul in the nearest big town.

Mushroom-picking is a much talked-about – and boasted-about – activity. From mid-summer on, one hears about this or that villager who claims to have picked 10, 20 or even 30 kilos of ceps (the suspiciously round figures suggest the weighing was done in the mind, not on scales). One man in my village even said he had gathered 50 kilos of chanterelles in an hour, a virtually impossible feat given the weight of an average chanterelle (15 grammes).

Ceps have become scarcer almost everywhere in the Châtaigneraie in the twenty years I have lived there. Bits of woodland where, when there had been enough rain, I could regularly rely on finding a few of them in the face of fierce competition from other gatherers are now barren. One does not need to look very hard to find a reason for this sad state of affairs. Ceps live in a particularly complicated form of symbiosis with trees and are extremely sensitive to any changes in the soil. Much of the Châtaigneraie consists of sensuously rounded little hills with steep sides that plunge down to a stream or river. Because of the steepness, all arable land and most pasture is located on the top of the hills, which were once covered with chestnut trees or heathland. Because of this configuration, the 'muck' spread on the scalped hilltops – and by 'muck' I do not mean manure, but fertilizers, pesticides and herbicides – gets washed down into the woods if a downpour occurs before it has had time to sink into the soil. The sad thing is that, as with trout and crayfish (p. 50), farmers lament the scarcity of ceps yet admit to being the culprits – vastly more 'muck' is spread on the land than twenty years ago. If proof were needed for this explanation of the cep decline, one need look no further than the fact that woods where ceps still grow in abundance, which are more and more fiercely guarded by their owners, all happen to be located on hilltops or on land that is not downhill from a field. Modern methods of logging have not helped either: when wood owners want to cut down trees nowadays, they blast a new or wider track through the woodland with a bulldozer, tearing down old drystone walls, all so as to let through a conveniently large vehicle that will take the timber away. The consequent churning up of the soil is fatal to the cep.

Although cep picking has become a rare pleasure, it is fortunately quite easy to come by the mushroom, as those with undamaged or unpolluted cep woods often sell some of their harvest at market. And there are still plenty of chanterelles and hedgehog mushrooms, both of which are less vulnerable to pollution.

⤙ Salade de responchons ⤚

Wandering through Villefranche-de-Rouergue market one spring morning I came across a bent old lady selling bunches of what she called '*asperges sauvages*'. As I was keen to sample a new vegetable, I bought a bunch ('Just boil them and eat them with a *vinaigrette*,' she advised). A little later that morning I was assailed by other market-goers who had spotted what I was holding in my hand and urgently wanted to know where I had bought my *responchons*, as they called them. When I went back a little later past the spot where the old woman had put down her carton of *responchons*, she had gone, no doubt after being cleaned out in next to no time. Little did I know then that the appearance of the young shoots of *Tamus communis* (black bryony, also known as lady's seal) in the hedgerows is a long-awaited moment for the people of the Aveyron.

The Aveyronnais will spend hours scouring the hedgerows for the difficult-to-see shoots, which have to be picked before the plant begins twining round any stems and branches within reach and quickly climbs to cover a considerable expanse of vegetation with its pretty heart-shaped leaves and white flowers.

Curiously, this passion for picking and eating *responchons* (or *respountsous*, *répounchous*, *respounjous* – words transcribed from Occitan (p. xxi) often have several spellings, which approximate to the Occitan pronunciation) is not shared by those who live in the neighbouring *département* of the Cantal. So the untouched Cantal hedgerows offer rich pickings for incoming Aveyronnais. This 'invasion' is resented by the Cantaliens, even if they do not themselves fancy the vegetable. '*Les douze*' – as people driving cars with number plates ending in 12, the figure that denotes an Aveyron registration, are known in the Cantal – are suspected of every crime, from foraging in mushroom woods to picking lettuces, snaffling the occasional chicken and stealing wood. One Cantal farmer I know once went so far as to booby-trap his wood-pile as a precaution.

This interdepartmental difference of taste is symbolized by the village of Saint-Santin, which is unique in France in that it is divided down the middle into two *communes*, Saint-Santin-d'Aveyron and Saint-Santin-de-Maurs. The boundary separates not only the two *communes* but two *départements* (the Cantal and the Aveyron) and two administrative regions (the Auvergne and the Midi-Pyrénées).

The village has two churches (one Romanesque, one Gothic) and two village councils (one left-wing, one right-wing). Until recently, it also had two primary schools (with different holiday dates) and two football teams. The schools have now been merged, and a single football team formed. It is called Entente and plays on a pitch where one goal is in the Aveyron and the other in the Cantal. Saint-Santin has to make do with a single curate for its two churches. To avoid antagonizing either camp, he holds mass alternately in each church.

Sylvie Roualdes, who works for Daniel Ville, the itinerant fruit and vegetable vendor (p. 143), was born in Saint-Santin-d'Aveyron and moved recently a few hundred yards down the road to Saint-Santin-de-Maurs. She tells me that the village's schizophrenia also extends to the eating of *responchons*: one half of the village eats the vegetable, the other does not. Around her new Cantal home, she has no difficulty in finding plenty of *responchons* to pick.

Does black bryony deserve the enthusiasm of the Aveyronnais? I have to say in all honesty that my great expectations of *responchons* were dashed when I tasted them: although they have a pleasant colour and texture, their taste is bitter and rather one-dimensional. To get rid of most of their bitterness, the Aveyronnais boil them in plenty of water, changing it at least once, and sometimes twice. They serve them, as in the recipe that follows, in salad with boiled potatoes, hard-boiled eggs and bacon, which further disguise any lingering bitterness.

Tamus communis, which belongs to the yam family, has apparently been eaten since Roman times. Yet Richard Mabey, in *Food for Free* (1972), describes it as poisonous 'when eaten in moderate amounts'. Mrs M. Grieve, in her *Modern Herbal* (1931), says 'death in most painful form is the result of an overdose, while the effect of a small quantity, varying not with the age only, but according to the idiosyncrasies of the patient, leaves little room for determining the limit between safety and destruction.' It is perhaps just as well that the Aveyronnais boil their *responchons* in several changes of water.

Poisonous or not, black bryony are reputed to have medical properties. *Potter's Cyclopaedia of Botanical Drugs and Preparations* (Potter &
Clarke, 1907) says: 'The fresh root is scraped and the pulp rubbed into
parts affected by gout, rheumatism, or paralysis . . . Black Bryony is a
popular remedy for removing discolouration caused by bruises, hence
its name – Blackeye Root.' This property also no doubt explains its
other Auvergnat name, *herbe aux femmes battues* (battered wives' herb).

[*For four*]
400g (14oz) black bryony tips about 15cm (6in) long
250g (9oz) potatoes
5 tablespoons salad oil
1 clove garlic, finely chopped
salt
freshly ground pepper
3 eggs, hard-boiled
100g (3½ oz) smoked bacon or *poitrine fumée*
1 tablespoon vinegar

Wash and boil the black bryony tips in salted water for 45 minutes,
changing the water once. Wash the potatoes, boil in salted water
(leaving their skins on if they are of a thin-skinned variety) and cut
into dice. Make a dressing with the oil, garlic, a large pinch of salt and
plenty of pepper. Put the black bryony and diced potatoes into a salad
bowl, add the hard-boiled eggs, chopped not too finely, pour the
dressing over them and mix well. Cut the bacon into strips and sauté
until crisp. Transfer to the bowl. Deglaze the pan with the vinegar,
pour sizzling over the salad and mix well.

‹‹ Salade de grelons ››

When the end of March comes round, Auvergnats with kitchen gardens
look forward to eating *grelons* (also known as *tanous* or *méquettes*), the
unopened flowering heads of cabbage, kale or turnip. And rightly so.
Their delicacy of flavour took me by surprise when I first ate them.
Perhaps I should not have been all that surprised: broccoli – 'little
shoots' in Italian – is simply a more developed form of the same thing.

I had gone to buy some eggs from Louise Aymar (who gave me the recipe for *fromage de tête*, p. 79). When she came back from the hen coop with the eggs, she was also carrying a bunch of *grelons*. 'Here, try these, I think you'll like them.' I asked her how she prepared them, and she gave me the simple recipe below. With *grelons* (pronounced *grélous*), as with asparagus, artichoke and corn on the cob, the shorter the period of time that elapses between picking and cooking, the finer the flavour and the tenderer the flesh.

[*For four*]
500g (1lb 2oz) *grelons* (unopened flowering heads of
   cabbage, kale or turnip)
salt
3 tablespoons salad oil
2 teaspoons vinegar
1 teaspoon Dijon mustard
freshly ground pepper
4 eggs, hard-boiled
1 spring onion, finely sliced
2 sprigs flat-leaf parsley, finely chopped

Wash the *grelons* and plunge them into plenty of boiling, salted water. Cook for 3–5 minutes. They should be removed while they are still *al dente*. Strain and refresh with cold water. Leave to drain. Make a salad dressing with the oil, vinegar, mustard, a pinch of salt and plenty of pepper. Put the *grelons* in a serving dish and dribble the dressing over them. Garnish with quartered hard-boiled eggs, spring onion and parsley.

✦ Tourte de pommes de terre ✦

The Hôtel de la Poste's menu was offering '*tourte de pommes de terre*'. Potato in pastry sounded a bit like stodge in stodge, but I ordered it because I was curious to see what it was like. When it came, it looked promising: its puff pastry casing had that slightly lopsided look that denotes a truly home-made pie. I dug my knife into it, releasing a tiny puff of aromatic steam that showed the pie was piping hot. It was excellent, well lubricated with cream and filled with tasty, waxy potatoes.

The pie is a speciality of the Bourbonnais, in northern Auvergne, where it can commonly be found in charcuteries, ready to heat up, as well as in restaurants. But I was sampling my pie farther south, in the cavernous dining-room of the Hôtel de la Poste in Massiac (Cantal). It is one of those big turn-of-the-century inns that have recently lost ground to the anonymous, if more comfortable, modern hotels in the Novotel, Sofitel and Campanile chains. With its geranium-decked covered terrace projecting out on to the pavement of Massiac's high street like the floral bust of a buxom middle-aged lady, Hôtel de la Poste is an establishment where size and clockwork efficiency do not preclude genuine friendliness from both the *patron* and his squad of energetic, strictly uniformed waitresses. Its reliable, unfussy cuisine and good value attract lunching office workers and, in summer, holiday-makers on half or full board. Such hotels often proudly maintain for decades the standards that their customers have come to expect of them. The 1950—51 English edition of *Auberges de France*, a fat 880-page gastronomic guide put out by Le Club des Sans-Club, 'the organizer of your gustatory joys and cordial welcome on the road', already listed the Hôtel de la Poste in Massiac. Its quaintly translated entry still holds true today: 'If the Cantal has a reputation for austerity it certainly does not refer to this laughing corner which will leave you a souvenir of a most delightful stop.'

[*For four to six*]
400g (14oz) waxy potatoes
250g (9oz) double cream
3 cloves garlic, finely chopped
2 tablespoons flat-leaf parsley, finely chopped
large pinch salt
freshly ground pepper
400g (14oz) chilled puff pastry
1 egg yolk, beaten

Wash, peel and steam the potatoes (if they are new potatoes of a thin-skinned variety, they need not be peeled). Cut them into not too thin slices and put them into a mixing bowl with the cream, garlic, parsley, salt and plenty of pepper. Mix well, but without breaking up the potatoes too much.

Divide the pastry into 2 pieces, one slightly larger than the other. On a lightly floured surface, roll out the larger piece to a circle about 6mm (¼in) thick and place on a lightly oiled baking sheet. Put the filling neatly and compactly on to the centre of the pastry, leaving a 4cm (1½in) margin free on the edge. Roll out the other piece of dough to the same thickness and place it over the filling; it should be large enough to cover it completely. Fold the edge of the bottom round of pastry back over the edge of the top round, fold again so the border rests against the enclosed filling and seal well by crimping with the thumb and fingers. Brush the surface with egg yolk, and cut one or two slits in it with a sharp knife. Bake in a fairly hot oven (200°C/ 400°F/Gas mark 6) for 45–60 minutes or until the pastry begins to turn golden brown.

Tourte de pommes de terre is best served hot, but also makes a nice cold picnic dish (the potatoes absorb all the cream as they cool).

↤ Gratin auvergnat ↦

Mashed potato is just as good with mashed chestnuts as it is in the classic combination of mashed potato and parsnip or celeriac. In all cases, the potato attenuates the sweetness and improves the texture of the accompaniment. This *gratin auvergnat* has the added attraction of a crisp, golden crust of Cantal cheese. It can be eaten as a first course or accompany *boudin* or roast meat.

[*For four*]
500g (1lb 2oz) potatoes
175–250ml (6–9fl oz) milk
500g (1lb 2oz) fresh or frozen chestnuts, or unsweetened
   tinned chestnuts, drained
30g (1oz) unsalted butter
salt
freshly ground pepper
100g (3½oz) grated or very thinly sliced young Cantal

Clean, boil, peel and mash the potatoes with about 100ml (3½fl oz) of hot milk until a smooth purée is obtained. Depending on the variety and age of the potatoes you may have to add a little more milk. If you have unpeeled fresh or frozen chestnuts, make a circular incision round each of them with a sharp knife, boil for 5 minutes, remove from the water and peel. Return the chestnuts to the water and continue boiling until they are soft. Mash the chestnuts (whether fresh or tinned) with about 75ml (2½fl oz) of milk until they have the same consistency as the potatoes. Beat the two purées together with the butter, salt and plenty of pepper.

Butter a gratin dish and fill with the mixture. Sprinkle with grated cheese or, if the Cantal is too soft to grate, cover the filling completely with thin slices of cheese. Put in a fairly hot oven (190°C/375°F/Gas mark 5) for about 30 minutes or until golden brown on top.

⤙ Chou farci ⤚

The second time I visited the Croutes family at their farm (for an account of my unusual first encounter with them, see page 76), the distinctive heady smell of frying cep mushrooms met my nostrils as I stepped out of the car in their courtyard. I was puzzled, as one has to climb a flight of stone steps to reach their front door. How had the smell travelled down so far? The answer was simple: Yvonne Croutes was cooking the mushrooms on a huge gas ring in a basement-cum-cellar, whose door gives directly on to the courtyard at the foot of the steps. She does much of her cooking there, I discovered – when, for instance, she wants to prevent droplets of frying fat from soiling her spotless kitchen. I know no one more house-proud. She polishes the impressive array of copper pans and pewter plates that adorn the walls of the dining-room at least once a month, applying so much elbow-grease, she admits, that her shoulders ache for days afterwards.

The other time she uses the basement kitchen annexe is when she needs sheer heating power. The gas ring, which is also used for heating pigswill, will bring a huge high-sided pot of water to the boil within a few minutes. This is ideal when, for example, she needs to blanch a mountain of cabbage leaves for her *chou farci*, which family, relatives and friends rightly revere.

Generations of Auvergnat cooks worked out from experience what American scientists discovered in the laboratory: that overcooked, unblanched cabbage of the kind regularly served to millions of wretched British schoolchildren is one of the most repellent things ever to have emerged from the kitchen. In his fascinating book *On Food and Cooking*, Harold McGee notes that during cooking 'the mustard oils and cysteine derivatives [in members of the cabbage group] break down to form various odoriferous compounds, including hydrogen sulphide (typical of rotten eggs), ammonia, mercaptans, and methyl sulphide; eventually these may react with each other to form especially powerful trisulphides. The longer the vegetable is cooked, the more of these molecules are produced.' Hence the need to blanch cabbage if it is to be cooked for a long time. Most of the things in the cabbage that can turn nasty are thus thrown away with the water.

Yvonne says the best *chou farci* is made with a large Savoy cabbage which has had a touch of frost (this makes it sweeter). Her version of the dish is a traditional one of the kind that would have been eaten at a time when the Auvergne was still very poor and almost no one could afford to eat meat. Although her stuffing is meatless (but not vegetarian, as it contains lard), plenty of flavour is provided by its mixture of Swiss chard tops, parsley, garlic, onion, bread, flour, cream, eggs and milk. But in our more affluent age most restaurants serve a version of *chou farci* that also contains sausagemeat, just in case their customers feel cheated.

Various versions of *chou farci* are found in other cabbage cultures, mostly located in regions with a harsh climate that the cabbage can contend with. On the whole they consist of large individual cabbage leaves, sometimes soured like sauerkraut, which are wrapped round their own dollop of stuffing and can thus sit snugly side by side in the casserole. They include the Serbian *dolma*, Hungarian *töltött kaposzta*, Romanian *sarmale* and Polish *gołabki* (literally 'little pigeons').

[*For six*]
1 large Savoy cabbage
8 cloves garlic, finely chopped
10 sprigs flat-leaf parsley, finely chopped
10 Swiss chard tops, chopped
2 large onions, chopped

small bunch chives, finely chopped
100g (3½oz) white bread without crust, crumbled
2 *biscottes* (rusks), crumbled
6 eggs
100ml (3½fl oz) cream
250ml (9oz) milk
175g (6oz) plain flour
70g (2½oz) lard
2 tablespoons vegetable oil
300g (10½oz) carrots

Bring a very large pot of water to the boil. Cut the cabbage in half and gouge out the tough central core from each half. Pull off the leaves and blanch for 5 minutes. Strain and refresh under the cold tap.

Put the garlic, parsley, Swiss chard tops, onions, chives, bread, *biscottes*, eggs, cream and milk in a mixing bowl and mix thoroughly. Gradually incorporate the flour, stirring all the time. Heat the lard and oil in a large casserole. Cut the carrots into thin slices lengthwise. Fry them gently in the fat until they brown very slightly. Remove from heat and spread the carrots evenly over the bottom of the casserole. Cover the carrots with several large cabbage leaves. Spread a layer of stuffing evenly over them. Repeat the operation until all the stuffing is used up, ending with a layer of cabbage.

Place uncovered in a moderate oven (180°C/350°F/Gas mark 4) for about 2½ hours. After about 1½ hours, check that the edges are not in danger of burning. If they are, pour a little water down the sides and reduce the heat slightly. When the stuffed cabbage is ready, take the casserole out of the oven, run a knife round the edge, and put its lid on for a few minutes (this operation makes it easier to unmould). Turn out on to a large serving dish.

There is a fancy, restaurant version of *chou farci* that is very rarely made in the home. In that version, the leaves of the cabbage are left on the central stalk and the stuffing is literally 'interleaved', i.e. pressed down between the leaves, and the whole thing tied up with string. It has the disadvantage of being much more difficult to execute, and of not acquiring the caramelly outside produced by Yvonne Croutes' recipe.

⊰⊱ Farcidures ⊱⊰

Farcidures – *farciduras* in Occitan (p. xxi) – is one of those dishes which you will find in several completely different guises depending on which part of the Massif Central you are in. It can mean a pancake made with wholemeal bread, or Central European-style dumplings, or a *galette* of grated potato with *lardons*, or cabbage leaves with potato and *lardons*. It is this last version which is the most specifically Auvergnat, the others being more specific to the Quercy and Limousin regions. It comes from *Recettes d'Auvergne* (Ostal del Libre, 1992), by Michèle Canet, who in this and her other books, *Lo Companatge* (Institut des Etudes Occitanes du Cantal, 1991) and *Recettes de Châtaignes* (Ostal del Libre, 1997) has done much to preserve the Auvergne's culinary heritage by her tireless research in the field.

[*For four*]
8 large cabbage leaves
1.2kg (2lb 10oz) potatoes
100g (3½oz) flat-leaf parsley, finely chopped
100g (3½oz) onion, finely chopped
salt
freshly ground pepper
50g (2oz) plain flour
100g (3½oz) salt pork belly or green streaky bacon, cut
    into *lardons*

Blanch the cabbage leaves in plenty of salted boiling water for 5 minutes, strain and refresh under the cold tap. Peel the potatoes and grate finely. Squeeze out excess moisture and put in a mixing bowl with the parsley, onion, a little salt and plenty of pepper. Sprinkle the flour over the mixture and mix well. Form balls the size of a potato. Push 2 or 3 *lardons* into each ball and close up the holes. Press each ball against a cabbage leaf and, using a slotted spoon, submerge gently in plenty of salted boiling water (*not* the water used for blanching the cabbage leaves). The starch in the potato causes the ball to adhere to the leaves. Simmer for 45 minutes. Remove with a slotted spoon and serve with a meat dish such as *civet de lièvre* or *petit salé*.

❧ Blettes au jus ❧

Swiss chard tops are used in a multitude of ingenious ways in Auvergnat cooking. They are an essential ingredient of *pounti* (p. 21), *falette* (p. 136), *poule farcie* (p. 116), *farçous* (p. 19) and *tourifas* (p. 75). The other half of Swiss chard leaves, the white stalk, is as far as I know traditionally cooked in only two ways, *au jus* or with a *béchamel* sauce – though restaurant chefs like Nicole Fagegaltier of Le Vieux Pont (p. 84) use it in other imaginative ways as a garnish. *Jus* means gravy – not of the unspeakable flour-thickened English kind, but simply the fat and juices that exude from meat when it is cooking or being carved.

It is vital that the Swiss chard be ultra-fresh. Paradoxically the stalk suffers more than the tops from a long sojourn at the greengrocer's. It becomes leathery and tasteless. But when freshly gathered and from not too large a plant, it has a pleasant and subtle flavour.

[*For four*]
4 Swiss chard stalks
salt
200ml (7oz) juice from a veal or pork roast
50g (2oz) unsalted butter, melted
freshly ground pepper

Cut the stalks into strips about 5cm (2in) long. Bring plenty of salted water to the boil, add the stalks and cook for 3–6 minutes. Strain, refresh under the cold tap, and transfer to a hot serving dish. Add the meat juice (reheated if necessary), the melted butter and plenty of pepper. Mix well, check seasoning, and serve immediately.

This dish is a natural accompaniment to the roast that produced the *jus*.

Desserts, Breads, Preserves and Confectionery

Desserts – or puddings, as purists insist that all sweets and afters should be called – do not play a prominent role in the Auvergnat kitchen. One could say, quoting one of the French food writer Robert J. Courtine's favourite epithets when describing dishes like grilled sole or a boiled egg, that traditional Auvergnat desserts have a 'Racinian simplicity'. They mostly call for very mundane ingredients, such as the classic canon of flour, egg, sugar and milk or cream, and when they venture beyond that spectrum they tend to call for locally available fruits and nuts such as wild cherries, apples, pears, plums/prunes, hazelnuts, walnuts and bilberries (which grow on mountains up to an altitude of 1,400 metres, and are gathered with huge metal combs that pull the fruit off the plant and into a box-like container).

The Auvergnats love baking – anything from the essential bread they used to bake themselves in their round bread ovens to the *fouaces* they make for christenings and weddings and the biscuits they offer you when they invite you in for a drink. And as in the rest of France, every self-respecting rural store cupboard is chock-a-block with preserves, of which I give two less well-known examples.

↤ Cornets de Murat ↦

My first experience of *cornets de Murat* was, aptly enough, in the small town of Murat, which nestles below the north-eastern flank of the extinct volcanoes that make up the Parc Régional des Volcans du Cantal. We had dropped our bags at the Hôtel des Messageries, one of those large old-fashioned hotels which, like the Hôtel de la Poste in Massiac (p. 149), seem to sail imperturbably down the decades, and decided to take pot luck for lunch before taking a walk on the Plomb du Cantal, the highest of the Cantal's extinct volcanoes. At the village of Albepierre, half-way up the mountain, the Restaurant du Plomb, whose terrace was packed with people, seemed a promising candidate. We had an excellent, simple lunch of the kind that the Auvergne offers so liberally. It included *tripoux* and delicious trout fished from the local stream, the Lagnon (back in the sixties restaurants could still serve locally caught fish; now it has to come from fish farms). The tables were decorated with bunches of wild flowers.

After working off lunch on the slopes of the Plomb du Cantal, we were prepared to tackle the cuisine of the Messageries. Its fare, much more 'sophisticated' than what we had eaten for lunch, included *cornets de Murat*, which were marked on the menu as a '*spécialité*'. They turned out to be wafer biscuits rolled into a cone shape and filled with Chantilly cream – a tasty enough variation on the classic *cornet à la crème* made with puff pastry, but not very high on the individuality scale. In contrast to the *truites au lard*, the sturdy product of a peasant tradition, that we had had for lunch, the cones were symptomatic of a bourgeois country table trying to give itself the trappings of '*grande cuisine*'. It was only next day, when I saw that all the *pâtisseries* of Murat sold *cornets* (empty and waiting to be garnished by the customer), that I realized they were indeed a speciality of the town as well as of the hotel. Who first invented them I was unable to find out. I give the recipe here because they have remained an Auvergnat speciality, and are fun for children to eat.

[*To make eight cornets*]
75g (2½oz) caster sugar
90g (3oz) unsalted butter, softened
2 egg whites
60g (2oz) plain flour
400ml (14fl oz) double cream
60g (2oz) icing sugar

Beat the sugar and 60g (2oz) of the butter in a bowl with a wooden spoon until pale. Add the egg whites and incorporate thoroughly. Put 40g (1½oz) of flour in a sieve and sift over the mixture, folding it in rapidly with a spatula. Place tablespoonfuls of the mixture on a buttered and floured baking sheet (or 2 sheets) and flatten with the spatula to make rounds about 12cm (5in) in diameter. Bake in a fairly hot oven (200°C/400°F/Gas mark 6) for 5 minutes or until the biscuits have brown edges or patches.

Place the baking sheet on the open oven door to keep warm, and slide a thin plastic spatula under one biscuit, lift it off the baking sheet and quickly roll it round a conical mould, making sure the pointed end of the cornet is closed. If you do not have a conical mould specially designed for this purpose, roll the biscuits round the top of a wine bottle, allowing the pointed end to protrude slightly so it can be pinched closed. Do the same with the other biscuits, proceeding as quickly as possible, since they soon become brittle as they cool and cannot then be moulded. If this should happen, put them back in the oven for a minute or two to become pliable again.

Whip the cream in a chilled bowl until it has doubled in volume, fold in the icing sugar and mix well. Put in a pastry bag with a cannelated tip and fill the cornets.

The biscuit dough can, if you wish, be flavoured with a teaspoonful of good rum or orange-blossom water. The cornets have more individuality, but are less orthodox, when filled with chocolate mousse.

⤛ Flognarde ⤜

It would be stating the obvious to say that wherever flour, eggs, sugar and milk are commonly available ingredients, some form of cheesecake-like preparation is likely to be made. The Auvergne is no exception. A variety of slightly differing recipes are found there, some calling for cow's milk, like this *flognarde*, others for curd cheese and a pastry crust, like *tarte à l'encalat* (p. 160). *Flognarde* (also spelt *flaugnarde*, *flangnarde* and *flougnarde*) has a similar balance of ingredients to the Breton speciality, *far*, and, curiously, to a recipe jotted down by my Scots grandmother in her manuscript cookbook under the name of 'French pancake'.

[*For four*]
180g (6½oz) flour

180g (6½oz) caster sugar
750ml (26fl oz) milk
6 eggs, beaten
zest ½ lemon, finely grated
30g (1oz) butter

Mix the flour and sugar in a bowl and stir in the milk until a smooth paste is obtained. Add the beaten eggs and the lemon zest. Butter a 25–28cm (10–11in) non-stick flan tin. Pour the mixture into the tin and bake in a hot oven (220°C/425°F/Gas mark 7) for about 30 minutes or until puffed up and well browned. If it seems to be browning too soon, protect by laying a sheet of aluminium foil on top. Sprinkle with sugar and serve.

↠ Tarte à l'encalat ↞

This rich yet curiously refreshing recipe was given to me by Germaine Lacoste. She makes *tartes à l'encalat* on a regular basis for the Relais du Heurtoir's Marché de Pays (p. 111). She and her husband, Robert, who have a large dairy herd, are a rarity among farmers round here in that they still make their own cream. And a delight it is too – thick, sweet and aromatic, and very different from the more acid *crème fraîche*, which is the only cream available in the great majority of French *crémeries*.

Encalat is the Occitan (p. xxi) word for curd cheese (*caillé* in French). In the south of the Auvergne (northern Aveyron) this dish is called *flaune* (or *flône* or *flausone*), a word of the same etymological origin as flan, and usually calls for Brousse (made from ewe's whey, like traditional Italian Ricotta) instead of cow's-milk curd cheese. *Flaune* is flavoured with orange-blossom water.

[*For four to six*]
300g (10½oz) chilled short pastry
650g (1lb 7oz) well-drained curd cheese
3 eggs, beaten
160g (5½oz) double cream
175g (6oz) caster sugar

On a lightly floured surface, roll out the pastry 3mm (⅛in) thick. Use it to line a 25–28cm (10–11in) flan tin, with a removable base if possible, and bake blind in a fairly hot oven (200°C/400°F/Gas mark 6) for 12 minutes. Put the cheese, eggs, cream and sugar into a mixing bowl and blend thoroughly. Turn the mixture into the pastry-lined flan tin and bake in a fairly hot oven (190°C/375°F/Gas mark 5) for 30–45 minutes, or until the mixture has set and its surface begun to brown. If it seems to be browning too soon, protect by laying a sheet of aluminium foil on top. Remove from the oven, leave to firm up for 5 minutes, then transfer to a hot dish and serve immediately.

⊰ Millard ⊱

Part of the charm of woodland in the Châtaigneraie is that it is not properly husbanded, partly because much of it lies on very steep slopes. As a result one finds a very wide range of tree varieties (sweet chestnut, horse chestnut, false acacia, oak, ash, elm, beech, silver birch, lime, medlar, white poplar, lombardy poplar, aspen, spruce, pine, wild pear, crab apple and wild cherry, among others). Each individual tree has to fight it out with its competitors in the eco-system. The result is a pleasing variety. In autumn, the respective trees' leaves turn many different hues of brown, yellow and russet as the days get shorter, sometimes producing an almost chocolate-box effect that has people rushing for their cameras – almost always with disappointing results. In spring, before any leaves come out, banks of woodland seen from a distance are dotted with what seem to be sparkler-like bursts of tiny white specks: these are wild cherry trees coming into bloom. Later they will bear very small dark cherries which, when fully ripe, become soft sacs of sweet juice that explode gratifyingly in the mouth (and less gratifyingly on one's clothes if one is not too careful). As with the wild strawberry, the wild cherry's flavour is 'gamier', more intense and more astringent than its cultivated version. The only problem is that the fruit is often inaccessible, since wild cherry trees grow to a respectable height. One can get round that by picking cherries from trees on steep inclines, where there are branches that can be reached from a higher bit of hillside.

One of the best uses for wild cherries, and one that exploits their

juiciness, is in a kind of baked cherry custard called *millard, milliard* or *clafoutis*. There are many versions of this farmhouse favourite. Those that date from hungrier days call for a high proportion of flour to egg. The version given below is the kind of *millard* you might get served in today's more prosperous farmhouses, where eggs are less of a luxury than they used to be. The word *millard* has largely fallen out of use in the Auvergne and been replaced by the Limousin term *clafoutis*. The legend goes that when the French Academicians were thinking of defining the word *clafoutis* as 'a kind of fruit flan' in their dictionary, the inhabitants of the Limousin protested that *clafoutis* was not a flan and that it could not be made with any old fruit, but only with small black cherries (wild if possible). As a result, the definition in the *Dictionnaire de l'Académie* now reads: 'pudding with black cherries'.

Clafoutis has an interesting etymology which backs up the Limousins' argument that only cherries should be used in the dish. The word comes from the Old French *claufir*, which derives from the Latin *clavo figere* ('to fix with a nail'), which is found in tenth-century *Passions* in the sense of 'fixing Christ to the cross with nails' and has survived in dialects in the sense of 'to stud, or cover with nail-like objects' – in this case small black cherries.

[*For four*]
30g (1oz) butter
80g (3oz) plain flour
500g (1lb 2oz) whole wild cherries or Morello cherries
100g (3½oz) sugar

4 eggs, beaten
300ml (10½fl oz) single cream or equal quantities of
  double cream and milk

Butter a shallow baking dish large enough to hold the cherries in a single layer. Sprinkle with 30g (1oz) of flour and shake vigorously so it spreads evenly over the surface. Tap out excess flour. Wash, stem and pat dry the cherries with kitchen tissue. Spread them in the baking dish.

Put the rest of the flour into a mixing bowl and stir in the sugar, then the eggs. Mix thoroughly. Warm the cream and gradually add to the mixture, stirring all the time until a smooth batter is obtained. Pour evenly over the cherries. Bake for 45 minutes in a fairly hot oven (190°C/375°F/Gas mark 5), or until well browned and puffed up. Remove from the oven, sprinkle with icing sugar if desired, and leave to cool slightly. The *millard*, which will subside slightly, should be served warm but not hot. It is also good cold.

You should warn your guests that the cherries have not been pitted, otherwise their teeth may get a nasty shock – or worse. The reason the cherries are left whole in this dish is that their pits, as they heat up, contribute a characteristic bitter–almond flavour.

⊰ Tarte aux pruneaux ⊱

Prunes used to play an important role in the Auvergnat diet. Every household had a plum tree or two in the orchard. Plums, mostly of the *prune d'Agen* or *prune d'ente* variety, were easily grown and easily dried (first in the sun, then in the bread oven during the last stages of its cooling). They were a useful storable source of energy and vitamins in the days before refrigerators came in. Hence the widespread use of prunes in Auvergnat recipes, some of them savoury: *pounti* (p. 21), some stuffings, one version of *farçous* (p. 53) and, of course, this prune tart.

The combination of prunes and short pastry can verge dangerously on the leaden, particularly when, in typical Auvergnat style, extra strips of pastry are laid, trellis-fashion, across the surface of the tart.

That is why, taking my cue from Yvonne Figeac (p. 21), I give a version which calls for a sweet flan pastry that includes egg and sugar. The result is a deliciously light and delicate crust that sets off the filling of sticky prune paste admirably.

[*For six*]
125g (4½oz) sifted plain flour
pinch salt
30g (1oz) caster sugar
60g (2oz) unsalted butter, diced and chilled
1 tablespoon iced water
1 egg, well beaten
400g (14oz) prunes
1 tablespoon milk

Mix the flour, salt and sugar in a mixing bowl. Add the butter. Holding a pair of table knives scissors-fashion, with their blades touching and your hands crossed over, pull them apart repeatedly so that the butter is cut into the flour. Continue until the mixture has the consistency of fresh breadcrumbs. Mix the iced water with the beaten egg and gradually pour over the mixture, quickly stirring all the time with a fork until the dough forms into a compact and unsticky mass (you may need to add a little more iced water). Shape the dough into a ball. If you have a blender that makes pastry, simply put the flour, salt, sugar and butter into it and blend for about 15 seconds. Add the egg and water, and blend for a further 15 seconds or until the mixture forms into a ball.

Wrap the dough in aluminium foil or clingfilm, and refrigerate for at least 30 minutes, and overnight if possible, before use.

Soak the prunes in hot tea for 30 minutes if they are of the unrehydrated type (i.e. very wrinkled and quite hard).

On a lightly floured surface, roll out the chilled pastry 3mm (⅛in) thick. Use it to line a 25–28cm (10–11in) flan tin, with a removable bottom if possible. Gather up the trimmings of pastry, compress into a ball, roll out to the same thickness and cut into strips about 1cm (½in) wide and 28cm (11in) long.

Pit and mash up the prunes to make a thick paste. Spread evenly over the pastry-lined flan tin, then lay 6 strips of pastry on top to form a criss-cross pattern. Brush the pastry with milk and bake in a moderate oven (180°C/350°F/Gas mark 4) for 30 minutes or until the pastry turns light brown. Remove the tart from the oven and leave to become lukewarm before serving. It is also good cold.

⤙ Cadet-mathieu ⤚

Intensively grown Golden Delicious, picked before they are ripe and still green when they go on sale, have flooded the British market. This has prompted some people to jump gleefully to the conclusion that all French apples are lousy. This is quite simply not true. While the range of varieties offered by most greengrocers is relatively small – though consumers have recently been won over by the excellent New Zealand variety, Royal Gala – there is a wealth of old and little-known varieties in farm orchards and alongside fields and hedgerows. In the Auvergne, they have intriguing names like Queue de Lièvre (Hare's Tail) and Pomme-Poire (Pear-Apple), which is so called not because of its shape but because its skin has a grainy, pear-like texture. But the best-liked apple in the Auvergne is beyond all doubt the Sainte-Germaine, a variety of russet that keeps extremely well. My first encounter with the apple was at a market stall in Brioude (Haute-Loire). Alongside the, yes, Golden Delicious and Starkings, there were some unprepossessing green apples with greyish blotches on them. The stallholder told me they were Sainte-Germaines and strongly recommended them. We agreed with her when, during a riverside picnic later that day, we sank our teeth into their crisp flesh, which was clean, aromatic and sweet, with just a touch of tartness.

Sainte-Germaine apples are the ideal variety for this Auvergnat version of apple pie called *cadet-mathieu*.

[*For four*]
30g (1oz) butter
400g (14oz) short pastry
90g (3oz) plain flour
500ml (18fl oz) milk
70g (2½oz) caster sugar
4 egg yolks

1 tablespoon orange-blossom water
1kg (2lb 3oz) Sainte-Germaine or similar tart and sweet
   apples, peeled, cored and finely sliced
1 egg, beaten

Butter a 20cm (8in) deep-sided round pie dish. Divide the pastry into 2 pieces, one weighing almost twice as much as the other. On a lightly floured surface, roll out the larger piece into a 28cm (11in) circle about 6 mm (¼in) thick and line the pie dish with it.

Mix the flour thoroughly with 150 ml (5½fl oz) of the milk. Put the rest of the milk in a heavy saucepan and bring slowly to just below boiling point. Remove from heat and stir in the milk-and-flour mixture until smooth. Add half the sugar and cook gently for about 10 minutes or until fairly thick, stirring all the time. Remove from heat. Beat in the egg yolks, one by one, and the orange-blossom water.

Pour the mixture into the pastry-lined pie dish. Cover evenly with layers of sliced apples and sprinkle with the rest of the sugar.

Using a pastry brush, moisten the rim of the pastry shell with beaten egg. Roll out the remaining piece of pastry into a 20cm (8in) circle. Roll it on to the rolling-pin and unfurl over the pie dish to form a lid. Press down to seal and knock up the edges. Make a central hole and ensure it stays open by inserting a small roll of card or aluminium foil folded double. Brush the surface well with beaten egg.

Bake in a fairly hot oven (200°C/400°F/Gas mark 6) for 25 minutes, then reduce the heat to moderate (180°C/350°F/Gas mark 4) and bake for another 20–25 minutes or until the pastry is golden brown. If it browns too soon, cover with aluminium foil. Remove the pie from the oven and allow to rest for 5 minutes before serving.

Charlotte de châtaignes et potimarron
↤ au coulis de coings ↦

This recipe for a chestnut and *potimarron* charlotte with a quince *coulis* was given to me by Jean-Pierre Courchinoux, of the Auberge Fleurie in Montsalvy, 23 kilometres from Mourjou. It won the cookery competition at Mourjou's 1994 Foire de la Châtaigne (Chestnut Festival). I include it not only because it offers a delicious and finely tuned

combination of autumnal ingredients (chestnut, *potimarron* – a small and flavoursome variety of pumpkin called onion squash – and quince), but because it allows me to say a word or two about the Foire de la Châtaigne. The festival, the brainchild of a Mourjou-born journalist, Pascal Piganiol, started quite modestly in 1989 as a village *fête* on the theme of the nut that gave the Châtaigneraie its name. But over the years it has become a major local event, held annually during the third weekend of October. In 1996, for example, it attracted some 12,000 visitors over two days, was the subject of a twenty-minute programme on the France 3 television channel, and was covered by a woman journalist from the Japanese daily *Asahi Shimbun* (circulation 8 million). The Japanese are big chestnut eaters, and in the summer of 1997 Piganiol was already getting phone calls from *Asahi Shimbun* readers inquiring about how to get to the festival. It may be only a question of time before coachloads of Japanese tourists spill out on to the village's small car-park.

What is it that attracts so many visitors – after all, surely a chestnut is a chestnut is a chestnut? With the benefit of professional help from the Institut des Etudes Occitanes (Institute of Occitan Studies) in Aurillac, the festival organizers decided to focus on every aspect of the chestnut culture that is a feature of the Châtaigneraie. Two criteria are used in the selection of the commercial stands, bands, singers, actors, painters and lecturers that are present at the festival: they must either offer a chestnut-related product or be based in the Châtaigneraie or another area with a similar chestnut culture (Catalonia, Ardèche, Corsica, Italy). Thus, attractions might include: a lecture on the history of the chestnut tree, a band that plays traditional Auvergnat dance music, a concert by the now celebrated Corsican *a cappella* singers, a commentated hike through chestnut woods with halts and refreshments at farms, a cookery competition for original recipes incorporating chestnuts, exhibitions of paintings or flower arrangements by local artists, and stands (no less than 85 in 1997, when the festival was attended by 15,000 people) selling anything from different varieties of chestnut saplings, chestnut baskets, chestnut furniture, chestnut walking-sticks, chestnut toys, chestnut-handled knives and large chestnut-gathering pincers to culinary specialities containing chestnuts (jams, *boudin*, preserved rabbit, venison stew, duck *civet*, chocolates) or chestnut flour (*beignets*, *croissants*, cakes). Each year the festival is rounded off in rumbustious style by a dinner consisting of an *aligot géant* (p. 32), a local dish which, perhaps thankfully, contains no chestnuts, followed by a dance.

No product-related festival in France would be complete without its *confrérie* (confraternity or guild), whose members dress up in quaint robes. I was honoured to be asked to become the Grand Maître of Mourjou's Confrérie du Pelou – the Occitan (p. xxi) word for the chestnut's prickly husk – in my capacity as a cookery writer and journalist who could spread the good chestnut word. I was a little apprehensive about my duties as Grand Maître, but they have now boiled down to opening the festival each year after a series of thunderingly boring speeches by local grandees. I have had two sticky moments, though: one occurred at a congress of *confréries* – which was attended, among others, by a Confrérie de l'Escargot, whose representatives, an extremely serious husband-and-wife team, marched about with staffs and wearing hats that had snail shells dangling from their rim, and by a Confrérie de l'Ail, whose contingent sported big white headdresses in the shape of heads of garlic – when I had to read out a long charter in Occitan which I had never set eyes on before; the other cold-sweat occasion came when a television camera was thrust in my face at thirty seconds' notice and I was asked the dauntingly vague question: '*Alors, Grand Maître, c'est quoi, pour vous, la châtaigne?*' (Which could roughly be translated as: 'What does the chestnut mean to you?')

A lot of eating goes on at the Foire de la Châtaigne, much of it in the form of snacks (roasted chestnuts with cider, sandwiches, *beignets*). Unfortunately for the public, the dishes entered for the 1994 cookery competition were tasted only by the panel of judges. The crowd watched stoically as we – I was on the panel – sampled mouthfuls of seven dishes and gave them marks for appearance, taste, balance, ease of execution and so on.

The president of the panel was the chef Michel Bras, whose restaurant in Laguiole (two rosettes in the Michelin guide and the top 19/20 rating in the Gault-Millau guide) is the pride of the Auvergne. Bras has written a massive and at times mystical cookbook of inventive recipes, many of which call for the wild plants and mushrooms he comes across as he goes on his daily jog across the high Aubrac plateau.

We all easily agreed that Courchinoux's charlotte was the best recipe. But nobody expected Bras, a thin, serious and almost clerical-looking man, to launch, in his prize-giving speech, into a scathing critique of most of the entries. 'Too much butter and cream went into the recipes, and I couldn't find the taste or texture of the chestnuts of my youth,' he said. This prompted one of the judges to mutter that the Aubrac plateau was too high and too cold in winter for there to be any chestnut trees there. Bras did, however, have time to praise Courchinoux's charlotte before he sprinted to his car and drove back to Laguiole.

That Courchinoux should have won the competition, which was reserved for professional chefs from the area, was no surprise. He has a very solid culinary training behind him. It started when he was ten and living in Arpajon, the village that has now been engulfed by the suburbs of Aurillac. He always watched and helped his mother when she made apple tarts. After a spell at Aurillac's catering school, he went on to its more prestigious equivalent in Toulouse. After graduation he worked as a chef at various restaurants in the provinces and in Paris (including Le Petit Riche, which has one of the most congenial Belle Epoque décors in the capital). He has run L'Auberge Fleurie since 1989 and has no intention of moving on: he loves the surrounding countryside and appreciates its wildlife – and abundant woodcock in particular.

[*For eight*]

15g (½oz) unsalted butter

50g (1½oz) plain flour

790g (1lb 12oz) caster sugar

4 eggs, separated

50g (2oz) chestnut flour

tiny pinch salt
200g (7oz) *crème de marrons*
500g (1lb 2oz) *potimarron*, peeled
250ml (9fl oz) double cream
500g (1lb 2oz) quince

Butter a round cake tin measuring 22cm (9in) in diameter and 4cm (1½in) deep. Add 1 teaspoonful of flour, shake around the cake tin and tap out any excess flour.

Put 40g (1½oz) of sugar into a mixing bowl with 4 egg yolks. Beat until the mixture thickens and forms a ribbon. Beat in 45g (1½oz) of plain flour and the chestnut flour. Put the egg whites and salt into a dry mixing-bowl and beat until stiff peaks are formed. Stir a large spoonful of the egg whites into the mixture, mix well, then fold in the rest. Turn into the cake tin, spreading the mixture well up against the rim with a spatula. Bake in a moderate oven (180°C/350°F/Gas mark 4) for 30–35 minutes, or until the cake has browned and has shrunk slightly away from the rim of the tin. Leave to cool for about 8 minutes. Run a knife round the edge of the tin and turn the cake out on to a rack. Turn back on to its flat side. Leave to cool for an hour.

With a very sharp knife, cut the cake into 3 discs horizontally. Trim one disc to fit the bottom of a charlotte mould, spread 100g (3½oz) of *crème de marrons* on it and place in the mould. Cut the rest of the cake into strips the size of lady's fingers and place them upright and tightly pressed together to line the sides of the mould.

Put 500g (1lb 2oz) of caster sugar into a saucepan with 500ml (18fl oz) of water, bring to the boil, and simmer for 15 minutes. Cut the *potimarron* into small pieces, add to the syrup and simmer until soft. Strain, reserving the syrup for some other use, and put the *potimarron* into a blender. Blend until a very fine purée is obtained. Incorporate the rest of the *crème de marrons*. Whip the cream until stiff and incorporate into the mixture. Turn it out into the charlotte mould. Refrigerate for 24 hours.

Peel and core the quinces. Cut into small pieces and cook in 1.5 litres (53fl oz) of water with 250g (9oz) of sugar. Simmer until the liquid has reduced by half. Push through a *chinois* sieve to make the *coulis*.

Unmould the charlotte by turning it over on to a serving plate and giving the mould a sharp tap. Pour the *coulis* around it and serve.

(L'Auberge Fleurie, Place du Barry, 15120 Montsalvy. Tel: 04 71 49 20 02.)

⊷ Pompe à l'huile ⊶

My first encounter with *pompe à l'huile*, a pastry almost as basic as *fogassons* (p. 177) and sometimes known as 'poor man's cake', was in the hidden village of Conques (Aveyron). I was wandering through the streets near its splendid Romanesque church when a little label bearing the words *pompe à l'huile* (literally 'oil pump'), stuck in what looked rather like a pizza without any filling, caught my eye in a *pâtisserie* window. I bought a small portion. It tasted surprisingly good, despite its off-putting name: the pastry had been drenched with a mixture of vegetable oil and walnut oil and dredged with sugar.

Like *fogassons*, the eggless *pompe à l'huile* was originally a Lenten dish, though it is now eaten throughout the year. It is a traditional accompaniment to Marcillac wine (p. 209). There are two versions of *pompe à l'huile*, one that uses white bread dough as a base, and the other a croissant dough (or yeast-leavened puff pastry). Here I have opted for the second, tastier version.

[*For four*]
250g (9oz) strong plain flour
7g (¼oz) salt
200g (7oz) caster sugar
7g (¼oz) baker's yeast
170ml (6fl oz) milk
110g (4oz) unsalted butter
80ml (3fl oz) vegetable oil
80ml (3fl oz) walnut oil

Put the flour, salt, sugar, yeast and milk in a mixing bowl and mix until a soft dough is obtained. Leave to rest for 30 minutes. Roll out the dough into a rectangle about 3mm (⅛in) thick. Cover half the surface with the butter, slightly softened. Fold the other half over the layer of butter and roll out to the same size. Refrigerate for 60 minutes. Fold the rectangle over and roll out to the same size again. Refrigerate for 60 minutes. Repeat the process once more. Leave the dough to prove for a further 60 minutes at room temperature. Prick the dough all over with a fork and bake in a hot oven (220°C/425°F/Gas mark 7) for about 20 minutes, or until golden brown. Mix the oils together. When the *pompe à l'huile* has cooled slightly, dribble evenly with oil and sprinkle with sugar. It is best eaten warm.

⪡ Gâteau aux noix ⪢

Walnuts are greatly appreciated in the Auvergne and are found all over those parts of the region where there is not too great a risk of late frosts. And if the flowering heads do get zapped – it is not unknown for the temperature to plummet to as low as −7−8° C in late April or early May even at moderate altitudes – walnut-tree owners can always fall back on the leaves, which can be used to flavour an aromatic apéritif, *vin de feuilles de noyer* (p. 211).

Walnut oil, too, is highly prized, especially in salad dressings. It is one of those products that are incomparably superior when home-made. There are still a few walnut mills operating in the Auvergne where people can take along their shelled walnuts and have them turned into oil. The resulting product has none of the slight bitterness of commercial walnut oil and a far greater walnut 'nose'. The *marc* (residue) left over from the pressing, once dried, is a great favourite with children.

A litre of walnut oil needs 2 kilos of shelled walnuts. As anyone who has shelled large amounts of walnuts knows, it is an activity that is highly labour-intensive. In pre-television days, people who turned their own walnuts into oil would organize a *veillée* (p. xvii), where a dozen or so people sat round cracking walnuts, littering the floor with fragments of shells, telling stories and singing songs. After pressing, the resulting oil would be distributed on a pro rata basis to those who had brought walnuts to the *dénoisillage* session.

This *gâteau aux noix* is more of a tart than a cake. Pastry goes very well with walnuts, as it offsets their almost cloying richness.

[*For four*]
320g (11oz) short pastry
3 eggs, separated
60g (2oz) caster sugar
3 tablespoons honey
110g (4oz) shelled and chopped walnuts
salt

On a lightly floured surface, roll out the pastry 3mm (⅛in) thick. Use it to line a 20cm (8in) flan tin. Beat the egg yolks vigorously into the sugar and honey, then add the walnuts. Mix well. Whisk the egg whites with a small pinch of salt until very stiff, and fold gently into the mixture. Pour into the pastry-lined flan tin and bake in a moderate oven (180°C/350°F/Gas mark 4) for 45 minutes or until the surface browns slightly. Serve warm.

⤙ Croquants aux noisettes ⤚

Fernande Faven, an accomplished cook who used to help out in the kitchen at three of Mourjou's now defunct restaurants, gave me the recipe for these pleasingly crunchy hazelnut biscuits.

Fernande and her husband Paul have the most impeccable kitchen garden in Mourjou. It has a line of small fruit trees (greengage, peach, pear and quince) down one side, and is surrounded by a privet hedge as neatly clipped as the hair Paul cuts for certain villagers and so dense that large green lizards like to bask on it when the weather is hot. There are only a few flowers in the garden (dahlias and lavatera for decoration, and French marigolds to keep away disease): pride of place is given, as it usually is in French rural areas, to the edible.

A garden of that kind, which outsiders to the village often stop to admire as they walk past, requires a great deal of effort: both Favens spend many hours digging, removing stones, spreading farm manure (they are organic gardeners in everything but name), removing weeds while they are still infant, yanking up garlic and shallots to dry out on the surface of the ground, picking raspberries, pruning the fruit trees, taking chicory down into the cellar to blanch it in sand, digging potatoes and performing the countless other tasks of the conscientious gardener.

Paul has never been work-shy. For years he was employed as a postman in the days before motorbikes, let alone vans, were used. He cycled the length and breadth of this very hilly commune with a mailbag on his back, sometimes tackling short cuts so steep he had to carry his bike as well as his mailbag up them.

In the sixties, he built his house with his own bare hands and the help of a few friends. This was in the days when builders had to lift massive granite cornerstones with pulleys, not mechanical lifts. After working as a postman he became the village *cantonnier* (roadman). His main task, as such, was to keep the verges of the communal, as opposed to departmental, roads well clipped. This he did by hand, kilometre after laborious kilometre, with his murderously sharp and regularly honed scythe and billhook.

The Favens are a living refutation of the Auvergnats' reputation for stinginess. As soon as there is a glut of lettuce or courgettes or raspberries, I will find a plastic bag full of goodies tied to the metal bar that runs across my front door. When the asparagus is pushing up, the plastic bag will contain little bundles of the vegetable, trimmed, washed and tied up ready for cooking. When, during a hot but well-watered summer, the French beans get out of control, it is they that find their way into the bag. If Paul finds some ceps – and he knows all the best '*coins à cèpes*' – he gives me one or two '*juste pour faire l'omelette*'. Once, when Fernande was making a large quantity of *chou farci* to put in the freezer, a surplus ended up on my front door in a soufflé dish, oven-ready. Occasionally I manage to catch Paul and inveigle him in for a drink just as he has furtively tied up a bag on my door and is about to make a getaway on his bicycle.

One day the bag contained hazelnuts which Paul had gathered from the hedgerows. Remembering that I had tasted some deliciously crunchy hazelnut biscuits at the Favens', I asked Fernande for the recipe.

[*To make about 18 croquants*]
130g (4½oz) hazelnuts
200g (7oz) plain flour
11g (½oz) baking powder
2 eggs
200g (7oz) caster sugar
salt

Put the hazelnuts in a large flan tin and toast in a hot oven (220°C/ 425°F/Gas mark 7) for about 10 minutes or until light brown (it is as well to use a timer for this, for a couple of minutes overtoasting will ruin them). Take them out of the oven and, while they are still hot, rub them vigorously until their skins come off. Pick them out of the debris of skins and crush them coarsely in a mortar.

Put the hazelnuts, flour, baking powder, eggs, sugar and a small pinch of salt into a mixing bowl and mix thoroughly. Using a teaspoon, spoon the mixture on to a lightly oiled baking sheet, leaving at least 2cm (1in) between dollops, and bake in a hot oven (220°C/425°F/ Gas mark 7) for 25 minutes, or until lightly browned. Cool on a rack.

⋯+ Fouace +⋯

Fouace (or *fougasse* or *fogassa*) is a very ancient kind of leavened semi-sweet cake. Its name derives from the Romans' *panis focacius* ('bread of the hearth'). It is found in various versions in many regions of France, from Caen and Chinon to Périgueux and Nice. Chapter XXV of the first book of Rabelais' *Gargantua et Pantagruel* describes how Gargantua's countrymen were so fond of *fouaces* that they forcibly seized 'four or five dozen' cakes from the bakers of Lerné and thus caused 'fierce wars'. Rabelais' *fouace* differed from the modern version in that it contained 'saffron and spices'. The *fouace* of the Auvergne is half-way between a brioche and a sponge cake and, particularly in the Aveyron, is often flavoured with lemon zest or orange-blossom water, and more rarely with crystallized citron peel. The erstwhile baking of *fouaces* in the family bread oven, after a batch of bread loaves had been taken out, is something that evokes fond memories in the older generation. They are usually associated with the deliciously yeasty smell given off by the *fouaces* as they baked. Big bakings of *fouaces* were undertaken for special occasions such as christenings and weddings, when *fouaces* were distributed to each household in the village. That tradition is still maintained today, though the baking is done in ordinary kitchen cookers.

Najac (Aveyron) has an annual *fouace* procession, when a beribboned and flower-decked mega-*fouace* 1.40 metres long, 70 centimetres thick and weighing 50 kilos is paraded through the streets, then cut up and handed out to all those attending the event. Patricia Auger-Holderbach, in *La Cuisine Paysanne en Rouergue* (Editions du Rouergue, 1992), tells us that the origins of the festival, which takes place on the last Sunday in August, are to be found in a dispute many centuries ago between the inhabitants of the upper and lower parts of the village (Najac is built on a rocky outcrop). The *fouace* ceremony is thought to commemorate a fleeting reconciliation between the two warring clans.

Even within the Massif Central, *fouaces* vary considerably in consistency and sweetness. As a general rule, those made by professional bakers tend to have a softer, more brioche-like texture, while home-made *fouaces* are usually sweeter, firmer and crumblier. *Fouaces* may be round, oval or crown-shaped. The version below, which was given to me by Sylvie Ratier of Les Feuillardiers (p. 45), is somewhere between the softer bakers' version and the firmer home-made version. You can, if you like, devise your own *fouace* by slightly varying the proportions of flour, butter, eggs and sugar.

[*For six*]

20g (¾oz) baker's yeast
100ml (3½fl oz) milk
250g (9oz) unsalted butter, softened
500g (1lb 2oz) plain flour
150g (5½oz) caster sugar
2 eggs
2 tablespoons orange-blossom water
50g (2oz) crystallized fruit (citron peel if possible), finely
  chopped
1 egg yolk, beaten

Dissolve the yeast in 25ml (1fl oz) of warm water. Heat the milk gently in a saucepan, add the butter, stir until melted and pour the mixture into a mixing bowl. Add 425g (15oz) of the flour, the dissolved yeast, 120g (4oz) of the sugar, the whole eggs, the orange-blossom water and the crystallized fruit. Knead this mixture vigorously with the hands. It will seem rather liquid to start with, but will gradually stiffen. After a minute or two, when your hands begin to ache, the dough is ready. Scrape any dough off your hands into the mixture, flour them, form the dough into a ball and place in a shallow circular ovenproof dish. Sprinkle liberally with flour to prevent a crust forming. Cover with clingfilm and leave to rise for 5 hours at room temperature (20°C/ 68°F), after which it should have doubled in volume.

Knead the dough, adding a little flour if necessary to prevent it sticking to your hands. Form into a ring and put back in the baking dish. Cover with clingfilm and leave to rise for a further 3 hours. Remove the clingfilm and bake the mixture in a fairly hot oven (190°C/375°F/Gas mark 5) for 25 minutes, or until well browned. Insert a small pointed knife into the *fouace*. If it comes out clean, the *fouace* is cooked. Brush lightly with egg yolk and sprinkle with the remaining sugar. Leave to cool on a rack.

Being a rather dry cake, *fouace* is a good accompaniment to breakfast coffee or tea, or an *apéritif*. In the Auvergne it is traditionally served with *îles flottantes*. It is also excellent with strawberries and whipped cream.

⊷ Fogassons ⊶

In the course of my conversations with them, several Mourjou people fondly recalled a treat they used to look forward to as children. They described it as consisting of a small ring-shaped piece of pastry, which was first boiled, then baked. It was heavenly, they said, when eaten just after it had been baked in the bread oven that every household used to have. It was clear from their description that the speciality belonged to the large family of *échaudés* (literally: 'scalded' things), which are found in many regions of France and traditionally eaten from Lent to Easter. The boiling/baking process apparently allows the pastries to keep better.

The trouble was that none of the people who so enjoyed the *échaudés* could give me a recipe for them or even remember their local name (they did not recognize the word *échaudé*). Someone who was bound to know, I was told, was ninety-three-year-old Marie Pétry, the extraordinarily youthful mother of Joseph Pétry, Mourjou's part-time baker (p. 182). And she did. 'They are called *fogassons*,' she said as she prepared to make a batch of them when I came to watch her son baking bread. 'I haven't made these in ten years,' she added. The *fogassons* were indeed delicious, if a little one-dimensional, when allowed to cool just long enough after being baked not to be mouth-burners. Since they contain no fat, they become very hard once they have cooled. The Occitan (p. xxi) word *fogasson* (which is pronounced *fouassou*) turned out, I discovered, to have the same root as *fouace* (p. 175), i.e. the Romans' *panis focacius* ('bread of the hearth').

[*To make 20 fogassons*]
500g (1lb 2oz) plain flour
3 eggs
50g (2oz) caster sugar

Put the flour in a mixing bowl, make a well, add 2 eggs and the sugar, and mix well. Form into little rings about 4cm (1½in) in diameter. Plunge into plenty of boiling water, making sure the *fogassons* do not stick to each other. Remove with a slotted spoon as soon as they rise to the surface and leave to drain on kitchen paper. When they are dry, brush with beaten egg and bake in a hot oven (220°C/425°F/ Gas mark 7) for about 15 minutes or until golden brown. Eat while still warm.

◄+ Brioche aux grattons +►

Anyone who likes crisp-fried bacon or pork fat (I insist on the word 'crisp', having once tasted and almost thrown up that British speciality, pork scratchings – sludgy, greasy and preservative-packed bits of inferior pork fat) will adore the complex and subtle flavour of these *brioches*. They make an excellent, unaggressive accompaniment for a wine-tasting. Curiously, a very similar, more scone-like pastry called *töpörtyüs pogacsa* is widely eaten in Hungary.

[*To make about 20 brioches*]
80ml (3fl oz) milk
12g (½oz) baker's yeast
300g (10½oz) salt pork belly or green streaky bacon

500g (1lb 2oz) plain flour
4 eggs
freshly ground pepper

Heat 50ml (2fl oz) of milk until tepid, and mix in the yeast until dissolved. Leave in a warm place for 30 minutes. Cut the salt pork or bacon into very small pieces (the size of green lentils), and sauté gently. When the pieces have turned light brown, strain off the lard and reserve. Leave the pieces for a minute or two more over a low heat to crisp up. Put the flour, the yeast and milk mixture, the eggs and plenty of pepper into a blender. Blend for 15 seconds, then, with the machine still on, pour in the melted lard and blend for a further 20 seconds. Mix in the *lardons*. If the mixture seems too liquid, add a little more flour and blend again until the dough forms a ball. Transfer the dough to a bowl, cover with a tea-towel and leave in a warm place or hot cupboard for 2 hours. Separate the dough into little balls about 5cm (2in) in diameter and arrange on a lightly oiled baking sheet. Brush with milk. Bake in a very hot oven (230°C/450°F/Gas mark 8) for 5 minutes, then reduce the heat to fairly hot (190°C/375°F/Gas mark 5) for a further 20 minutes or until the brioches are golden brown. Cool on a rack.

⤛ Bread ⤜

When I bought my house in Mourjou from Jeanne Chabut (p. 7) and her children, they generously left many pieces of furniture in it as part of the deal: twenty-four chairs (it had been a café-restaurant), six tables and three beds, among other things. Various other pieces – rustic antiques like fireplace benches, a huge Art Deco mirror and a grand-father clock – had been stolen by two young Parisiennes who had earlier rented the café for a couple of years. They told a friend in the area afterwards that they regarded the theft as a 'liberation of property'. The Chabut family never saw their antiques again: although everyone knew who the thieves were, there was no proof of theft as the Chabuts had been too trusting to draw up an inventory.

One of the pieces of furniture the thieves spurned was a large, though not antique, kitchen table whose most striking feature was a huge bread drawer measuring 57 × 70 centimetres. I could tell from the dimensions of the drawer – and from the semicircular bread ovens that nestled against the sides of almost all the older houses in the area – that the people of the Châtaigneraie took their bread very seriously.

And so it turned out. As in the rest of the Auvergne, almost every farming household in Mourjou used to make its own bread, usually with flour from wheat and rye grown on the farm itself. Up until the introduction of the potato in the late eighteenth century (p. xv), bread occupied an even more important place as a staple foodstuff than it did later. In years of crop failure and severe shortage in the nineteenth century (in 1817–18 and in 1848), bread was made from any grain farmers managed to grow, sometimes even with an admixture of potato or pounded bracken roots. At such times peasants eked out their flour with bran, which they normally held in low regard. Brown bread was seen as inferior to refined white bread, which was the food of aristocrats and feast days. Today, of course, attitudes have changed. (A similar reversal has also occurred in the case of attitudes to sun-tan: at the turn of the century, a tanned skin was seen as evidence of toil in the open air, while a 'porcelain' complexion betokened a life of leisure indoors or beneath parasols on the lawn or beach.)

Pierre Besson, whose memoirs, *Un Pâtre du Cantal* (1914), are an

invaluable record of what life was like in a very poor peasant community at the turn of the century, quotes an old cowherd who could remember the years of shortage: 'We only ate barley and oat bread, from which we were careful not to remove the bran – to the point where, if you'll excuse the term, you couldn't distinguish a man's '*estroun*' [turd] from a mare's droppings.' During the Second World War, when there was again a shortage of flour because much of it was requisitioned by the Germans, the Vichy authorities ordered the population not to remove bran from their flour. It is only relatively recently in France, with mounting interest in health food and organic produce, that 'bran' loaves (*pains au son*) have caught on and become widely available in bakeries.

In Mourjou – as in countless other villages all over France – a bread van does its rounds twice a week. It brings bread baked by the bakery in the next village, Calvinet. The loaves, often still warm from the oven and audibly crunchy when squeezed, range from the familiar *baguette* and its variant, *épi* (literally 'ear of corn' – a *baguette* with a succession of points up each side) to *boules* and *tourtes*. These are round, flattish loaves. A *boule* is about 20 centimetres in diameter and weighs about 500 grams, while a *tourte* has twice the diameter and weighs up to 2.5 kilos. The *tourte* is the sort of loaf my bread drawer was designed for. Even in our less devout times, most heads of household make a sign of the cross over the loaf before cutting it. The loaf is placed vertically in the drawer, which is then half closed in such a way as to wedge the loaf against the table top. Slices are then cut with a Laguiole knife (p. 193). *Boules* are usually made of maslin (a mixture of rye and wheat flour), while *tourtes* may be made of either pure wheat flour or maslin.

Bread still looms very large in the Auvergnat diet. Substantial quantities of it are eaten not only with *charcuterie* and cheese, but with main courses. It is the basis of the *casse-croûte* (literally: 'break–crust'), a snack taken at various times of the day, sometimes at home, sometimes in the fields. Bread goes into a number of soups, and indeed was the original meaning of the word *soupe*, and of the English 'soup' (p. 1).

The quality of bread is the subject of much keen debate locally. Each time the bakery in Calvinet changes hands (as it has done twice in the last ten years), the new baker's bread is pitilessly assessed for crispness, degree of baking, evenness of texture and keeping qualities.

This is undoubtedly because, although almost no one bakes their own bread any more, most inhabitants of Mourjou aged over fifty can remember the time when they or their parents put the family bread oven into use once a fortnight. People who have tasted home-baked bread feel entitled to set themselves up as judges.

It was around the turn of the century that commercial bakers first began to set up business in the Auvergne. To start with, families would supply the baker with flour made from their own grain. They would get it ground at one of the many mills that straddle rivers and streams all over the Auvergne. Millers had a particularly bad reputation because they were suspected of adulterating flour. The baker would turn the flour he was given into bread, keeping back about 20 per cent of the flour as his remuneration. As years went by, the system whereby people supplied the baker with their own flour died out, and they began simply to buy loaves as they do today. But a number of families continued to bake bread in their own bread ovens, in Mourjou at least, until well after the Second World War, particularly in households with many mouths to feed. Gradually, the practice came to be seen as backward, and almost all such non-professional baking has now died out. But Mourjou is fortunate in having a man who feels strongly enough about bread quality to continue to use his oven. He bakes loaves for his family (mother, wife, daughter, son-in-law, grandchildren and, during the holidays, assorted other relatives) and, each Wednesday in summer, for a *marché de pays* at the tiny village of Saint-Parthem on the river Lot. He is the aptly named Joseph Pétry (*pétrir* means to knead).

When I asked if I could watch him bake a batch of loaves, he was delighted to oblige. He uses the sourdough method: he mixes a portion of leaven held over from the previous baking, the *levain de chef*. This is left to ferment overnight. When I went round very early one Wednesday morning, he took me into a little shed with a bread oven at the back and proudly showed me his second-hand kneading machine. This consisted of a deep and very thick cast-iron revolvable bowl measuring 104 centimetres across, with a large kneading paddle fixed at such an angle as almost to scrape the sides and the flared central spindle of the bowl, thus gathering up all the dough when in movement.

Joseph slipped a conveyor belt over the end of the paddle and hitched it up to a little electric motor mounted on a kind of wheelbarrow. First

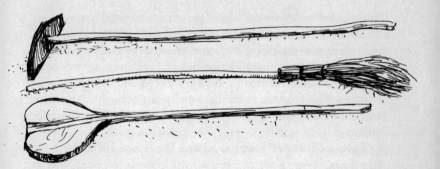

to go into the kneading bowl was the *levain de chef*, some flour and water (one and a half times as much flour as water), as well as a little baker's yeast and some salt. Joseph then set in motion his Heath-Robinson contraption, which he described as '*vieux comme Hérode*': the paddle revolved slowly, the force it exerted causing the kneading bowl to revolve. When the paddles had dissolved the leaven in the water, he added about 850 grammes of salt, two 10 litre buckets of water, and roughly 30 kilos of flour, a mixture of ordinary white and stoneground white.

Meanwhile Joseph's wife – and sternest judge – Lucienne prepared the *paillassons* into which the dough would be put to rise. These are large flat baskets made of straw bound together with coils of split, flattened and dried stems of bramble, an extremely tough material. She lined the baskets with multicoloured tea-towels, apologizing for their patina of earlier flour and dough and explaining that they could not ever be washed (if they were, the dough would stick to them).

Joseph stopped the machine when he judged the dough to be of the right consistency, yanked a double handful of it out of the kneading bowl and carried it, like a drooping skein of wool, to a little table where he folded it and knocked it into shape, then deftly transferred it to a basket Lucienne was holding ready. Soon the whole floor of the little shed was covered with twenty-two loaves nestling in their baskets. The air was heavy with yeasty, almost winery smells.

Joseph now started heating the bread oven, an igloo-shaped brick construction with a flat floor and an opening measuring about 70 centimetres across. He inserted a bundle of twigs and fairly slender branches and set fire to them. As they burned, long and strangely beautiful flames rose up the sides of the oven. Their beauty came from the sensual slowness with which they licked the bricks; yet at the same time there was something awesome about them and their intense redness – something vaguely suggestive of a firestorm. A jokily acrimonious discussion started up between Joseph and Lucienne, who warned her husband not to overbake the bread this time. 'It's not nice when it's black on the bottom,' she said. 'I like it that way,' he muttered.

'How about a bite?' Joseph suggested. We repaired to the kitchen-cum-living room of the farmhouse, which was as spick and span as the kneading shed was dusty and floury. The snack, at 9 a.m., consisted of homemade *pâté*, Cantal cheese, some wine and his own bread, which had a remarkably even and close texture and an off-white colour that made it look like the more commonly found maslin loaf. Joseph explained that the bran in the stoneground flour was responsible for this. The bread was quite springy and unstale after a week of careful keeping in the bread drawer, and had an excellent and distinctive flavour. 'Bread baked in the baker's electric oven doesn't taste like that,' Joseph said proudly.

After that Joseph went back to stoking his oven. An hour and a half and several bundles of wood later the oven was hot enough for baking. Joseph raked out the hot ash with an implement that looked like a larger version of a croupier's rake. The loaves were ready for baking, Joseph said, because they had doubled in size and when you prodded them with your finger they returned to their original shape. I prodded one: it had a startling, almost buttock-like springiness.

The crucial question now was to determine whether the oven was not too hot. This Joseph did, not with anything as sophisticated as a thermometer, but with an ear of corn which he wedged into a crack at the end of the flat, long-handled peel (baker's shovel) that he was about to use to feed loaves into the oven. He stuck the peel into the oven for a few seconds. The ear of corn came out charred: the oven was still too hot. A few minutes later, he repeated the operation. This time the ear of corn had turned golden-brown: the oven was ready.

Joseph and Lucienne had to move quickly now. She brought up one of the baskets and expertly tipped the loaf of soft dough out on to the peel. Joseph gave the top of the loaf four quick slashes of his Laguiole knife (p. 193), forming a noughts-and-crosses grid, inserted

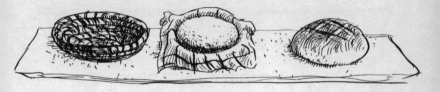

the loaf, pushing it right to the back of the oven, and, with a very abrupt backward movement of the long handle, caused it to slide off the peel. He told me afterwards there was a proverb in Occitan (p. xxi) that warned against the perils of the backward-jerking peel handle: '*Val mièlhs se téner darrièr un cagaire que darrièr un enfornaire.*' ('You're better off standing behind a crapper than behind an oven-man'.)

When all twenty-two loaves had been evenly distributed around the surface of the oven, Joseph closed the opening with a large charred piece of chipboard. The loaves would be ready in an hour and a half. It was noon, and we repaired once again to the kitchen. Apéritifs were brought out, and, with typically Auvergnat generosity, Joseph said: '*Vous allez manger avec nous.*' Suspecting that just such an unrefusable invitation was on the cards, I had earlier nipped home while he was stoking the oven to get a couple of bottles of wine as a contribution. We sat down to an excellent simple lunch of soup, *crudités*, *pâté*, roast beef (one of their own animals), sautéd potatoes, salad, cheese, fruit and home-made *marc* flavoured with wild pears.

We went to inspect the loaves. The chipboard was removed, and Joseph and Lucienne both agreed they were ready. 'Not too black,' she remarked contentedly, prompting a shrug and a clacking of the tongue from her husband. He skilfully slid the peel under the loaves, drew them out of the oven and put them vertically into *paillassons* to cool, before loading them into his van.

Naturally I was not allowed to leave without taking a loaf with me. Payment was politely but firmly refused. I accepted the gift on condition that next time I would feel free to drop by on a Wednesday and buy a loaf. This I have since done many times in summer, when Joseph bakes for the St Parthem market. I find his bread particularly tasty not only because it is baked in a wood-fired oven, but also, I suspect, because it seems to provide a direct link with the Auvergne's culinary past – a bit like Proust's madeleine, except that in this case the automatic mechanism of memory is replaced by an effort of the imagination.

⊰ Confiture de châtaignes ⊱

In chestnut-growing areas like the Châtaigneraie, there used to be only three ways of preserving the bounty of the chestnut crop: drying the chestnuts in *sécadous* (p. 9) and then sometimes turning them into flour, sterilizing them in jars, or making chestnut jam or, in its puréed form, *crème de marrons*. Nowadays, of course, there is a fourth possibility – freezing – which best preserves the flavour of the fresh chestnut.

But chestnut jam can be deliciously aromatic, too, on bread or toast, or else as a dessert ingredient, if a tasty variety of chestnut is used, such as Paquette.

[*To make 1kg (2lb 3oz) of jam*]
650g (1lb 7oz) whole chestnuts, fresh or frozen
500g (1lb 2oz) caster sugar
1 vanilla pod

Make a circular incision round each of the chestnuts with a sharp knife. Bring a large saucepan of water to the boil, put in the chestnuts and simmer for 5 minutes. Remove from the heat. Take out the chestnuts one by one, peel off their outer and inner skins (they have to remain hot for this to be easy; you may need to wear gloves) and return them to the water when done. When the peeling process has been completed, bring the water back to the boil and cook the chestnuts for 20 minutes or until soft.

Transfer to a thick pan (made of copper if possible), add the sugar and vanilla pod, and place over a very low heat. Stir constantly, breaking up the chestnuts into lumps, until the mixture produces large bubbles and comes away from the sides of the pan. It will be dark brown by now. Remove the vanilla pod, pot, leave to cool and cover.

To make *crème de marrons*, push the cooked chestnuts through a sieve before proceeding to the jam-making stage.

✦ Gelée de fleurs de pissenlit ✦

Another recipe, given to me by Yvette Gazal, that exploits the wild larder. This dandelion-flower jelly is supposed to be good for the throat and lungs; it is also startlingly tasty.

[*To make 2kg (2lb 3oz) of jelly*]
400 newly opened dandelion flowers
2 oranges
2 lemons
1kg (2lb 3oz) caster sugar

Trim all the leaves off the dandelion flowers so only the yellow petals are left. Cut the oranges and lemons, unpeeled, into slices and put in a large saucepan. Add the dandelion flowers and cover with 2 litres (70fl oz) of water. Bring to the boil and simmer for 1 hour until half the liquid has evaporated. Strain the liquid into a bowl, pressing down to extract every drop. Put through a very fine sieve or jelly bag into another saucepan. Add the sugar, bring to the boil, stirring all the time, and simmer gently for 45 minutes.

Test the jelly by dropping a small amount of the liquid on to a cold plate. If it sets, the jelly is ready to pot; if it does not, continue cooking for a few more minutes. Allow to cool, and pot.

✦ Caramels de miel ✦

These honey caramels are so irresistibly good that they are snapped up in a trice whenever they appear on sale – at Mourjou's annual chestnut festival (p. 166) and, just occasionally, at the *superette* in nearby Calvinet where their inventor, Colette Rouquier, works as a sales assistant. Fans would like to be able to get more of the caramels, whose flavour has more than a hint of top-quality butterscotch. But Colette says they are a terrible slog to produce by hand in very large quantities.

Colette grew up surrounded by huge drums of honey. Her father, Roger, in addition to running a traditional farm, owns 350 hives, which are dotted around Mourjou and beyond at twenty-five different sites. The honey they produce is excellent, which is not surprising given the abundance of chestnut trees in the area. The honey is given a particularly rich, almost gamey flavour by chestnut blossom, whose huge creamy-white plumes make the woods round Mourjou look as if they are illuminated by shafts of sunlight even when the sky is overcast.

[*To make 40 caramels*]
100g (3½oz) honey
100g (3½oz) unsweetened cocoa powder
100g (3½oz) caster sugar
100g (3½oz) unsalted butter

Put the honey, cocoa, sugar and butter in a thick-bottomed enamel or copper saucepan and place over a low heat. Stir constantly until all the ingredients have amalgamated and form a smooth mixture. Simmer gently for a few minutes. The mixture is ready to be turned out when it reaches a temperature of 157°C (315°F). If you do not have a sugar thermometer, test by removing a tiny amount of the mixture in a teaspoon and dropping it into a glass of cold water. If the mixture immediately turns into a hard ball, remove the pan from the heat at once and turn the caramel out on to a non-stick flat surface (a frying-pan or, better, a rectangular oven tray). When the caramel has cooled to lukewarm, cut into rectangular shapes measuring about 2 × 1cm (1 × ½in). Store in a tin.

Cheese

On my first visit to the Auvergne I was woken, in my hotel room, by a gentle clunking of cowbells filtering through the window. I looked out along the steep east-west valley in which the hotel was located. There, in fields dotted with trees whose early morning shadows pointed pleasingly in the opposite direction from those cast by the previous evening's setting sun, ambled a herd of Salers cows. I was immediately struck by the beauty of the animals, with their slightly curly chestnut coats, light build, broad faces and slender, elegantly curved horns, some lyre-shaped, others pointing forwards like those of Spanish fighting bulls. I did not realize at the time that, quite apart from their unusual appearance, these were cows extraordinary, totally different in their behaviour, character and milk-producing quality from such hobbling milk factories as Friesians. Those very characteristics are partly responsible both for the very high standard of Auvergne cheeses and for some of the problems encountered by the industry.

Before explaining why this should be so, I should perhaps say a word or two about the origins of the Salers breed. It was the creation

of a man from a family of aristocratic lawyers in the large medieval village of Salers, Ernest Tyssandier d'Escous (1813–89). From 1840 on, he developed from the ancient Auvergnate breed a nimble and hardy animal that was ideally suited to the difficult environment surrounding Salers – an altitude of 1,000 metres and more, steep and often waterlogged terrain, long winters and considerable temperature fluctuations. Tyssandier d'Escous naturally called the animal after the village where he was born. He was by all accounts a persuasive and charismatic man, who from 1853 on organized Salers shows that encouraged local farmers to improve their stock. Salers cows have other qualities in addition to their hardiness: they are strong and docile draught animals (which was important before tractors came in), they are long-lived, they have a broad pelvis and thus encounter few problems when calving, and their milk, although not very abundant, is very rich in proteins and therefore makes excellent cheese. Salers cattle are now exported all over the world.

They have another trait, which is both a quality and a drawback: they are extremely maternal. This means, among other things, that they will defend their calves ferociously. Two farmers in my part of the Châtaigneraie have been killed by Salers cows in the past thirty years. In one case, a cow had just calved next to an electric fence. The farmer, worried that the calf would struggle to its feet and get a shock from the live wire, began to drag it clear when its mother gored him in the ribs. In the other case, a cow was about to calve – a time when cows are notoriously unpredictable – and the farmer was scything some grass near her. She took fright and charged him, assisted in her task by three other cows. They tore off practically all his clothes and dumped him, dying, in a nearby river. In both cases the crucial factor that triggered such behaviour in an otherwise docile animal was the presence of a barking dog. Salers have an atavistic fear of dogs which, it is persuasively claimed, goes back to the time when wolves were common in the Auvergne. Legrand d'Aussy (p. xiv), writing towards the end of the eighteenth century, says that when a mountain cow is faced with a wolf she emits a special sound that alerts the other cows, which then form a circle and gradually close in on the wolf and kill it. Whether or not he was repeating legend or actual fact, such behaviour seems in character.

On top of being maternal and 'sisterly', Salers are intelligent (as cows go). Until fairly recently, many herds of Salers cows and calves used to be driven over a distance of up to 30 kilometres to their highland summer pastures as soon as the snows on the Monts du Cantal and Monts Dore had melted in spring. Those animals that had already been on such a *transhumance* would get excited at the prospect of all that fresh grass and variety of mountain plants and, when the herd set off in the small hours, sometimes after being blessed by the local priest, they were eager to lead the way. Herds from farther afield were taken up by train to stations like Allanche or put on lorries, but still had to walk the last few kilometres to the tract of mountainside that was the property of, or had been rented by, their owner.

The pasture's focal point was the *buron*, a stone hut half sunk into the ground and often surrounded by trees. It is there that the *buronniers* lived and worked from about 1 May to 15 October. This trio of usually unmarried men – a *vacher* (the boss), the *boutilier* (his first assistant) and the *pastre* (a younger man who did the more menial jobs), sometimes also accompanied by a *bédelier* (who dealt with the calves) – spent those months milking the cows twice a day by hand and making Cantal cheese. The Salers's maternal instinct is such that she will not give milk unless she is in contact with her own calf. This complicated the task of the *buronniers* considerably. It meant they had to identify the cows by giving them names to which they would answer – often sarcastic names like Bourgeoise, Marquise, Perle, Poupée, Champagne or Comtesse, while the bull might be called Utilitaire. The *buronniers* rose at four and prepared the first milking at 5 a.m. (the second one came in mid-afternoon). The *vacher* and the *boutilier* each strapped a *selon* – a stool with a single central prong not unlike a low shooting-stick – to their backside (if they had used a three-pronged stool, they would have toppled over on the bumpy, chewn-up terrain). The *pastre* or *bédelier* went to the pen where the calves were enclosed and called out the name of a calf's mother, adding the diminutive Occitan suffix -*òt* (pronounced *ou*) to her name. Having learnt to recognize its mother's name, the calf came running to the pen's entrance. The *pastre* led it to its mother, got it to 'start' the udder by letting it suck a teat for a minute or two, then tied it to the cow's left front leg, out of reach of the udder. The milker then took a handful of coarse salt out of a horn container attached to his belt and rubbed it on to the calf's back. This allowed the mother to lick the salt, thus further exciting her maternal, milk-producing feelings and calming the calf down.

The *vacher* and the *boutilier*, sometimes assisted by the *pastre*, would milk up to thirty cows each at each of their two sittings. The buckets of milk were poured through a fine sieve into a large cylindrical wooden container, slightly narrower at the top than at the bottom, called a *gerle*. A pine pole threaded through the holes of its two handles at the top enabled it to be carried, like a sedan chair, to the *buron*. Then there began the tricky process of turning the milk into cheese – which is of course the same as the one used today in mountain farmhouses. After making a sign of the cross, the *vacher* stirs rennet into the milk while it is still warm; when it curdles, the whey is baled out by pressing down a special circular ladle with a central handle, rather like an upturned mushroom, on to the curds; the curds are then wrapped in a cloth, pressed, milled and pressed again eight or nine times. The end product of this process – during which the amount of rennet used, temperature and timing are all crucial – is Tomme fraîche de Cantal, a cheese that resembles an unsalted cow's milk mozzarella in its consistency and properties, and is used in a number of dishes. If not set aside for use as Tomme fraîche, the cheese is milled again, salted and packed into a cylindrical stainless-steel cloth-lined mould. It is then pressed into its final Cantal shape. After several changes of cloth, the cheese is unmoulded and put to ripen in the coolest part of the *buron*, at which point it weighs up to 45 kilos. There it is turned over every other day and brushed once a week. After a month it becomes Cantal *doux* (a wonderfully creamy-flavoured cheese), after two months Cantal *entre-deux* (which can sometimes have a surprisingly tangy aftertaste), and after six months Cantal *vieux* (a pungent and excellent – when carefully ripened – cheese with an impressively thick rind). Cheese made from the unpasteurized full-cream milk between 1 May and 31 October in the Cantal and a few *communes* in neighbouring *départements*, and ripened for at least three months, qualifies as Salers. A sister cheese, Laguiole, is made on the high Aubrac plateau, which occupies much of the part of the northern Aveyron that sticks up into the Cantal.

Life was very hard for the *buronniers* in the days when they spent the whole summer up in the mountains. Arthémy Mazars of Montsalvy, in the Châtaigneraie, remembers going up several summers running during the last war to work in a *buron* in the valley of Lavigerie. When he was a *pastre*, on the bottom rung of the ladder, he had to put up with a particularly tyrannical *vacher*, who, like many of his kind, regarded himself as '*maître après Dieu*'. When the *vacher* snapped his Laguiole folding knife★ shut, that was the end of the meal – and too bad for Arthémy or anyone else who still had some food left on his plate. Just as child abusers are often people who have themselves been abused in their youth, so a large proportion of brow-beaten *pastres* later turned into overbearing *vachers* (though I cannot believe this was the case with the gentle Arthémy). In the *vachers'* defence, it should be pointed out that they carried a very heavy responsibility: any mistake in the Cantal-making process – too much rennet, curds at the wrong temperature, wrong timing, uneven salting, too much heat in the *buron* during hot weather – could be disastrous. The cheese would swell, crack and/or crumble during ripening, with the result that a whole 40–45-kilo cheese might have to be written off. The *vacher* could lose all his wages if his cheeses were badly made; but if they were particularly good and fetched a higher price, he did not benefit. One *vacher* was so ashamed at having been shown to be an incompetent cheese-maker after five or six cheeses went wrong that he hanged himself.

There was scarcely a spare moment in the life of the *buronniers*: when not milking, carrying the milk to the *buron* or making the cheese,

---

★ This is the folding knife with an elegantly curved handle that any self-respecting Auvergnat male farmer carries in his trouser or jacket pocket. Usually kept extremely sharp, it performs all sorts of everyday tasks. On the farm, it is used to sever anything from string to a small branch; at table, it is the implement with which the head of the household – if male – cuts up the food on his plate, or slices bread (whether he holds the loaf against his chest, leaving traces of the flour with which it is dusted on his jacket or pullover, or wedges it in the end drawer of the table, he will always cut the bread by starting at the farthest point and slicing towards him; if a new loaf is being broached, he will often make a sign of the cross before cutting it).

Laguiole knives are made in the small town of the same name on the windswept Aubrac plateau, which lies at the meeting point of the Aveyron, Cantal and Lozère *départements*. At one time, this cottage industry almost disappeared and only two knife shops remained in Laguiole. It looked as though Thiers (Puy-de-Dôme), France's capital of knife manufacture and Laguiole's long-standing rival at the top end of the market, was going to have a clear run. Then Laguiole knives suddenly came into fashion and reached a wider clientele than the local population. It became the done thing for teenage kids at posh Paris *lycées* and dynamic young executives (all male) to carry and flash a Laguiole knife. France's leading designer, Philippe Starck, got interested, designed his own version of the knife and even opened a boutique in Laguiole. Over a dozen shops in the town now sell the knives, mostly to tourists. Some knives boast fancy (and unauthentic) extra trappings of the Swiss-army-knife type, or are given sandalwood, mahogany or teak handles instead of the traditional horn. But the basic design – a curved handle to provide plenty of grip on the blade when the knife is opened, and a very pointed blade – has remained unchanged.

the three men had to look after the pigs that lived in sties next to the *buron* on a diet that consisted partly of whey, a by-product of cheese-making (Arthémy remembers how the pigs screamed for their food when they heard the whey plopping into the bucket); they had to dig the small kitchen garden which was also next to the *buron*, where they would grow radishes, lettuces, potatoes and cabbages; they had to move the calves' pens from one patch of pasture to another – patches known as *fumades*, because the cows and calves usefully fertilized each patch with their manure (*fumier*). Milking thirty cows each twice a day was bad enough. Arthémy remembers with a wince how he practically lost the use of his arms when one of his team was mobilized in 1939 and he and a colleague spent a fortnight milking ninety-three cows between the two of them. He also recalls without any nostalgia how it once got so cold in October that the milk which dribbled from the teat on to his hands froze instantly. Not surprisingly, *buronniers* did not suffer from insomnia in their dark, dank and cramped sleeping quarters.

I have used the past tense when describing the life and work of *buronniers*, because the vast majority of *burons* are no longer used for cheese-making. Some have even been turned into *gîtes*. At the time of writing eight *burons* in the Cantal are still in operation with a live-in *vacher*, *boutilier* and *pastre*. But for how long? As the demand for veal and beef guaranteed free of 'mad cow' disease (BSE) continues to increase, what used to be called *montagnes à lait* have turned into *montagnes à viande* (not meat mountains, but meat-producing mountains). The high pastures are now inhabited during the summer mainly by Salers cows, their offspring and the occasional bull (Salers or the white Charolais, which produces buff-coloured calves). As long as the money is good (which it is, as there is a premium on Salers meat), most farmers prefer to produce beef and veal, because it requires much less labour and risk than the complicated process of cheese-making.

Complicated and not always properly remunerated: throughout its history, mountain-produced Cantal cheese has been regularly faced with the problem of whether or not it can be made profitably, and if so, profitably for whom. Its history is perhaps worth looking at in some detail. Cantal is a very old cheese. Pliny the Elder mentions cheeses from the regions of Nîmes, Lozère and Gévaudan being taken to Rome, where they compared well with cheeses from other parts.

But there is no way of ascertaining if those cheeses were the forerunners of Cantal or Laguiole.

In his *De re cibaria*, written in Latin in 1560, Jean Bruyerin-Champier mentions cheeses he calls *formagines* made in the region of Allanche that would seem to be similar to modern Cantal. He describes how he went up a mountain and found 'a large number of huts where many children, barely aged fourteen, were busy making cheese. Bare-armed up to the elbow, they pressed the cheese with their hands into a strainer.' He was told that no children with scabies or with 'hot hands' were chosen for the job – hot hands were thought to cause the cheese to ripen unevenly and form holes, which diminished its value.

Two centuries later, the value of Cantal was apparently not very high, to judge from Panckouke's *Encyclopédie méthodique* (1783), which describes it as 'one of the least esteemed of all the kinds of cheese so far mentioned', and one eaten mainly by 'humble folk and religious communities' because of its very low price.

There is much evidence that the Cantal made in the eighteenth century was often of poor quality, which could explain its low price. On 4 March 1733, the Controller General of Finance, Orry, told the Administrator Trudaine that Paris grocers were rejecting Auvergne cheese because of its unpleasant taste and bad smell, defects ascribed to a lack of cleanliness during its manufacture, 'with the result that we often find it contains pebbles, wood and other infinitely more disgusting dirt'. They preferred Dutch cheese, which travelled better and was cheaper.

Dutch cheese enjoyed a virtual monopoly in Paris. Cantal cheese faced a number of handicaps: makers had to pay heavy salt taxes, the cheeses were too large, the duty on taking them out of the Auvergne province was high (whereas Dutch imports carried no duty), the region was geographically hemmed in and had poor roads, and the softer texture of Cantal made it vulnerable to long and bumpy journeys and to temperature fluctuations.

In an extraordinary episode that was to last nearly 200 years (and which is meticulously charted by Marie-Christine Zelem in her paper *L'Evolution des techniques fromagères dans le Cantal: petite histoire d'un conflit entre savoir local et savoir idéal*), a series of attempts were made to produce Swiss and Dutch cheese in the mountains of the Auvergne. In the early eighteenth century, 'enlightened' men wanted to banish outdated structures and old-fashioned practices by introducing scientific rigour into the manufacture of cheese. Trudaine himself encouraged the setting up of '*établissements pour la fabrication des griers* [*sic*]' by offering such incentives as tax reductions and exemption from military service to those who agreed to take part. In 1736, some big landowners invited fourteen Swiss cheese-makers to the Cantal to teach the *vachers* how to make Gruyère. The opinion of the *vachers* on the matter had not been sought, and they not unreasonably felt that their traditional skills, passed on from generation to generation, were being disparaged. As was only to be expected, they reacted with hostility. Legrand d'Aussy wrote: 'These uncouth and stupid people, of more limited intelligence than the animals among which they live, stubbornly refused to be taught . . . Far from listening to the Swiss cheese-makers, they so taunted them that they [the Swiss], after much harassment, abuse and ill-treatment, were forced to leave the Auvergne and go home.'

The experiment was called off after the Revolution. But in 1810, the Société Centrale d'Agriculture advocated a return to Dutch and Swiss cheeses. But they never really caught on. The only people who stood anything to gain from the operation were the big landowners, who acquired kudos when they won cheese competitions but ran no risk if things went wrong (that was the Sociétés d'Agriculture's responsibility). The prizewinners in 1829, for example, all had a handle to their name: MM. de la Tour, de Marenzac, de la Farge, de Lamarge, de la Bastide, de Tournemire, Lescurier d'Espérières and Tyssandier d'Escous.

It turned out that more Cantal could be made with a given quantity of milk than Gruyère. On top of that, the Swiss cheese needed to be heated during manufacture and therefore required firewood, which was expensive at the time as a result of deforestation. It therefore cost more to make. In 1844, the journal *Le Propagateur Agricole* compared the respective costs of the two cheeses and concluded that it would be a better idea to improve existing methods of making Cantal rather than borrow techniques from others. Cantal was 'eaten more often off the pauper's horny hand than off the rich man's porcelain' and should set out to conquer the tables of the wealthy. The manufacture of Auvergnat Gruyère and Dutch cheese gradually petered out.

One improvement in cheese-making methods which was based on a Dutch technique, but encountered little resistance from the *vachers* because it made life easier and did not offend their pride, was the *catseuse*, a mechanical press to squeeze whey out of the drained curds, which was introduced towards the turn of the century. Up until then, the *buronniers* used to press the curds to reach the Tomme fraîche stage by rolling their trousers up to mid-thigh and kneeling on the cheese. This technique of *genouillage* was inefficient (because the pressure exerted was uneven). It also alarmed one observer, who, writing in *L'Indépendant*, wondered whether consumers might not be put off by the fact that their cheese had received a 'seasoning' from the *vacher*'s knees even more repugnant than the 'Spartans' celebrated black broth'. Curiously, no doubt because of the quaintness of *genouillage*, postcards of about 1910 regularly depict *vachers* kneeling on their *tomme*, well after the mechanical *catseuse* had come in.

As the twentieth century advanced, the number of *burons* steadily diminished and that of dairies and co-operatives increased. Salers cows were less and less used for cheese-making. *Vachers* preferred to work for dairies, where they enjoyed decent wages and easier working conditions. In the 1960s, overproduction led dairies to look once again at the possibility of making 'foreign' cheeses. With the help of modern technology, they started making, and indeed still make, Auvergnat versions of such Italian cheeses as Fontina, Asiago, Taleggio and Parmesan. Up until fifteen years ago, they also made what was marketed in Britain as French Cheddar. (I once asked a cheese-maker in the Cantal if he made any other type of cheese apart from Cantal. '*Oui, le "shtarre"*,' he replied. It took me a few seconds to realize what he meant.)

Farmers and dairies went all out for quantity rather than quality, and in the 1970s the *appellation d'origine contrôlée* (AOC) criteria for Salers were relaxed. The cheese still had to be made from unpasteurized full-cream milk between 1 May and 31 October and matured for at least three months; but it could be made anywhere in the Cantal production area, even at an altitude of only 200 metres, and thus lost its denomination Salers Haute Montagne; and instead of having to be made from the milk of 'mountain breeds' of cattle, it could now consist entirely of milk from specialized milk-producing breeds such as Friesians and Montbéliardes.

Attitudes have fortunately shifted since then. The Comité Interprofessionnel des Fromages du Cantal realizes that there is a new opening at the top of the market, and that people are prepared to pay more for a top-quality product that tastes better and is perceived to be 'organic'. Plans to introduce a new AOC category called Tradition Salers are in the pipeline. Cheese bearing that label will have to be made from the milk of Salers cows only, which have grazed on mountain pastures and whose only feed supplement is grain (not silage, let alone meat-and-bone meal).

The question of the breed of cow whose milk is used to make Salers is a nature/nurture issue, and therefore more complex than it might seem at first sight. I have talked to mountain cheese-makers who swear that their product, made from Friesians' milk (before the Tradition Salers AOC was introduced), is just as good as that made from Salers' milk because of the quality of the herbage (the sum of grasses and plants growing on a given pasture) which their Friesians eat. And it certainly tastes good, especially when matured, as it occasionally is, for twelve months rather than the statutory three. It is true that the mountain and subalpine flora of the Monts du Cantal is extraordinarily rich in aromatic grasses and other plants which affect the flavour of cheese to good advantage (including downy oat, oxe-eye daisy, crested dogstail and sweet vernal grass, the grass that gives new-mown hay its distinctive smell). Some people wax over-enthusiastic and claim to be able to detect hints, in mountain Salers cheese, of gentian (which cows in fact scrupulously avoid because of its bitterness) and liquorice (they imagine this to be the same plant that produces liquorice sticks, which is unable to survive at such heights; the plant concerned is *Trifolium alpinum*, sometimes called liquorice clover because of its sweetness, which is greatly appreciated by cows). But in my experience, when put out on mountain herbage, Salers cows produce a superior cheese to Friesians on the same diet. A blind tasting was organized at the 1994 Fête du Fromage d'Appellation Salers at Saint-Martin-Valmeroux (Cantal). Of the seven cheeses tasted, I rated two as distinctly superior. They had a richer, much more complex flavour than the rest, with a subtle bouquet that is difficult to describe, except that it had very faint, and therefore pleasant, overtones of sulphur. The two turned out to be the only cheeses in the selection that had been made from pure Salers milk.

The breed/milk problem is not so acute in the case of Laguiole, which is made mainly with the milk of Simmental cows (a Swiss breed), with the addition of a little Aubrac milk. Laguiole is a cheese that not so long ago virtually disappeared: only 25 tonnes were produced in 1960. It has fortunately made a comeback since then, and annual production now stands at 750 tonnes. Another 180 tonnes are marketed as Tomme fraîche de Laguiole to cater for the Aveyron's big demand for *aligot* (p. 32). A really mature four-month Laguiole is very similar to a Salers of the same age, but slightly blander. Plans are in the pipeline to produce a special version of Laguiole using Aubrac milk only. Aubrac cows are delightful buff-coloured animals with black-tipped horns and a white ring round their dark eyes that gives them almost a Joan Blondell come-hither look. They certainly succeeded in seducing the conductor John Eliot Gardiner, who has imported a number of Aubrac cattle to his Dorset farm. They are smaller, hardier and even more docile draught animals than Salers, and can be ridden safely by small children. Unfortunately they give very little milk, albeit of superb quality.

The quantity of milk available daily to cheese-makers has a bearing on the size and therefore the type of cheese they make. A herd of thirty Salers cows on the high mountain pastures produces about 400 litres of milk per day, or exactly the amount required to make one 40-kilo cheese.

The situation is very different in the area where that second great – if not greatest – Auvergne cheese, Saint-Nectaire, is made. The AOC area covers the south-west of the Puy-de-Dôme and the north of the Cantal. Although part of the terrain (around the Monts Dore) is similar to the Monts du Cantal, there is now no *transhumance* of cows. The rest of the area consists of high hills and plateaux rather than mountain, and is dotted with mostly small farms. The restricted size of herds is ideal for Saint-Nectaire: each cheese, which weighs about 1.75 kilos, requires about 17 litres of milk, and can therefore be made on farms with only a few cows. Because of the lower quantities of milk and smaller cheese size, the making of Saint-Nectaire demands much less physical strength and is therefore often performed by women. François Greliche, in his *Science et tradition du Saint-Nectaire*, argues that women are particularly skilled at making Saint-Nectaire, 'a complex process which requires cleanliness and meticulousness'. Complex is an understatement: it has more to do with alchemy than manufacture. And that alchemy is wholly dependent on the milk used being unpasteurized.

The first stages of the making of a Saint-Nectaire are similar to those of Cantal. Again, renneting, temperature, timing, salting, the absence of draughts and so on are all crucial. After being pressed into a flat circular mould about 21 centimetres in diameter and 5 centimetres high, the cheeses, now known as *blancs*, are either ripened in cellars on the farm or, much more often, bought by *affineurs*, who ripen them in former wine cellars, chiefly in and around Clermont-Ferrand. The *affineurs* mostly buy them at the big *blancs* markets in Besse-en-Chandesse or Egliseneuve, but they also collect them directly from some farms. The finest Saint-Nectaire is ripened on a bed of rye straw. What goes on during the process is best left to Patrick Rance's description in *The French Cheese Book* (without any doubt the best book on French cheese in any language, and the fruit of enormous enthusiasm and an incredible amount of legwork; his chapter on Saint-Nectaire is a classic of its kind):

Within a fortnight the cheese gradually acquires its first, white-mould coat, *Geotrichum candidum*, and often some grey *mucor*. The unwelcome black *Mucor-aspergillus* is carefully removed by brine-washing and rubbing with a jute rag . . . It should [after two months in the *cave*] have developed clusters of the charming yellow petit mimosa of *Sporotrichium aureum*, and brilliant red patches of *Oïdium auranticum*, without which two adornments no Saint-Nectaire *de bonne famille* is considered properly dressed.

Greliche describes how the good and bad germs fight it out in the cheese during ripening, in a passage that is pure scientific poetry:

Although present in an amount 25 times less than that of lactose, citrate is metabolized by leuconostocs, heterofermentative lactobacilli, and Lactococcus lactis var. diacetylactis into acetaldehyde, CO_2 and above all 2,3-butanedione, which play an important role in the flavour, aroma and 'openness' of the cheese.

Greliche says there are 150 different yeasts – the list of which I shall spare you – at work in the cheese, as well as many moulds in addition to those mentioned by Rance. Humidity levels and the amount of aeration have a crucial effect on the balanced growth of desired flora – which means that the ripening cellars are as vulnerable to human breath as the Lascaux caves and therefore cannot be visited by tourists.

This whole process is anathema to the brigades of blinkered microbiologists who are urging Brussels to ban the use of unpasteurized milk in cheese-making. Pasteurization prevents the development of Saint-Nectaire's useful microbes, moulds and yeasts and thus robs the cheese of its very essence. Pasteurized (*laitier*) Saint-Nectaire, which is recognizable from its square green casein implant on the rind, is as dead and as tasteless a cheese as Saint-Paulin. Its unpasteurized (*fermier*) version, which has an oval implant, is, when properly ripened (with a soft-to-runny *pâte*), one of the gastronomic glories of France. Attempts to describe its flavour – sweet, nutty, aromatic, lingering, fragrant – fall at the first hurdle of its complexity. As for its smell, which can only be described, approximately, as pleasantly musty or cellary or earthy, it is so insistent that I have more than once caught a whiff of it in the open air, wafting out of a cheese shop door or off a market stall. Unlike the smell of, say, a Munster or a ripe Camembert, it does not aggress the nostrils but, like some pheromone, gently alerts one to delights in store. I am glad to report that sales of Saint-Nectaire *fermier* rose by 43 per cent from 1986 to 1996, and are now roughly equivalent to those of the *laitier* version.

The Auvergne produces several kinds of cylindrical blue cheese which can be excellent at their best. Unfortunately, Bleu d'Auvergne is often sharp, over-salty and one-dimensional (the result of pasteurization and the use of industrial powdered mould). Except for unpasteurized Bleus d'Auvergne made by a handful of producers, they cannot compete with the creamier-tasting, ivory-coloured Bleu des Causses, made in the southern Aveyron (and therefore strictly speaking not an

Auvergne cheese), or Fourme d'Ambert, from the Forez in south-east Auvergne. This last very ancient cheese (it is represented by a ninth-century sculpture in the Chapel of La Chaulme, near Saint-Anthème) has suffered greatly in recent decades. It used to be made with the unpasteurized milk of *transhumance* cows and ripened in *jasseries*, the Forez equivalent of *burons*, where it was naturally blued by resident moulds. Now only seven producers persist in using unpasteurized milk, but for reasons I fail to understand do not qualify for the Fourme d'Ambert AOC. The grey-rinded Fourme d'Ambert is reminiscent in flavour of Stilton, but has a more 'farmyardy' nose; and, as with Stilton, its flavour is less harmed than most by the pasteurization process. In other words, a pasteurized Fourme d'Ambert can be a respectably flavoursome cheese, though it cannot compare with its unpasteurized version. It has a sister blue cheese, the blander Fourme de Montbrison, which has an orange-coloured rind and is produced in such small quantities (about 10 per cent of that of Fourme d'Ambert) that it is rarely found outside the Forez and Lyon areas.

Monkeying about with traditional techniques has always, as we have seen, been a constant temptation for Auvergne cheese-makers. And they are always quick to come up with good excuses such as marketability, cost and the need for uniformity. Take the small dome-shaped Gaperon (or Gapron). Originally made from buttermilk (*gape*), it was an aromatic, creamy, crumbly cheese flavoured with garlic and pepper. The effect of the naturally fermented (i.e. un-renneted) cheese on the garlic over a period of three months produced a distinctive taste that bore no resemblance to that of the much better-known garlic-flavoured cheese, Boursin à l'ail. The trouble with the old-fashioned low-fat Gaperon was that it was unstable and did not travel well. So the manufacturers changed the cheese, using full or lightly skimmed milk instead of buttermilk, and bumping up the fat content from 30 per cent to 45 per cent. They were thus able to market the cheese throughout France (and Europe), but in the process of so doing transformed its piquant, almost wild flavour into something bland and much less interesting. Fortunately there are one or two makers who still produce the old low-fat version.

One Auvergnat cheese that has remained unchanged for decades is Cabécou, probably because it is mainly marketed locally. Almost always made from unpasteurized goat's milk, it varies in size from a large medal to a thicker, almost *crottin*-like cheese. The excellent Cabécou I buy locally (from Isabelle Fau in Vieillevie) is a very lightly salted cheese with a startling ability to ripen very fast: bought in a moist, lactic state, the six cheeses in the packet will, when laid out on a plate, covered with a cloche and left in a coolish place (15°C), develop a wrinkled skin within three or four days. Between that and the Cabécou's crumbly centre a thin layer of glossy cream has magically formed. The overpoweringly goaty smell when you lift the cloche can create a Bateman cartoon effect ('The man who lifted the cloche in front of the EU hygiene inspector . . .') on fellow diners, but they soon discover that, as with a number of cheeses (Munster, Epoisses, Reblochon), its bark is worse than its bite – and its taste delectable. If one puts the same cheese into the refrigerator for three or four days, as the food-safety fundamentalists would have one do, it will not only not develop in any way, but will emerge smelling of wet dog – and with a bite just as bad as its bark.

I am all in favour of food hygiene, but a recent episode showed how wary we should be of bowing uncritically to the latest scientific opinion. Brussels has ruled that food should no longer come into contact with wood, which must be replaced by PVC or stainless steel. This means that, if Brussels has its way, the wooden *gerles* in which the first stage of Cantal-making takes place will eventually be banned. This is a preposterous enterprise. Quite apart from the fact that consumers of Cantal have not been dying like flies over the many centuries that Cantal has been made in wooden *gerles*, their replacement by stainless steel containers would affect the quality of the cheese: the milk reacts badly to the 'shock' of coming into contact with cold steel.

Following EU legislation, butcher's shops now boast deeply scored and virtually uncleanable PVC chopping blocks, whereas in the old days the butcher would clean his block by scraping off the top layer of wood and all the dried blood with it. In 1992 Dean Cliver and Nese Ak, two researchers at the University of Wisconsin-Madison, tried to find a way of decontaminating wooden kitchen surfaces. They spread *Salmonella*, *Listeria* and *Escherichia coli* on various samples of wood and plastic, which they left overnight at room temperature. By next day the bacteria on the plastic had multiplied, whereas none at all could be found on the wood. As the *Economist* magazine wittily noted when reporting on their findings:

At first sight these results seem astonishing. But, unlike polymer chemists, plants have spent hundreds of millions of years fighting off bacteria. They should, by now, be pretty good at it. And trees might be expected to be the best of the lot . . . Even when a tree is dead, its wood can hang around for decades, resisting the attacks of micro-organisms. Slaughtering a few Salmonella should be child's play. [The researchers'] guess is that the porous structure of the wood is soaking up the fluid with the bacteria in it. Once inside, the bacteria stick to the wood's fibres and are 'strangled' by one of the many noxious anti-microbial chemicals with which living trees protect themselves.

It looks, then, as though the Euro-chemists will have to go back to their drawing-boards. Let's hope that as a result Vacherin Mont d'Or, the wonderful Alpine cheese made on both sides of the Franco-Swiss border, whose inimitable flavour is imparted by a ring of spruce bark running round it, will be saved from the death sentence it currently risks.

At the same time one cannot but welcome improved hygiene in the making and keeping of Auvergne cheeses, particularly now that our digestive systems are in danger of becoming more sensitive to germs as a result of eating increasingly sanitized food. The Auvergnats almost certainly had more robust stomachs in the pre-refrigeration era than they do now. They, at least, were convinced of that. Jean-Marie Gaston, a Châtaigneraie poet, possesses a copy of Pierre Besson's *Un Pâtre dans le Cantal* (p. 180) annotated by the author. One of the handwritten notes in the margin reads as follows:

In 1890 I attended a lecture at which the head of the Aurillac Dairy School and the agriculture teacher told some *vachers* about the pernicious germs to be found in cheese. You should have seen the mocking reception they got. What? How could such tiny creatures be harmful? Why, they ate shovelfuls of germs every day and were in wonderful health! *Di masclis qui poujiou mistresa un braou, n'abiou pas pour di ta pétiotas bistounellos* [this passage in Occitan (p. xxi) could be translated as follows: We men who can master a bull are not afraid of such tiny creepy-crawlies].

The *vachers* were clearly confusing germs with cheese mites, similar if not identical to those found on Stilton, which are responsible for the thick pitted rinds of old Cantal, Salers or Laguiole. Some people, particularly of the older generation and male gender, are very partial to cheese mites and prize the rind more than the cheese itself. The creature concerned, *Tyroglyphus siro* (literally: pit cheese-carver), so tiny it looks like dust, burrows into the rind of the cheese and, by oxidizing it, changes its flavour. I myself find that the fresh tang of an old cheese that has been brushed regularly to get rid of the mites is far preferable to the rather stale tang of one that has been allowed to become deeply pitted. However that may be, the mites are definitely frowned upon by microbiologists. Or rather: officially at least. Jean-Pierre Morin, Aurillac's finest cheesemonger (p. 28), tells me that he once provided the cheese platter for a lunch that followed a morning of lectures by hygiene experts, one of whom launched a virulent attack on cheese containing *Tyroglyphus siro*. The cheese platter sported, among other things, a young Cantal and a very old Salers, with a thick but not too pitted rind which nonetheless contained some mites. When the scientists got to the cheese course, guess who unhesitatingly went for the old Salers and munched the mites with visible delight: the very man who had earlier sounded the alarm.

Since it is unlikely that any readers of this book are sufficiently equipped or self-confident to attempt to make Cantal, Salers, Saint-Nectaire, Bleu d'Auvergne, Fourme d'Ambert or Gaperon, I shall not provide indications on how they should be made.

Curd cheese, on the other hand, is easy to make. In both its strained and unstrained form (junket), *caillé*, or *encalat* in Occitan (p. xxi), used to be very commonly eaten on farms, especially for breakfast and for supper. It was even carried out to haymakers and threshers in the fields. People in the Châtaigneraie still eat it from time to time in the evening, with sugar or jam, when they are not feeling hungry enough for a full-blooded meal.

[*To make about 1kg (2¼lb) of well-drained curd cheese*]
4.5 litres (160fl oz) whole milk
2 tablespoons live (cultured) buttermilk

Half-fill a large saucepan or casserole with water. Heat until the water reaches blood temperature (about 37°C/98°F), then remove from the heat. Pour the milk into a china bowl and place in the pan. When the milk reaches a temperature of 27°C (81°F), add the buttermilk and stir thoroughly. Leave the mixture at about 20°C (68°F) for 18–24 hours or until it sets to curds and whey. You can tell when it is ready as follows: place the back of your hand on the surface; if it picks up milk and/or fragments of curd, the coagulating process has not been completed; if it is simply moistened with whey, you can proceed to the next stage.

Place a sterilized piece of muslin, folded double, in a large colander. Spoon the curds gently into the muslin. Leave to drain for a few hours in a cool place. Scrape the curds down towards the centre of the muslin, tie it up into a bundle and suspend over a bowl or sink. Leave for about 10 hours. Untie the bag, peel off the muslin and turn the curd cheese out into a bowl. It is now ready to use. If fairly liquid curd cheese is called for, leave the bundle suspended for only 5 hours.

Wine

Talk about wine to more or less any member of the older generation in the Cantal, and it will soon become clear that the most important criterion used when judging whether a wine is worth buying or not is not so much its quality, but its price and, even more so, its alcoholic strength. This is probably a hangover – if you will excuse the term – from the time when the only wine available was to a large extent *piquette*, a mean wine which easily turned vinegary because of its low alcoholic strength. The indication '11°' or '12°' used to be a guarantee of drinkability. Attitudes have now begun to change, though, with the increasingly high standard of wines available in the cheap to middle price range. And as people, particularly the younger generation, drink less wine nowadays, they are more interested in quality – an interest that has been fuelled in recent years by the hypermarkets' annual 'wine fairs', which offer a wide range of regional wines as well as top clarets and burgundies, all very moderately priced.

I have tasted the old-fashioned *piquette*, and most unpleasant it was. In 1979, on a walk to the village of La Vinzelle (p. 9), which is perched spectacularly on a rocky outcrop high above the Lot valley, I and some friends halted at the village café, whose terrace was shaded by a vine-covered pergola. It was run by a charming old lady, Lucie Delagnes, and her son, Germain. Her other son had gone to university and become a senior hospital doctor in Paris (he sent his daughter to holiday at La Vinzelle). But Germain, an amiable, bear-like man, had done less well at school, so stayed behind to help his mother out (this pattern of divergence in siblings' careers is not uncommon in the Auvergne). We got talking about his small vineyard, which was ideally situated facing the south-west and arranged in terraces on the steep terrain around La Vinzelle. Grape-picking was going to start in a few days: would I be interested in lending a hand?

I duly turned up at 8 a.m. at the beginning of my two-day stint. Germain immediately handed me a tumbler of a deep purple liquid so opaque it looked like undiluted Ribena. It turned out to be last year's wine, drawn from a huge barrel that was nearly empty and therefore full of air: the wine was perilously vinegary, tasted horrible and stained my lips purple. This was, without any doubt, the legendary 'gros rouge qui tache' of the French popular novel.

Except for the succession of proffered glasses of wine – which I could not systematically refuse – the grape-picking was most enjoyable: the vineyard was dotted with fig trees, pêchers de vigne, and rare apple varieties, whose clean-flavoured fruit banished the wine's aftertaste. It has to be said that Germain, as a wine-drinker, was more interested in quantity than quality. He had planted his vineyard with one of those French hybrid vines, now banned by the European Union, whose poor flavour is offset by their extremely high yield. For that very reason, they cannot manage an alcoholic strength of more than 9°.

Germain had no tractor and drove no car, but had a pair of docile Aubrac cows, which he yoked up to a cart after the morning and afternoon grape-picking sessions to take the harvest back to the café. Even back in 1979, it was extremely rare for cows to be used as draught animals. Sadly, while on a rare trip to Paris some years later, Germain was knocked down by a car that suddenly loomed out of the night in a Pigalle street – a lifetime spent in La Vinzelle had left him with no traffic sense whatsoever – and died in hospital a few days later.

A few kilometres east from La Vinzelle, also high above the Lot valley, is the village of Le Fel, which, with neighbouring Entraygues, qualifies for France's interim wine quality designation, VDQS (Vin délimité de qualité supérieure). The climatic conditions are similar to those of La Vinzelle, but the vineyards are planted with a mixture of Fer Servadou (known locally as Mansois), Cabernet Franc and Cabernet Sauvignon, the wines are scientifically made, and the result is in a completely different league from Germain's dark brew. A particularly attractive, light and fruity red is made by a young Le Fel vigneron, Laurent Mousset.

Estaing, a VDQS wine like Vins d'Entraygues et du Fel, is produced in the vicinity of the small town of the same name a little farther up the Lot. A rustic picnic wine, it is made from Gamay and Mansois (red), and Chenin and Mauzac (white).

The monks of Conques introduced vines not only to Entraygues, Le Fel and Estaing, but to Marcillac, 30 kilometres south of the Lot on the Rodez road. In 1990 Marcillac wine succeeded, after much lobbying, in securing the higher-quality *appellation d'origine contrôlée* (AOC). It is the only Auvergne wine with an AOC. The extraordinary magenta soil known as *rougier*, which lends the landscape around Marcillac – and indeed its buildings, built of locally quarried soft sandstone of the same colour – a startlingly unreal air, combines with the Mansois grape (the only one used) to give Marcillac wine its utterly individual character. It is the only wine I would be confident of identifying without fail at a blind tasting. Its tannic, spicy and almost peppery qualities come as a surprise after its raspberry nose, and it goes best with dishes that have plenty of character. The best Marcillac growers are Claudine Costes, Philippe Teulier and Jean-Luc Matha. The Cave Co-operative also produces a decent wine. Those wishing to discover more about the wines of the southern Auvergne should refer to Paul Strang's highly readable *Wines of South-West France* (Kyle Cathie, 1994), undoubtedly the most thoroughly researched book on the subject in either French or English.

Wine is also made in the northern Auvergne. The VDQS Côtes d'Auvergne, from the area around, and sometimes in the suburbs of, Clermont-Ferrand, is sold either simply under that name or more specifically as Côtes d'Auvergne Boudes, Chanturgue (p. 122), Chateaugay, Corent and Madargue. The main grape used to make the reds and *rosés* is Gamay, along with a little Pinot Noir. There are a few white Chardonnays. Côtes d'Auvergne can be disappointingly thin, with little of the nose of that most famous of all Gamays, Beaujolais. The strikingly pale *rosés*, or *vins gris*, are more reliable than the reds. Considerable efforts have, however, been made recently to improve quality, particularly by Michel Bellard, Henri Bourcheix (who makes a superb Chanturgue), and Jean-Pierre and Marc Pradier.

The Auvergne's oldest and best-known wine is Saint-Pourçain (Allier), which graced royal tables in the Middle Ages. It has come down a notch or two since then, and as with Côtes d'Auvergne your best bet is not to take pot luck, but to go for the very best growers, particularly when buying white, which is made with Chardonnay, Sauvignon, Tressalier and Aligoté grapes. The more reliable *rosés* and reds are made with 100 per cent Gamay or a combination of Gamay and Pinot Noir. The growers to look out for are Domaine de Bellevue, Famille Laurent and GAEC Nebout.

⊰⊱ Three apéritifs ⊰⊱

It is a curious fact that the leaves of certain plants and trees yield up, when macerated, a flavour that recalls the taste of the fruit that grows on those very same plants and trees. Bramble shoots and the leaves of cherry trees and walnut trees are cases in point. The Auvergnats, always on the lookout for ways of exploiting the wild larder, make unusually delicate and delicious *apéritifs* from those three ingredients.

⊰⊱ Vin de pousses de ronce ⊰⊱

Anyone who has picked blackberries from a sun-drenched bank of brambles will have noticed the distinctive fragrance that the plant gives off when it bakes in the sun – a fragrance reminiscent, in a way, of the bouquet of certain oaky Rioja red wines. That fragrance is magically, almost alchemically captured in this *apéritif* made from young bramble tips, the recipe for which was given to me by a Mourjou man, Théodore Carrière. The tips should be harvested in the spring when, much cursed by gardeners, they set out on their invasive forays.

[*To make 8 × 750ml (26fl oz) bottles of apéritif*]
300g (10½oz) bramble tips
1 litre (35fl oz) fruit spirit
750g (1lb 10oz) caster sugar
4 litres (140fl oz) good red wine
250ml (9fl oz) *crème de cassis*

Immediately after picking the bramble tips, which should be cut off about 10cm (4in) from their tips, chop them up coarsely and put them to macerate in the fruit spirit in a glass, china or enamel container which can be closed hermetically. Leave for 10 days in a cool place. Strain the liquid through a very fine sieve into a mixing bowl, add the sugar, wine and *crème de cassis*, and stir well. Leave for an hour or two. Stir again until all the sugar has dissolved. Bottle, leaving almost no air in the neck of each bottle, and seal tightly with conical corks. Like most *apéritifs*, it is best served chilled.

⤙ Vin de feuilles de cerisier ⤚

The leaves of the cherry tree, believe it or not, give this apéritif a hint of the distinctive astringent flavour of kirsch (the spirit that is made from cherries).

[*To make 8 × 750ml (26fl oz) bottles of apéritif*]
300g (10½oz) young cherry-tree leaves
1 litre (35fl oz) fruit spirit
750g (1lb 10oz) caster sugar
4 litres (140fl oz) good red wine
250ml (9fl oz) *crème de cassis*

Immediately after picking the cherry-tree leaves, chop them up coarsely and put them to macerate in the fruit spirit in a glass, china or enamel container which can be closed hermetically. Leave for 10 days in a cool place. Strain the liquid through a very fine sieve into a mixing bowl, add the sugar, wine and *crème de cassis*, and stir well. Leave for an hour or two. Stir again until all the sugar has dissolved. Bottle, leaving almost no air in the neck of each bottle, and seal tightly with conical corks. Like most *apéritifs*, it is best served chilled.

⤙ Vin de feuilles de noyer ⤚

This is a variant of the more usual *vin de noix* found all over south-west France, which is made from walnuts picked at the unripe stage when their shells are still soft. As you will know if you have crushed walnut leaves in your hand, they possess almost the same strongly aromatic fragrance as the unripe fruit.

[*To make 8 × 750ml (26fl oz) bottles of apéritif*]
300g (10½oz) young walnut-tree leaves

1.25 litres (44fl oz) fruit spirit
750g (1lb 10oz) caster sugar
4 litres (140fl oz) good red wine

Immediately after picking the walnut-tree leaves, which should be as young as possible, chop them up coarsely and put them to macerate in the fruit spirit in a glass, china or enamel container which can be closed hermetically. Leave for 10 days in a cool place. Strain the liquid through a very fine sieve into a mixing bowl, add the sugar and wine, and stir well. Leave for an hour or two. Stir again until all the sugar has dissolved. Bottle, leaving almost no air in the neck of each bottle, and seal tightly with conical corks. Like most *apéritifs*, it is best served chilled.

Select Bibliography

Affre, Henri, *Dictionnaire des institutions, mœurs et coutumes du Rouergue*, Rodez, Carrère, 1903; reprint: Marseille, Editions Jeanne Laffitte, 1974.

Ajalbert, Jean, *En Auvergne*, Paris, Dentu, 1893.

Alalain, André, *La Haute-Loire gourmande*, Le Puy, L'Eveil de la Haute-Loire, 1965.

Alibert, Louis, *Dictionnaire Occitan-Français*, Toulouse, Institut d'Etudes Occitanes, 5th edition, 1993.

Almanach Gourmand de l'Allier, Contigny, Noir sur Blanc, 1990.

Amé, Emile, *Dictionnaire topographique du département du Cantal*, Paris, Imprimerie Nationale, 1897.

Amicale des Cuisiniers et Pâtissiers Auvergnats de Paris, *Cuisine d'Auvergne*, Paris, Denoël, 1979.

Amicale du Canton de Montsalvy, *Le Pays d'où l'on vient*, Montsalvy, Amicale du Canton de Montsalvy, 1991.

Andraud, Alexandre, *Paysan et maître d'école: mémoire d'un pays au pied du Puy Mary*, Nonette, Editions Créer, 1995.

Anglade, Jean, *La Vie quotidienne dans le Massif Central au XIXe siècle*, Paris, Hachette, 1971.

Anglade, Jean, *La Cuisine d'Auvergne et du Limousin*, Paris, Presses Pocket/Cadif, 1982.

Annuaire du département du Cantal pour l'année 1849, Aurillac, P. Pieut, 1849.

Ardouin-Dumazet, *Voyage en France*, 32e série, *Haut Quercy-Haute Auvergne*, Paris and Nancy, Berger-Levrault, 1903.

Audigier, Camille, *Quelques coutumes et traditions de la Haute Auvergne*, Aurillac, Bancharel, 1892.

Auger-Holderbach, Patricia, *La Cuisine paysanne en Rouergue*, Rodez, Editions du Rouergue, 1992.

Auvergne, Paris, Guides Michelin Régionaux, 1932–3.

Auvergne, La France à table, Paris, Imprimerie Aulard, 1953.

Auvergne, Bourbonnais, Velay, ed. Pierre Mazataud, Paris, Guides Bleus, 1997.

Basserre, Madeleine, *Le Cantal – Economie agricole et pastorale*, Aurillac, Imprimerie Moderne, 1928.

Besson, Pierre, *Un Pâtre du Cantal*, Paris, Delagrave, 1914; reprint: Aurillac, Editions de la Butte aux Cailles, 1989.

Béteille, Roger, *La Vie quotidienne en Rouergue avant 1914*, Paris, Hachette, 1973.

Bigay, Jean-Claude, *Secrets gourmands d'Auvergne et du Bourbonnais*, Beaumont, La Française d'Edition et d'Imprimerie, 1982.

Bonis, Georges, *Un Pitsou tour o lo Costognaou*, Aurillac, Malroux-Mazel, 1985.

Borgé, Jacques, and Viasnoff, Nicolas, *Archives d'Auvergne*, Paris, Editions Michèle Trinckvel, 1993.

Bosc, Zéfir, *La Vigne et le vin du Fel et d'Entraygues*, Rodez, Bauguil & Bordes, 1995.

Breuillé, Luc, Dumas, Richard, Ondet, Roland, and Trapon, Patrice, *Maisons paysannes et vie traditionnelle en Auvergne*, Nonette, Editions Créer, 1987.

Brimo de Laroussilhe, Albert, *Les Paysans de la Châtaigneraie devant la vie quotidienne à l'aube du XXe siècle*, Aurillac, Editions de la Butte aux Cailles, 1988.

Bruneton-Governatori, Ariane, *Châtaignes et marrons*, Paris, Messidor, 1991.

Bruneton-Governatori, Ariane, *Le Pain de bois, ethnologie de la châtaigne et du châtaignier*, Toulouse, Eché, 1984.

Bruyerin-Champier, Jean, *De re cibaria*, Lyon, Sébastien Honoré, 1560.

Canet, Michèle, *Lo Companatge*, Aurillac, Institut d'Etudes Occitanes du Cantal, 1991.

Canet, Michèle, *Recettes d'Auvergne*, Aurillac, Ostal del Libre, 1992.

Canet, Michèle, *Recettes de châtaignes*, Aurillac, Ostal del Libre, 1997.

Cantal, Paris, Hachette, 1925.

Chabrol, Etienne, *Coutumes générales et locales de la province d'Auvergne*, Riom, Martin Dégoutte, 4 vols., 1784.

Charbonnier, Paul, 'La Consommation des seigneurs auvergnats du XVe au XVIIIe siècle', in *Annales, Economies, Sociétés, Civilisations*, Paris, Armand Colin, March–June 1975.

Charet, J. Maruéjouls, M., and Parisot, Ch., *L'Economie laitière et techniques fromagères du Cantal*, Aurillac, Imprimerie Moderne, 1947.

Châtaigneraie, La, Aurillac, La Maison des Volcans.

Châtaigneraie, Vallée du Lot, Clermont-Ferrand, Chamina, 1989.

Chaz Monsur: secrets, préceptes, remèdes & recettes d'une famille d'Auvergne avant la Révolution, Paris, Berger-Levrault, 1979.

Claustres, Francine, *La Cuisine aveyronnaise*, Bordeaux, Editions Sud Ouest, 1996.

Collignon, Jane, *Les Temps des châtaignes*, Aix-en-Provence, Edisud, 1986.

Couffignal, Huguette, *La Cuisine rustique Auvergne-Rouergue-Limousin*, Forcalquier, R. Morel, 1970.

Cuisine traditionelle d'Auvergue, La, Ytrac, Editions Bos, n.d.

Découverte d'une région naturelle: la Châtaigneraie, Aurillac, La Maison des Volcans, n.d.

Decuq, François, *Cent et une recettes de cuisine aveyronnaise*, Saint-Affrique, Imprimerie Nouvelle, 1969.

Delbos, M., and Pouget, G., *Dans un buron du Cantal*, Cannes, Bibliothèque de travail, 1971.

Delcher, Pierre, *Souvenirs d'un petit pâtre du Cantal*, Aurillac, Editions Gerbert, 1991.

Delmas, Jean, *Autour de la table, recettes traditionnelles du Rouergue*, Rodez, Editions Françaises d'Arts Graphiques, 1983.

Déribier du Châtelet, *Dictionnaire statistique du département du Cantal*, Aurillac, Picut et Bonnet, 1852−7; reprint: Mayenne, Joseph Floch, 1964.

Desdevises du Dézert, *L'Auvergne pittoresque*, Clermont-Ferrand, Syndicat d'Initiative d'Auvergne, 1898.

Doisneau, Robert, and Dubois, Jacques, *Les Auvergnats*, Paris, Nathan Image, 1990.

Durand, Alfred, *La Vie rurale dans les massifs volcaniques des Dores, du Cézallier, du Cantal et de l'Aubrac*, Aurillac, Imprimerie Moderne, 1946.

Durif, Henri, *Guide historique, archéologique, statistique et pittoresque du voyageur dans le département du Cantal*, Aurillac, Ferary, 1861.

Fau, Jean, and Fay, Joan, *Forma e masuc*, Aurillac, Imprimerie Gerbert, 1974.

Faure, Odile, *Quelque part, le Cantal . . .*, Montsalvy, Editions Quelque Part sur Terre, 1996.

Fête du cochon en Auvergne, La, Aubespeyre, Groupe de Femmes d'Aubespeyre, 1990.

Fontaine, Jacques, *La Cuisine auvergnate traditionnelle et moderne*, Lyon, Editions Horvath, 1995.

Garnier, Henri, *Autour de la ferme dans le Cantal*, Aurillac, Imprimerie Terrisse, 1896.

Gaston, Jean-Marie, *Un Village de Haute-Auvergne: Calvinet*, Aurillac, Editions Gerbert, 1965.

Gaston, Jean-Marie, *Cantal, mon beau pays*, Aurillac, Imprimerie Moderne, 1981.

Gaston-Crantelle, Raymonde, *Femme. . . et notaire*, Montsalvy, L'Oustalet, 1986.

Gault, Henri, and Millau, Christian, *Guide gourmand de la France*, Paris, Hachette, 1970.

Girard, Roger, *Quand les Auvergnats partaient conquérir Paris*, Paris, Fayard, 1979.

Graham, Peter, *Classic Cheese Cookery*, London, Penguin, 1988.

Greliche, François, *Science et tradition du Saint-Nectaire*, Bresse, Imprimerie Morillat, 1993.

Guide touristique gastronomique du Cantal, Paris, Havas, 1948.

Guillemard, Colette, *Ethnocuisine de l'Auvergne*, Avallon, Civry, 1980.

Hewitt, H. J., *The Organization of War under Edward III*, Manchester, Manchester University Press, 1966.

Inventaire du patrimoine culinaire de la France: Midi-Pyrénées, L', Paris, Albin Michel/Conseil National des Arts Culinaires, 1996.

Jabinet-Roy, Marie-Françoise, *Le Carnet de Mita*, Saint-Pourçain-sur-Siole, Editer en Bourbonnais, 1986.

Jalenques, Roger, *Maurs au fil des siècles*, Maurs, Syndicat d'Initiative de la Région de Maurs, 1976.

Joberton, Gérard, Perret, Yves, and Dalbavie, Thierry, *Arbres et fleurs de nos montagnes: Massif Central*, Lyon, Editions de Borée, 1991.

Joubert, Chanoine, *Les Vieilles pierres de la Châtaigneraie*, Aurillac, Imprimerie Moderne, 1968.

Laforce, Edouard, *Essai sur la statistique du département du Cantal*, Aurillac, P. Picut, 1836.

Lallemand, Roger, *La Vraie cuisine de l'Auvergne et du Limousin*, La Rochelle, Quartier Latin, 1973.

Lallemand, Roger, *Le Bourbonnais*, Paris, Editions Lanore-CLT, 1979.

Lauras-Pourrat, Annette, *Guide de l'Auvergne Mystérieuse*, Paris, Club Princesse, 1976.

Leclère-Ferrière, Catherine, *Auvergne: carnet de cuisine*, Sommières, Romain Pages Editions, 1996.

Legrand d'Aussy, Pierre-Jean-Baptiste, *Voyage fait en 1787 et 1788, dans la ci-devant Haute et Basse Auvergne*, Paris, Imprimerie des Sciences et Arts, 1794.

Maillebouis, Christian, *La Lentille verte du Puy*, Aurillac, Ostal del Libre, 1995.

Mallouet, Jacques, *Jours d'Auvergne*, Châteauroux, Badel, 1973.

Marchi, Christian, *Le Cantal autrefois*, Lyon, Editions Horvath, 1993.

Marre, E., *La Race d'Aubrac et le fromage de Laguiole*, Rodez, E. Carrère, 1904.

Mathieu, Georges, *Guide pratique de la fabrication du cantal et du bleu d'Auvergne*, Aurillac, Office Départemental Agricole du Cantal, 1929.

Mergoil, Guy, 'Un îlot insolite de consommation du stockfisch: les confins du Rouergue-Quercy', in *Alimentation et régions*, ed. Jean Peltre and Claude Thouvenot, Nancy, Presses Universitaires de Nancy, 1989.

Merlin, Annie, and Beaujour, Alain-Yves, *Les Mangeurs de Rouergue*, Paris, Editions Duculot, 1978.

Mesnagier de Paris, Le, ed. Georgina E. Brereton and Janet M. Ferrier, trans. and notes Karin Ueltschi, Paris, Le Livre de Poche, 1994.

Meynier, André, *Ségalas, Lévézou, Châtaigneraie*, Aurillac, Editions USHA, 1931.

Monteil, Amans-Alexis, *Description du départment de l'Aveiron*, Villefranche-de-Rouergue, Société Anonyme d'Imprimerie de Villefranche-de-Rouergue, 1884.

Morgan, Bryan, *Fastness of France: a Book about the Massif Central*, London, Cleaver-Hume Press, 1962.

Nadeau, Louis, *Voyage en Auvergne*, Clermont-Ferrand, Barot-Duchier, 1865.

'Notes sur la région de Maurs', in *Revue de la Haute-Auvergne 1970*, Aurillac, Revue de la Haute-Auvergne, 1970.

Oliver, Raymond, *Quand L'art et la magie de la cuisine fusent du pays des volcans éteints . . . et dansent la plus froumageuse des bourrées d'Auvergne*, Paris, Comité Regional Interprofessionnel des Productions Fromagères du Cantal et Haute-Auvergne, 1969.

Paysan, Le, Actes du 2ème Colloque d'Aurillac, Aurillac, Editions Christian, 1989.

Piganiol de la Force, *Auvergne*, vol. II of *Nouvelle description de la France*, Paris, Théodore Legras, 1754.

Raflin, Claire, *Almanach auvergnat 1993*, Chamalières, Editions Canope, 1992.

Raison-Jourde, Françoise, *La Colonie auvergnate de Paris au XIXe siècle*, Paris, Ville de Paris, Commission des Travaux Historiques, 1976.

Rance, Patrick, *The French Cheese Book*, London, Macmillan, 1989.

Reports of the Club des Sans-Club (English edition), The, ed. O. Poulgy, Paris, Club des Sans-Club, 1950.

Robaglia, Suzanne, *Margaridou: journal et recettes d'une cuisinière au pays d'Auvergne*, Nonette, Editions Créer, 1977.

Roc, Jean-Claude, *Le Buron de la Croix Blanche*, Brioude, Editions Watel, 1989.

Rocher, Jean-Claude, *L'Art de la fourme*, Aurillac, L'Ostal del Libre, 1990.

Roque, Monique, *Auvergne, terre de fromages*, Montsalvy, Editions Quelque Part sur Terre, 1997.

Roque, Monique, *Estives et transhumance*, Aurillac, Ostal del Libre, 1996.

Rouergue et causses, La France à table, Paris, Imprimerie Aulard, 1953.

Rouquette, J., *Le Rouergue sous les Anglais*, Millau, Imprimerie Artières et J. Maury, 1887.

Sand, Christine, *A la table de George Sand*, Paris, Flammarion, 1987.

Saveurs, essences et sens, Rodez, Mission Départementale de la Culture/ Bibliothèque Départementale de Prêt, 1991.

Sérieys, Jules, *Un Mot sur la race de Salers*, Aurillac, Imprimerie Terrisse, 1905.

Société Amicale des Originaires du Canton de Montsalvy, *Annuaire*, Paris, Amicale du Canton de Montsalvy, 1936.

Strang, Jeanne, *Goose Fat and Garlic*, London, Kyle Cathie, 1991.

Strang, Paul, *Wines of South-West France*, London, Kyle Cathie, 1994.

Tijms, Wigbolt, *Le Saint-Nectaire*, Groningen, Rijksuniversiteit te Groningen, 1976.

Tourret, Marissou, *La Cuisinière auvergnate*, Nonette, Editions Créer, 1990.

Trin, Antoine, *Petite histoire de l'élevage cantalien*, Rodez, Editions Subervie, 1983.

Trin, Antoine, *Les Routes de la Châtaigneraie*, Aurillac, Imprimerie Gerbert, n.d.

Vence, Cécile, *Auvergne – Rouergue*, Tokyo, Japon & Cil France, 1971.

Victoire, Honorin, *Autour des Monts d'Auvergne*, Rodez, Editions Subervie, 1996.

Villatte des Prûgnes, Robert, *La Cuisine bourbonnaise*, Moulins, Crépin-Leblond, 1949.

Visser, Margaret, *Much Depends on Dinner*, Toronto, McClelland & Stewart, 1989.

Volcan Cantalien, Clermont-Ferrand, Chamina, 1987.

Weber, Eugen, *Peasants into Frenchmen*, London, Chatto & Windus, 1977.

Zelem, Marie-Christine, 'L'Evolution des techniques fromagères dans le Cantal: petite histoire d'un conflit entre savoir local et savoir idéal', in *Actes du colloque de Saint-Martin Valmeroux*, Institut d'Etudes Occitanes, 1992.

Index

Page numbers in **bold type** refer to recipes.

Index